Software Transparency

Software Transparency

Supply Chain Security in an Era of a Software-Driven Society

Chris Hughes
Tony Turner

WILEY

This is dedicated to my children, Carolina, Calvin, Callie, and Clayton, as well as my wife, Kathleen, for their unwavering love and support which serves as motivation to always strive to be my best. I also would like to dedicate it to my mother Dawn and grandfather Bill, who always taught me the importance of hard work.

— Chris Hughes

This book marks a transition point of so many things in my life, and throughout it all, my wife Becki, and my two sons, Alex and Gavin, have patiently supported me. I'd like to thank them from the bottom of my heart for always being there to remind me of what is most important in life.

— Tony Turner

About the Authors

 **Chris Hughes** currently serves as the co-founder and CISO of Aquia. Chris has nearly 20 years of IT/cybersecurity experience, ranging from active duty time with the U.S. Air Force, as a civil servant with the U.S. Navy and General Services Administration (GSA)/FedRAMP, as well as time as a consultant in the private sector. In addition, he is an adjunct professor for M.S. Cybersecurity programs at Capitol Technology University and University of Maryland Global Campus. Chris also participates in industry working groups such as the Cloud Security Alliances Incident Response and SaaS Security Working Group and serves as the Membership Chair for Cloud Security Alliance D.C. Chris also co-hosts the Resilient Cyber podcast.

Chris holds various industry certifications such as the CISSP/CCSP from (ISC)[2], as well as holding both the AWS and Azure security certifications and Cloud Security Alliance's Certificate of Cloud Auditing Knowledge (CCAK). He holds a B.S. in Information Systems, an M.S. in Cybersecurity, and an MBA. He regularly consults with IT and cybersecurity leaders from various industries to assist their organizations with their digital transformation journeys, while keeping security a core component of that transformation. Chris has authored many articles and thought pieces on software supply chain security, as well as presenting on the topic at industry events such as Carnegie Mellon's DevSecOps Days Washington, D.C. among others.

 **Tony Turner** is the founder and CEO of Opswright, a software company focused on security engineering for critical infrastructure. With over 25 years' experience in cybersecurity, Tony has worked as an internal security engineer, developer, network and systems administrator, security consultant, architect, and managed professional services for security vendors. Most recently he functioned as the VP of Research and Development for the Fortress Labs team at Fortress Information Security, where he spearheaded their software transparency and vulnerability management product research and roadmap. Tony also founded and leads the OWASP Orlando chapter since 2011, focused on improving the visibility of application security; is the project leader for WAFEC, a web application firewall documentation project; and co-founded the Security BSides Orlando conference. He sits on multiple trade organizations and industry groups from MITRE, ISA, OWASP, CISA, GlobalPlatform, and others, largely focused on the topics of software transparency, and software and product security within critical infrastructure.

Tony graduated with a B.S. from Hodges University in Naples, Florida, and holds several industry certifications, including the CISSP; CISA; six credentials from SANS/GIAC, OPSE, CSTP, and CSWAE; and multiple vendor certifications from F5, Imperva, and others.

Additionally, Tony has been involved with the certification exam writing process for GIAC and F5 ASM web application firewall certification and is a course author for SANS on Defending Product Supply Chains, to be released in 2023.

Tony lives in Indialantic, Florida, with his wife, Becki; two sons, Alex and Gavin; five cats; three lizards; two guinea pigs; and an army of squirrels in his backyard that demand their morning tribute.

About the Technical Editor

Steven Springett has over 25 years leading product development teams and has spent over 14 years focused on supply chain security. Currently, Steve is the director of secure development at ServiceNow, where he leads application security architecture, threat modeling, security champions, and developer enablement across the organization. Steve is passionate about helping organizations identify and reduce risk from the use of third-party and open source components. He is an open source advocate and leads the OWASP Dependency-Track project, is a coauthor of the OWASP Software Component Verification Standard (SCVS), and is the chair of the OWASP CycloneDX Core Working Group, a bill of materials standard that provides advanced supply chain capabilities for cyber-risk reduction. Steve holds a CSSLP and CCSK, among other industry certifications. Steve lives in Chicago's North Shore with his wife, Vera, and daughter, Aryana.

Acknowledgments

We would like to acknowledge the countless industry professionals who we have worked with, for, and learned with over our several decades of combined cybersecurity experience.

This includes industry thought leaders on the topic of software supply chain security, such as Allan Friedman, Joshua Corman, Robert Wood, Virginia Wright, Jason Weiss, and, of course, Steve Springett, who, in addition to serving as an industry leader on the topic of software supply chain security, also served as our technical editor and sounding board. We would also like to thank the countless public and private sector leaders who have participated in working groups and efforts associated with software supply chain security through groups such as OWASP, the Linux Foundation, OpenSSF, Department of Defense, NTIA, CISA, Carnegie Mellon's Software Engineering Institute (SEI), and others. Without the community's collective expertise, knowledge sharing, and collaboration, we would not be able to produce this body of knowledge to give back to the industry. Software is critical to nearly every aspect of our society, and we're in this fight together.

Contents at a Glance

Contents

Foreword

Many of us will remember December 2021 as a time spent hunched over small travel laptops in relatives' guest rooms, dealing with the Log4j crisis. That vulnerability in an open source Java-logging framework developed by The Apache Software Foundation was scored as severe by both official metrics and software experts. It was not the hardest vulnerability to address, either through patches or other inline mitigations. Yet, the real challenge most organizations faced was location: Where is this darn thing? Buried deep in countless modern applications' supply chains, both producers and users of software simply didn't have a usable roadmap of where to focus.

The hard part of security should be in identifying vulnerabilities and discovering attackers sneaking into our supply chains. Instead, we've discovered that understanding what's in the software we make has required a nontrivial amount of work.

The idea of tracking what goes into software isn't new. Academics have been talking about it since the 1990s. Early idea discussions were happening in disparate corners of the software world in the 2000s. Failure to account for the open source licenses got a number of large companies into serious legal trouble. Collecting and leveraging supplier data formed an integral part of the revolution in heavy industry quality that dates back to the late 1940s, with the Deming and the "Toyota revolution" that inspired the DevSecOps and modern software revolution decades later.

Indeed, it's quite remarkable that we don't have better transparency in our software supply chains. I often use the example of a Twinkie (first advanced by Audra Hatch and Josh Corman) to raise the question of why we have a better understanding of what is in a nonbiodegradable snack than what is in the software that runs in our companies, governments, and critical infrastructure.

As we embark on our journey to understand how to implement software bill of materials (SBOMs), it's useful to take a moment to understand why we didn't have this capacity at the beginning, how we're beginning to make progress, and what the value of this transparency is. There are some less-flattering reasons why few organizations wanted to share, including not wanting to be exposed to the previously mentioned open source license compliance risks. Frankly, many organizations did not want to admit to the scale of technical debt or incur the costs of having to set up the basic internal infrastructure and processes to track their dependency data. Moreover, it should be acknowledged that starting this SBOM journey hasn't been easy—it has required bringing together technical expertise, an understanding of the diverse software ecosystem, and an appreciation of incentives. But a massive amount of progress has been made in the last five years.

The first thing we needed was a shared vision of what an SBOM is. Many experts had a general idea; these were debated and refined from 2018 to 2020 in the open, international, "multistakeholder process" that the National Telecommunications and Information Administration (NTIA) convened. The community defined the basics of an SBOM and laid out its core use cases. We then needed a machine-readable means to convey this information across the supply chain. Fortunately, some across the software world were ahead of us, so we were able to align the Linux Foundation's Software Package Data Exchange (SPDX) and Open Worldwide Application Security Project's (OWASP's) CycloneDX to meet these models.

The next step was creating tools to generate and use this machine-readable data. Great progress has been made across the software world in implementing SBOM generally, with new tools emerging across the ecosystem. We're seeing more sector- and technology-specific tools, because the needs of the industrial control systems (ICSs) and operational technology (OT) firmware world are somewhat different from traditional enterprise software, which, in turn, have unique features and integrations compared to the cloud-native world. Generation tools have begun to mature and new tools emerge all the time to help organizations use this data, both operationally and strategically. (It's been one of the perks of my job, first at the NTIA and now at the Cybersecurity and Infrastructure Security Administration [CISA], to meet with start-ups and open source innovators to find ways to meet real needs across the software marketplace.)

Of course, the third leg of the tripod, along with technology and markets, is government. The U.S. government has focused on securing the supply chain in recent years, but there has been strong interest as well as policy innovations by our partners around the world. SBOMs moved to the main stage of cybersecurity policy in May 2021, when the President's Executive Order (EO) on Improving the Nation's Cybersecurity declared, among other things, that suppliers to the U.S. government will provide the purchaser with an SBOM. As this book goes to press, the final details of those regulations are expected. This goes along with regulations of medical devices in the United States by the Food and Drug Administration (FDA), activity from other U.S. regulators, and proposed regulations emerging around the world.

Because you have this book in your hands or on your screen, you probably don't need to be convinced of the value of transparency across the software supply chain. But you may have to convince others, evangelize across your organization or corner of the software ecosystem, argue for a budget, or convince your suppliers to share data. Despite the usual infosec vendors' hyperbole, the "SB" in SBOM doesn't stand for "silver bullet." SBOM is a data layer. We are still building the tools and processes to the turn that data into intelligence and, ultimately, into action. Just like a Common Vulnerabilities and Exposures (CVE) identifier doesn't actually fix a vulnerability on your network—and CVEs are now an indispensable part of our global vulnerability ecosystem—so, too, will SBOMs become an integral part of the software security and quality world.

Transparency in the software supply chain aids across the life cycle of software. For those of us who build software, SBOMs are a powerful tool to understand our processes and to ensure that we're not building things that are not secure-by-design or shipping with known risks. For those of us who choose or buy software, why would we use a supplier who doesn't understand what they are delivering? Why would we potentially adopt software that was outdated before its use? For those of us who operate software, without an SBOM, how can we respond to newly identified risks or make plans for systems that are built on end-of-life or end-of-support software? Of course, many of us occupy all three roles. It seems inevitable that more uses of this data will be identified and built as SBOMs become more ubiquitous.

There have been a lot of incredible contributions to the software transparency movement, championing the idea of SBOMs, building tools, and debating vital edge cases. Authors Hughes and Turner do a great job of capturing these advances—including some of their own—and explaining the details and nuances as we go from the idea of SBOM to the practice of SBOM. While I expect practitioners around the world to pick up and use this volume to incredible success for their organizations and their customers, it is my paradoxical wish that this book's critical value is actually short-lived. As more of us start to build and manage our software with the types of interoperable automation the authors so helpfully envision and follow the course they lay out, SBOMs will cease to be new and shiny and become a natural, automated part of how all software is made, sold, and used.

It's then we can turn to the next challenge.

Dr. Allan Friedman

Allan Friedman is Senior Advisor and Strategist at the Cybersecurity and Infrastructure Security Agency. He coordinates the global cross-sector community efforts around software bill of materials (SBOM). He was previously the Director of Cybersecurity Initiatives at NTIA, leading pioneering work on vulnerability disclosure, SBOM, and other security topics. Prior to joining the federal government, Friedman spent over a decade as a noted information security and technology policy scholar at Harvard's Computer Science department, the Brookings Institution, and George Washington University's Engineering School. He is the co-author of the popular text *Cybersecurity and Cyberwar: What Everyone Needs to Know*, has a C.S. degree from Swarthmore College and a PhD from Harvard University.

Introduction

We are living in a time where software touches every aspect of our society. Software is involved in everything from critical infrastructure, digital commerce, and national security. In fact, as of this writing, the World Economic Forum (WEF) predicts that by the end of 2022, 60 percent of global gross domestic product (GDP) will be tied to digital systems (`www3.weforum.org/docs/WEF_ Responsible_Digital_Transformation.pdf`). However, that same WEF report found that only 45 percent of people trust the technology that powers our modern economies and society. Part of that lack of trust can be traced to many years of notable digital data breaches and a long-standing issue with transparency when it comes to the software supply chain.

Software supply chain attacks are far from a new phenomenon, and concerns about trusting code have origins dating back to Ken Thompson's famous "Reflections on Trusting Trust" paper in 1984, where Thompson discussed the inability to trust code you did not create yourself. While the idea that code consumed from external sources could be untrustworthy or downright malicious, the manifestations of that statement have only been exacerbated in recent years as software supply chain attacks accelerate. Malicious actors, driven by a variety of motives, have realized that rather than targeting a single entity, they can compromise widely used software (whether proprietary or open source) and have a cascading impact across an entire ecosystem of consumers.

As these incidents have accelerated, organizations have increased their efforts to both understand software supply chain challenges, complexities, and incidents, and have implemented security measures to mitigate their associated risks. The Cloud Native Computing Foundation (CNCF) has compiled a catalog (`http://github.com/cncf/tag-security/tree/main/supply-chain-security/ compromises`) of supply chain compromises dating back to 2003. This catalog captures supply chain compromises from a variety of methods, such as exploited developer tooling, developer negligence, malicious maintainers, or even attack chaining (i.e., several compromises chained together to enable an attack).

Before some of the landmark cases discussed in this text, such as SolarWinds, Log4j, and others, the Office of the Director of National Intelligence (ODNI) published a paper (`http://dni.gov/files/NCSC/documents/supplychain/20190327-Software-Supply-Chain-Attacks02.pdf`) in 2017, calling it a watershed year for software supply chain attacks. The document laid out several significant software supply chain attacks in 2017, which impacted organizations supporting the U.S. government in addition to commercial leaders, several of which originated from nation-state actors. The ODNI paper points out that many software development and distribution channels lack proper security. ODNI also described some malicious actors going upstream due to better cyber hygiene among some organizations. It is often more efficient for malicious actors to go upstream and compromise downstream software consumers at scale, rather than targeting one individual organization. Some software supply chain attacks may be indiscriminate, targeting any consumers, while others may seek out specific upstream software producers knowing who some of their downstream consumers are.

There is no denying that digitally enabled systems have led to unprecedented efficiency, productivity, and innovation. That said, these same digitally connected software-empowered systems have now created levels of systemic risk that are only beginning to be fully understood. It is said that complex interdependencies can heighten systemic risk, and it would be hard to argue that the current state of the software ecosystem and modern digital systems are anything but complex. Malicious actors are realizing the value of targeting the software supply chain as well, with Gartner, an industry leader in technology research, predicting that by 2025, some 45 percent of organizations will experience a software supply chain attack. Some argue that estimate may be low, with organizations such as Sonatype producing a 2022 report (`http://sonatype.com/state-of-the-software-supply-chain/introduction`) showing a 742 percent annual increase in software supply chain attacks over the past three years.

As notable software supply chain attacks have increased, we have now seen ambitious efforts on behalf of governments as well as private sector organizations. In the United States, the White House issued Executive Order 14028, "Improving the Nation's Cybersecurity" (`http://whitehouse.gov/briefing-room/presidential-actions/2021/05/12/executive-order-on-improving-the-nations-cybersecurity`), which has a section dedicated to enhancing software supply chain security. This order includes a section about a common lack of transparency as it relates to software being consumed by organizations, including the federal government.

In this book, we will discuss in more detail relevant software supply chain incidents, industry activities, emerging solutions, as well as the significant challenges that remain when it comes to securing the software supply chain.

Why Is This Critical?

Before we dive into the specifics of software supply chain threats and emerging frameworks and guidance, we should initially discuss why this is such a critical issue that impacts every aspect of modern society. As mentioned previously, digital platforms are quickly on pace to touch over half of the global economic output. Powering those digital platforms and systems is software, much of which is open source software (OSS) components. OSS use is ubiquitous across much of the modern software ecosystem. A recent study (`http://synopsys.com/content/dam/synopsys/sig-assets/reports/rep-ossra-2022.pdf`) found that 97 percent of modern software codebases contain OSS, and not only do they contain OSS, but over half of the codebases are OSS.

OSS is now fundamentally integrated into some of society's most critical infrastructure and systems. Research has shown that over 90 percent of codebases for industries such as transportation, financial services, and manufacturing contain OSS. The same trends exist across industries such as telecommunications and health care as well. In the United States, the Department of Defense (DoD) released a memo titled "Software Development and Open Source Software" (`http://dodcio.defense.gov/Portals/0/Documents/Library/SoftwareDev-OpenSource.pdf`). The memo, which is part of their broader Software Modernization Strategy (`https://dodcio.defense.gov/portals/0/documents/library/softwaredev-opensource.pdf`), calls OSS "the bedrock of the software-defined world and is critical in delivering software faster, resiliently, as is key to their software modernization efforts." The Software Modernization Strategy states that "the ability to securely and rapidly deliver resilient software capability is a competitive advantage that will define future conflicts."

Innovative use of software is not just critical for national security purposes, as emphasized by the DoD, but is pivotal for society at large. In a hearing as part of the U.S. House of Representatives Committee on Science, Space and Technology titled "Securing the Digital Commons: Improving the Health of the Open Source Software Ecosystem" (`www.congress.gov/event/117th-congress/house-event/114727`), several elected officials as well as industry experts testified to the importance of a resilient OSS ecosystem. Congressman Bill Foster called OSS the "hidden workforce of the digital ecosystem." Congresswoman Haley Stevens stated that "a vibrant open-source ecosystem is an engine for U.S. competitiveness and growth." In an Open Source Software Security Summit hosted by the White House in 2022, it was emphasized that most major software packages include OSS, including software that is used by the national security community (`www.whitehouse.gov/briefing-room/statements-releases/2022/01/13/readout-of-white-house-meeting-on-software-security`).

Many are beginning to make the case that OSS is such a vital aspect of society that it should be considered critical infrastructure as well, comparing it to interstate highways, power grids, water treatment, and other fundamental aspects of our society (`http://hbr.org/2021/09/the-digital-economy-runs-on-open-source-heres-how-to-protect-it`). The argument also claims that designating OSS critical infrastructure would lead to additional resources, cross-sector coordination, public awareness, and dialogue.

Despite the ubiquity of OSS and its importance to national security, commercial industry, and society, it can be argued that its security concerns have been neglected. In an article titled "Open-Source Security: How Digital Infrastructure Is Built on a House of Cards" (`http://lawfareblog.com/open-source-security-how-digital-infrastructure-built-house-cards`), researcher Chinmayi Sharma makes the case that OSS and its associated vulnerabilities are pervasive across all critical infrastructure sectors and, due to a lack of resources and incentives, pose a systemic risk to society.

This lack of attention is not lost on malicious actors either, as some studies state we have seen software supply chain attacks experience as much as a 650 percent year-over-year (YoY) increase in 2021. This is not a unique phenomenon, with 2020 seeing an over 400 percent increase. These stark increases are also reflected in sources such as the Cloud Native Computing Foundation's (CNCF) Catalog of Supply Chain Compromises.

This uptick in software supply chain attacks is also supported by research from organizations such as the Atlantic Council, in their "Breaking Trust: Shades of Crisis Across an Insecure Software Supply Chain" white paper (`http://atlanticcouncil.org/wp-content/uploads/2020/07/Breaking-trust-Shades-of-crisis-across-an-insecure-software-supply-chain.pdf`). Their research shows a sharp increase in software supply chain attacks, with third-party applications among the primary attack vectors, along with OSS. The report documents more than 100 software supply chain attacks over the last decade, through a myriad of vectors such as hijacked updates, malicious dependencies, compromised software development platforms, and account compromises. This demonstrates not just the consistent and increasing use of software supply chain attacks by malicious actors, but also the diversity of attack vectors that malicious actors can use to compromise downstream software consumers due to the complexity of the modern software ecosystem. As demonstrated by the report, not only are these attacks impacting millions of users, but they are also quickly becoming a standardized method of nation-state conflict and engagement in the modern digital society. The attention from malicious nation-state actors was also emphasized by ODNI in its 2017 publication (`http://dni.gov/files/NCSC/documents/supplychain/20190327-Software-Supply-Chain-Attacks02.pdf`).

It is not just OSS components that are being targeted. Malicious actors are also targeting managed service providers (MSPs), cloud service providers (CSPs), and several other entities, all of which play various roles in the modern software ecosystem.

Malicious actors have realized the fruitfulness of targeting software supply chain components or suppliers and causing a massive downstream impact, which is more efficient than individually targeting the same number of victims. In this book, we will discuss everything from the background on software supply chain threats, notable incidents, emerging guidance, technical capabilities, and best practices, as well as where we are headed in the future.

What Does This Book Cover?

This book covers the topics relevant to the emerging discussion and challenges associated with software transparency and software supply chain security. This includes a detailed background on software supply chain threats, existing approaches, and the rise of innovative tools, technologies, and processes to address this exponentially relevant threat. Discussions will include the impact these threats have on nearly all aspects of society and practical guidance for various stakeholders on how to address these threats. It will cover emerging regulations and their impact, as well as predictions on where we as an industry and a society go from here moving forward.

Chapter 1: Background on Software Supply Chain Threats This chapter outlines core topics such as the incentives for attackers and the anatomy of a software supply chain attack as well as relevant landmark cases.

Chapter 2: Existing Approaches—Traditional Vendor Risk Management This chapter reviews existing approaches to software security, such as traditional vendor risk management, application security models, and methods such as hashing and code signing.

Chapter 3: Vulnerability Databases and Scoring Methodologies This chapter discusses existing and emerging vulnerability databases, as well as common methods used for scoring and prioritizing vulnerabilities in software and applications.

Chapter 4: Rise of Software Bill of Materials This chapter discusses the origins of the SBOM concept, including early failures and successes and the U.S. federal and industry organizations that have contributed to its maturity.

Chapter 5: Challenges in Software Transparency This chapter focuses on challenges related to software transparency, such as differences between open source and proprietary code as well as firmware and embedded software.

Chapter 6: Cloud and Containerization This chapter reviews the evolution of IT, including the cloud and containerization, as well as the complexity associated with software transparency in the realm of software-as-a-service (SaaS). The chapter also covers efforts associated with DevSecOps.

Chapter 7: Existing and Emerging Commercial Guidance   This chapter discusses existing and emerging commercial guidance related to software transparency and software supply chain security from both public and private sector organizations.

Chapter 8: Existing and Emerging Government Guidance   This chapter discusses existing and emerging government guidance related to software transparency and software supply chain security from the governmental sector.

Chapter 9: Software Transparency in Operational Technology   This chapter discusses some of the unique aspects related to software transparency and operational technology (OT) as well as implications for broader software supply chain efforts.

Chapter 10: Practical Guidance for Suppliers   This chapter focuses on practical guidance for software suppliers to help them meet emerging guidance and best practices and to facilitate their role in bolstering software supply chain security.

Chapter 11: Practical Guidance for Consumers   This chapter features practical guidance for software consumers, including whether an SBOM is actually needed, what to do with it, and how to mature organizations' software supply chain risk management efforts.

Chapter 12: Software Transparency Predictions   This chapter covers software transparency predictions moving forward, including emerging regulations and their impact on broader markets, promising emerging technologies, and where we go from here as an industry and a society.

Who Will Benefit Most from This Book?

This book will benefit various technology and cybersecurity professionals such as chief information security officers (CISOs), chief technology officers (CTOs), senior technology and security leaders, security engineers and architects, software developers, and open source software enthusiasts. It will also benefit acquisition professionals concerned with secure software acquisition and procurement and auditing professionals aiming to understand emerging software supply chain guidance and requirements. Researchers and policy makers interested in best practices and threats related to software and society will also benefit.

Special Features

DEFINITION   Throughout the book, we'll explain the meanings of terms that may be new or nonstandard in this special feature.

NOTE   In-line boxes are used to expand further on some aspect of the topic, without interrupting the flow of the narrative.

Small general discussions that deserve special emphasis or that have relevance beyond the immediately surrounding content are called out in general sidebar notes.

How to Contact the Authors

Chris Hughes can be contacted via email at `chris.matthew.hughes@gmail.com` as well as via LinkedIn at `http://linkedin.com/in/resilientcyber` or on Twitter `@ResilientCyber`.

Tony Turner can be contacted via email at `tony@opswright.com` as well as via LinkedIn at `http://linkedin.com/in/tonyturnercissp` or on Twitter at `@tonylturner`.

If you believe you have found a mistake in this book, please bring it to our attention. At John Wiley & Sons, we understand how important it is to provide our customers with accurate content, but even with our best efforts an error may occur.

In order to submit your possible errata, please email it to our Customer Service Team at `wileysupport@wiley.com` with the subject line "Possible Book Errata Submission."

Software Transparency

Background on Software Supply Chain Threats

This chapter outlines core topics such as the incentives for attackers, anatomy of a software supply chain attack, and relevant landmark cases. Let's begin by discussing the incentives for attackers to perform a supply chain attack.

Incentives for the Attacker

Supply chain attacks circumvent traditional perimeter defenses in ways that make them very attractive for the attacker. Organizations have invested heavily in firewalls, intrusion prevention, and access controls. These protections are defensive measures against a "push" style of attack that directly targets an organization's infrastructure. Supply chain attacks foster a scenario that is more of a "pull," where legitimate users of information technology (IT) request software updates that are malicious, causing the user to knowingly compromise their organization. Because the request originated from a trusted user and came from inside the corporate perimeter or was sent to a trusted entity already cleared by a third-party risk management process, these updates were trusted. Organizations simply compromise themselves.

When you are exploring the controls necessary to defend against attacks, it is not sufficient to consider a single layer as an effective defensive measure. In much the same way that network infrastructure administrators have realized they need to monitor outbound traffic or implement host-based controls, this move toward defense in depth, and especially looking beyond the perimeter, is crucial. For a variety of reasons, including cloud, mobile, social media, and modern application infrastructures, the concept of the perimeter must also evolve. It is no longer a static boundary but needs to be thought of as the separation layer between trust zones, whether they reside at your network's edge or as a logical barrier within your application or access control mechanism. As such, our controls and resultant threat modeling must consider the entire attack surface and explore each interaction point and trust relationship.

Supply chain attacks function as a force multiplier as well. By identifying key dependencies or widely used software, an attacker can inject malicious code into any environment that then utilizes that code. This has been seen time and time again and is similar to the concept of a watering-hole-style attack, where an attacker compromises a widely used website used by a target group, such as a programmable logic controller (PLC) web forum used by industrial control systems (ICS) integrators. If an attacker can compromise every user who visits the forum, they can theoretically gain access to any critical infrastructure entity that those integrators do work for. Likewise, any software used by those integrators that has been compromised may introduce unwanted and malicious functionality into the environments this software is installed in, even long after those consultants have moved on to their next project.

All of this means that software supply chain attacks are highly lucrative for the attacker. There is an economic factor to cyber-espionage that greatly benefits from reusable exploits and the low entry cost for supply chain attacks. Also, many recent attacks are seeing a combination of ransomware deployed via software supply chain, which not only makes for ease of compromise but a direct financial gain for ransomware operators and an increasing level of concern for organizations concerned with business interruption.

Threat Models

The topic of threat modeling is one that is frequently cited and, in the authors' experience, rarely performed in practice by most organizations. As an industry, we frequently discuss threats in fairly generic ways without ever exploring the context of the software or systems necessary to properly model those threats. At the core of these activities, however, is a definition of the attack surface—the points of interaction—and an exploration of what could go wrong.

To ensure that we provide maximum clarity, we'll define a few key terms:

Threat   A threat is a negative event that creates an undesirable outcome. Threats may be naturally occurring, benign in nature, or overtly malicious. An example might be that the billing system for your business fails to capture transactional entries or the datacenter is destroyed by a tornado.

Threat Agent   A threat agent is the entity responsible for causing the threat to occur. Examples include hacktivists, malicious insiders, a disgruntled business partner, a consultant who has been compromised, or even a weather pattern. It has been noted that threat attribution is frequently wrong, and assumptions made about an attack pattern's specific threat agents might lead to wrongful assumptions in protection characteristics. For instance, if you think a nation-state prone to ransomware is a likely threat agent, but you are instead faced with one more focused on espionage, how does this change your security posture? Does the actual country of origin matter, or is it creating undue bias?

Threat Action   This is the action taken by the threat agent that ultimately causes the threat to occur. For instance, a threat agent such as a hacktivist might bribe your system administrator to reconfigure the billing system, resulting in a threat that ultimately creates a financial impact.

Threat Model   This is the process of documenting systems and threats in such a way that we can model certain types of decisions related to risk management for the system because of a threat. There are different objectives for threat modeling, including general cyber risk management, systems design and analysis, and even information-sharing models.

Threat Modeling Methodologies

There are several types of threat modeling methodologies. Let's begin by discussing STRIDE.

Stride

STRIDE is a very common threat methodology used to help determine what can go wrong, although it is not the only methodology in use. STRIDE is broken up into a mnemonic aligned with the acronym:

Spoofing: Impersonating another user or system component to obtain its access to the system

Tampering: Altering the system or data in some way that makes it less useful to the intended users

Repudiation: Plausibly denying actions taken under a given user or process

Information Disclosure: Releasing information to unauthorized parties (e.g., a data breach)

Denial of Service: Making the system unavailable to the intended users

Elevation of Privilege: Granting a user or process additional access to the system without authorization

Most supply chain attacks are a result of operating a system, and traditional models such as STRIDE are designed for more direct attacks against a system, as opposed to the indirect impacts that occur when an administrator requests an update to their application, previously known as good, which then winds up being malicious.

Stride-LM

Researchers at Lockheed Martin have expanded the STRIDE methodology by adding a seventh dimension known as *lateral movement*. Although STRIDE is useful for systems design, it does not meet the needs of network defenders. STRIDE-LM provides a mechanism for defenders to design controls that allow for greater efficacy in defending beyond the point of initial compromise.

When evaluating threat models for applicability to software supply chain attacks, ask yourself what the model was designed for and how it will apply to the scenario in question. For instance, many supply chain attacks abuse maintenance phases through malicious updates or abuse of trust that circumvents controls designed to detect an initial software entry point. Likewise, due to the single point of failure inherent in software supply chains, the downstream impacts of these actions might not be effectively modeled in the original STRIDE methodology. As we explore the landmark cases in this book, you will begin to see how the use of lateral movement provides additional context to modeling and makes STRIDE-LM far more applicable to supply-chain-oriented attacks.

Open Worldwide Application Security Project (OWASP) Risk-Rating Methodology

The OWASP methodology is used as a quantitative scoring model to evaluate specific risks by leveraging technical threat and business impact criteria to derive the score. At its core, it uses a fairly standard impact × likelihood calculation, but where it gets interesting is how those two sides of the equation are created. The following description attempts to capture the basis of this formula, but it should be noted that in practical usage it is not uncommon for the factors to be changed or for weighting to be applied to specific factors that are very important. For instance, in critical infrastructure, we find many entities desire to add a fifth "safety" factor to the business impacts and will often weight it heavier than the others.

$$\textbf{Likelihood} = \textbf{AVG}\left(\textbf{Threat Agent} + \textbf{Vulnerability}\right)$$

where Threat Agent = skill, motive, opportunity, and size; and Vulnerability = ease of discovery, ease of exploit, awareness, and intrusion detection.

$$\textbf{Impact} = \textbf{AVG}\left(\textbf{Technical Impact} + \textbf{Business Impact}\right)$$

where Technical Impact = loss of confidentiality, integrity, availability, and accountability; and Business Impact = financial damage, reputation damage, noncompliance, and privacy.

$$\text{Risk Score} = \text{Likelihood} \times \text{Impact}$$

OWASP is useful for evaluating an identified risk and prioritizing it for actioning, but it is less useful as a threat modeling technique to identify unknown risks. It might make sense to work OWASP into your process *after* other threat modeling techniques have been applied. In our experience, it is far superior to prioritization mechanisms such as Common Vulnerability Scoring System (CVSS) scoring, but it does require context to be useful.

DREAD

DREAD was a legacy technique created by Microsoft, but we rarely see it used today and it is often considered to be a "dead" methodology. DREAD utilized a mnemonic similar to STRIDE's:

Damage: How bad would an attack be?

Reproducibility: How easy is it to reproduce the attack?

Exploitability: How much work is it to launch the attack?

Affected users: How many people will be impacted?

Discoverability: How easy is it to discover the threat?

Using Attack Trees

Attack trees (see `http://schneier.com/academic/archives/1999/12/attack_trees.html`) are a visual way to work backward from an unintended or undesirable consequence (so that you can understand how that event could occur and the most likely vectors of attack), and a way to create a prioritized list of controls to implement to prevent that consequence. In Figure 1.1, you can see the cheapest path for the adversary is to just cut open the safe. It might make sense to prioritize physical security controls to prevent access to the safe in the first place or to spend more money on a safe resistant to such attacks. While internal threats are a viable attack vector, the economics of the attacker make it far less likely they will choose this approach.

This can be an effective way to begin to understand a supply chain attack and to see how easy it is to carry out as opposed to more conventional attacks. With conventional attacks, half of the battle is gaining physical access to even attempt to bypass access controls. In a supply chain attack, a trusted entity is engaging in the actions necessary to compromise the system. However, there

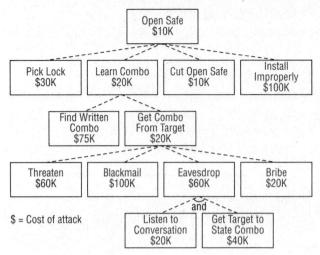

Figure 1.1

are far fewer barriers to pass through. Let's look at a sample attack in Figure 1.2, using a typosquatting attack, which is when attackers offer up malicious packages with names similar to real packages to masquerade a malicious component as a legitimate library on GitHub. This is by no means a complete example.

To put this in perspective, think about the steps required to execute an attack. Lockheed Martin developed a methodology referred to as the Cyber Kill Chain (http://lockheedmartin.com/en-us/capabilities/cyber/cyber-kill-chain .html), which describes the phases of attack. There are many nuances, but these are the basic steps in the adversary's approach (see Figure 1.3).

What if the adversary can skip most of these steps and go straight to Command & Control? It is extremely attractive to an adversary to reduce the cost and complexity of carrying out an attack, and by understanding the pathways they can accomplish those objectives.

Threat Modeling Process

In this section, we'll describe a typical threat modeling process. First, you must define the system or application you are building or updating. Determine its components and how these components interact with each other. This begins laying the groundwork to identify the attack surface for the system. Perhaps it is an externally consumable application programming interface (API) or Hypertext Transfer Protocol (HTTP) service. Maybe there are other dependencies, such as a middleware or database server that needs to communicate to execute application logic or authentication services that utilize federation, but the need for core architectural understanding is the foundation for starting this process.

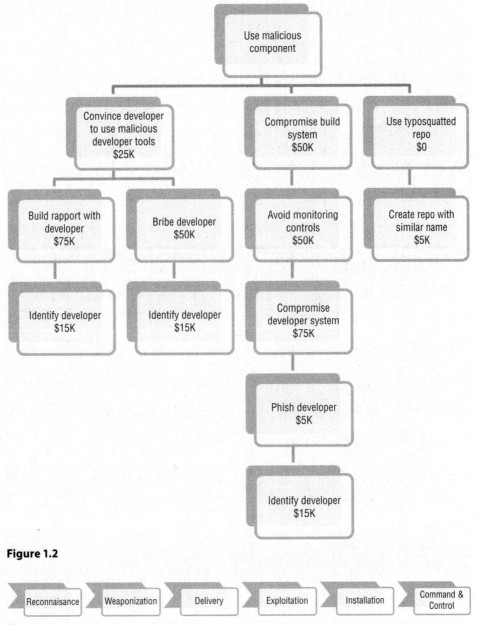

Figure 1.2

Figure 1.3

The OWASP Application Security Verification Standard (ASVS; http://owasp
.org/www-project-application-security-verification-standard) defines
this basic architectural understanding as a foundational requirement, including
the need to conduct threat modeling in design and future change cycles.

The OWASP Software Component Verification Standard (SCVS; `http://owasp` `.org/www-project-software-component-verification-standard`) extends this concept even further by calling for a software bill of materials, which we will explore further later in this book. It is clear, however, that a firm grasp of what needs to be protected is necessary to understand threats and how to defend against them.

Many tools can be used to document your system; one commonly referenced is the Microsoft Threat Modeling Tool. For many years it was the only viable option, but this space has evolved quite a bit over the last few years. The Threat Modeling Tool allows software architects to identify threats early in the development process, before it becomes too costly to remediate them. It uses the STRIDE model to document threats.

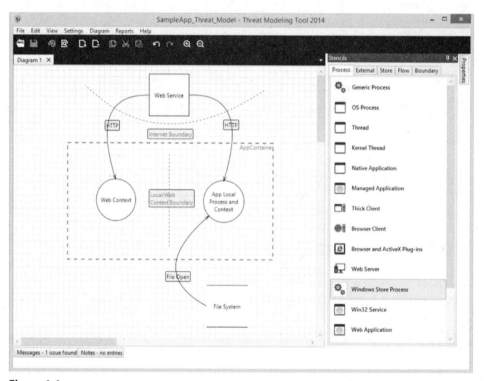

Figure 1.4

In Figure 1.4, you can see a simple application container, which separates the contexts of Internet access to an exposed web service and local access down to a filesystem level that compartmentalizes these application constructs using trust boundaries. By dissecting your system in this way, you can determine how a potential threat agent might interact with your system and can begin to answer the questions in the second part of this process. There are other free tools, such as pytm from OWASP, which is a Python-based way to automate threat modeling using Common Attack Pattern Enumeration and Classification (CAPEC) definitions, which we will explore later in this chapter, as well as Threat Dragon, which is more similar to the Microsoft tool. There are also very robust commercial tools available, such as Threat Modeler and IriusRisk, which also embrace the previous concepts in ASVS design principles.

The next step in the threat modeling process is to determine what could go wrong. This might be as simple as an error condition or a user who has not been trained to use the application correctly, or it can be as significant as an adversary seeking to cause harm. For our purposes, we will focus on malicious cyber sabotage scenarios to explore this topic.

To illustrate a potential software supply chain threat scenario, consider Figure 1.4, where a malicious actor has injected malicious log entries into the web service, which, when consumed locally and opened by a log viewer, executes a malicious JavaScript in the user's browser. If this web service is consumed by many downstream users, that one log injection attack could result in many downstream users who rely on this service to all become compromised. It then creates a scenario where the adversary has compromised a single web service, uses it to compromise many other organizations, and has now established a beachhead to conduct further attacks against those organizations or their downstream customers who trust them as part of their supply chains. Such a data-tampering attack can have tremendous downstream impacts.

Once you know what can go wrong, you then need to understand what controls can be implemented to minimize the threat. Part of this stage will likely include a prioritization exercise, as it might not be possible to eliminate every potential threat; however, focusing on the most impactful scenarios that also have a reasonable chance of success might help guide the control conversation.

For instance, in the previously described scenario, perhaps sanitizing log inputs or escaping characters might result in additional protections against this attack. Because there are many ways attackers can bypass traditional protections, such as those implemented to prevent cross-site scripting (XSS), it might be beneficial to look at similar protections, such as those documented in the OWASP XSS Prevention Cheat Sheet, which provides guidance to prevent XSS vulnerabilities. The cheat sheet is a list of techniques to prevent or limit the impact of XSS attacks (`http://cheatsheetseries.owasp.org/cheatsheets/ Cross_Site_Scripting_Prevention_Cheat_Sheet.html`).

The final stage of threat modeling typically involves evaluating the threat model's completeness and asking yourself if the diagram is complete enough to run through all your scenarios and if it clearly identifies trust boundaries. First, determine if you have covered all the threat actions defined in the model you are using, such as STRIDE, and if all the data flows have been explored. Lastly, determine if all identified threats have had a risk outcome or plan of action established, even if it has been determined to be non-feasible to worry about whether the mitigations required are outside of your control and cannot be acted on. You should close the loop on the model and revalidate the model every time major architectural changes are introduced into the system.

Additionally, we find that the following concepts play heavily in the topic of software supply chain threats, and as such, will take a moment to define them:

Provenance   Provenance is the concept of where an artifact came from. It is commonly confused with pedigree (see the next item). Provenance, as applied to software, might include where a specific software component came from or who contributed code to a specific library. It is uncommon for organizations to track at the individual contributor level, but for high-security scenarios this may be a worthwhile endeavor. We have seen through experience that almost every widely used open source library will have contributions from countries of origin that might be thought of as adversarial, so for organizations that choose to go to this level of detail, additional mitigating controls might be called for or deeper security analysis might be needed to determine if these contributions are problematic.

Pedigree   The concept of "track and trace" is not new, and in fact, is a core concept in forensics sciences and closely related to the application of a "chain of custody" log that identifies anyone who touched an artifact from creation through delivery. Tracking indicates the movement of the artifact, and chain of custody attributes the individual or organization who touched the artifact. The concept of secure equipment delivery has likewise emerged to track how physical assets transit the globe and includes the use of unique identifiers such as a Lot ID and Global Trade Identifiers via the GS1 family of standards and protections such as physical unclonable functions (PUFs). As we are primarily describing a digital artifact as it relates to software transparency, the use of cryptography and transparency logs satisfy these requirements. Pedigree, as it relates to software transparency, might indicate the history of a software package or a security patch for that piece of software, and it is a concept that can be documented in some software bill of materials formats. Likewise, pedigree can also track where a point of origin has changed over time, such as a GitHub repository that has changed from one maintainer to a new maintainer, or a supplier who has divested a product line and sold it to a third party. These are concepts we will explore further later in this book.

Many threat modeling frameworks such as DREAD and STRIDE are used today for various purposes. Such frameworks are commonly used to describe security design and analysis. The Consequence-Driven Cyber-Informed Engineering (CCE) framework from Idaho National Labs (INL) focuses on controlling threats aligned to specific business consequences and not necessarily every point in an attack surface. Then there are frameworks like STIX and PRE-ATT&CK, which are designed for information sharing and other preparatory phases.

Frameworks such as CAPEC and MITRE ATT&CK have a specific technology or situational focus. Organization-specific frameworks include the NIPRNet/SIPRNet Cyber Security Architecture Review.

Likewise, one key focus of threat modeling at scale tends to be a focus on attack patterns. The reason organizations do not perform threat modeling correctly is because it's difficult to do at scale. The Microsoft Security Development Lifecycle (SDL) lists threat modeling as activity #4 out of 12—just after defining security requirements and key performance indicators (KPIs) and just before defining design. This makes a lot of sense when designing a new system, but how do we threat-model hundreds or thousands of applications across our environment at scale? Typically, we wind up taking shortcuts. This is why attack patterns are so popular, especially if we can reduce the number of attack patterns based on identified adversaries or identified target groups for those adversaries.

CAPEC is a publicly available catalog of attack descriptions hosted by MITRE and originally created by the Department of Homeland Security. This catalog includes an entry for *supply chain* (`http://capec.mitre.org/data/defini tions/437.html`), which helps defenders understand how these attacks are constructed in order to better identify defensive measures. This CAPEC entry for supply chain attacks describes this category of attacks as captured below

---

Attack patterns within this category focus on the disruption of the supply chain lifecycle by manipulating computer system hardware, software, or services for the purpose of espionage, theft of critical data or technology, or the disruption of mission-critical operations or infrastructure. Supply chain operations are usually multi-national with parts, components, assembly, and delivery occurring across multiple countries offering an attacker multiple points for disruption.

Also included in this family of attacks patterns are the following:

- Excavation
- Software integrity attacks
- Modification during manufacture
- Manipulation during distribution
- Hardware integrity attacks

Additionally, references to MITRE ATT&CK can also be helpful, such as the *Supply Chain Compromise* entry (`http://attack.mitre.org/techniques/T1195`), which also captures three additional sub-techniques as well as some mitigation that might be helpful for defenders:

- Compromise software dependencies and development tools
- Compromise software supply chain
- Compromise hardware supply chain

Unfortunately, their coverage of supply chain is fairly basic at this stage, and it might make more sense to combine this approach with more specialized work, such as that of the Cloud Native Computing Foundation (CNCF), that might provide far more of the specificity needed to defend against these threats.

CNCF's catalog of software supply chain compromises also includes an index (`https://github.com/cncf/tag-security/blob/main/supply-chain-security/compromises/compromise-definitions.md`) defining several types of attacks. We will discuss those attack types in order to have a shared lexicon of some of the primary attack vectors in the software supply chain. The index of attack types includes:

- Development tooling
- Negligence
- Publishing infrastructure
- Source code
- Trust and signing
- Malicious maintainer
- Attack chaining

It is worth noting that several attack types map to existing frameworks such as MITRE's ATT&CK, which has sections (`http://attack.mitre.org/techniques/T1195`) dedicated to supply chain compromise, including software dependencies, development tooling, and the software supply chain itself.

Developer tooling attacks are a compromise of the tools used to facilitate software development. This might be the developers' end device, software development toolkits (SDKs), and toolchains. MITRE recommends using integrity-checking mechanisms such as validation and scanning downloads for malicious signatures. If a malicious actor can compromise development tooling, they are able to introduce potentially malicious code from the onset of the software development life cycle (SDLC) and tarnish all subsequent application development activities and consumers.

Negligence is a failure to adhere to best practices, which is common, given that there are so many applications security best practices to know and that we live in an increasingly complex digital ecosystem. Something as simple as neglecting to verify the dependency name can have a major impact on an organization. Malicious actors have increasingly been using an attack method known as *typosquatting*, which, as mentioned earlier, takes advantage of lack of attention to detail of dependency names. Attackers typically will target a popular framework or library, add their malicious code under a name similar to the original library, and then wait for unsuspecting victims to download and use it in their applications.

Publishing infrastructure has become increasingly critical as organizations now commonly utilize continuous integration/continuous delivery (CI/CD) pipelines and platforms to deliver software artifacts. One mitigation technique is code signing, which helps ensure the integrity of the published code. However, as you will see in our first landmark case, a compromise of the CI/CD infrastructure itself can allow malicious actors to legitimately sign software artifacts that present them as trusted to downstream consumers. This attack method can be devastating and nefarious, and it emphasizes why the publishing infrastructure must be secured as production environments are and that they must align with emerging frameworks like Supply Chain Levels for Software Artifacts (SLSA), which we will touch on in upcoming chapters.

Source code attacks involve the compromise of a source code repository, either directly from a developer or through the compromise of a developer's credentials. The 2022 Verizon Data Breach Investigations Report (DBIR; `http://verizon .com/business/resources/reports/dbir`) found that credential compromise was involved in over 80 percent of data breaches. This included situations impacting source code or source code repositories. Malicious actors targeting source code and repositories will often try to introduce vulnerabilities or backdoors into the source in order to later exploit them or impact downstream consumers.

Integrity is critical to trust in the software supply chain. This is typically facilitated by activities such as digital signing and attestations. Signing code gives downstream consumers a level of assurance regarding the provenance of code and its integrity. That said, compromising signing can enact software supply chain attacks. Therefore, fundamental security concepts like defense in depth remain key. *Defense in depth* is a long-standing cybersecurity practice of using multilayered defenses so that no single vulnerability or weakness leads to an entire system or organizational compromise. Malicious actors need to exploit several layers of defenses and security measures to achieve their objectives, rather than a single vulnerability or weakness. In the previous example, using only digital signing is insufficient and can be exploited. This is among the attack types listed in the CNCF index and cited by MITRE in their supply chain compromise section of the ATT&CK framework. Potential threats include activities such as theft or private keys, misplaced trust, and abuse of certificate issuance, among others, as cited by the National Institute of Standards and Technology (NIST) in their "Security Considerations for Code Signing" white paper (`http://csrc.nist.gov/CSRC/media/Publications/white-paper/2018/01/26/ security-considerations-for-code-signing/final/documents/security- considerations-for-code-signing.pdf`). Mitigation techniques involve such activities as establishing trusted users, separating roles, using strong cryptography, and protecting the signing keys.

Given the complexity of the software supply chain and the often voluntary nature of maintainer activity, not all threats originate from outside a project either. The malicious maintainer attack vector is among the threats listed in the CNCF index and involves a maintainer, or someone posing as one, deliberately injecting malicious software or vulnerabilities into the supply chain or source code. This can occur due to a maintainer deciding to act maliciously or because their account or credentials has been compromised by an external entity. Motivations for these sorts of attacks range from hacktivists to those posing as involved maintainers who only abuse their permissions and access for nefarious purposes.

Lastly, attacks and vulnerabilities don't occur only in isolation. Malicious actors may chain together several vulnerabilities and attack vectors to carry out their activities and desired intent. Looking at some of the attack types we've mentioned, a hypothetical scenario could involve a malicious actor posing as an interested contributor or maintainer only to abuse their access, insert malicious code, abuse signing, and so on. Stringing together several attack vectors can have a devastating impact and is often referred to as attack chaining, which has been researched and spoken about by researchers such as Dr. Nikki Robinson.

There are also other emerging methodologies and frameworks that can secure the software supply chain and threat-model ways it can be exploited by malicious actors, such as the Supply Chain Levels for Software Artifacts (SLSA), which we will be discussing in depth in upcoming chapters.

Landmark Case 1: SolarWinds

No discussion of modern software supply chain security incidents would be complete without discussing the SolarWinds cyberattack. SolarWinds is one of the largest digital system management tool providers in the market. In 2019, SolarWinds began experiencing cyberattacks that have now been attributed to Russian Foreign Intelligence Services. At the time of the attack, SolarWinds had 300,000 clients, including many U.S. government agencies and most of the Fortune 500 companies as well. It was estimated that of those 300,000 clients, 18,000, including federal government agencies and customers, had received a compromised software update. It is said that the malicious actors then specifically targeted a subset of the compromised clients whom they deemed high-value targets.

While not very much was clear in the initial stages of the attack, there have now been many post-incident reports that have shed light on both the technical sophistication of the malicious actors and the downstream impacts across the ecosystem of affected organizations in both the public and private sectors. One of those reports, created by the U.S. Government Accountability Office (GAO), has called the cybersecurity breach of SolarWinds "one of the most widespread and sophisticated hacking campaigns ever conducted against the federal government and private sector" (`http://gao.gov/blog/solarwinds-cyberattack-demands-significant-federal-and-private-sector-response-infographic`).

The GAO also produced the report shown in Figure 1.5 (http://gao.gov/products/gao-22-104746) to help communicate the high-level timeline of activities associated with the SolarWinds attack.

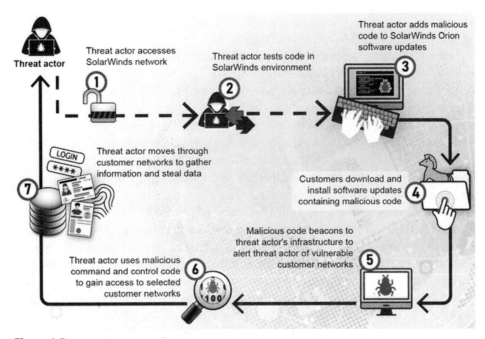

Figure 1.5

SolarWinds made an enticing target and quintessential software supply chain attack because it is unlikely that the malicious actors were interested in Solar-Winds as the end target but instead were interested in SolarWinds' customers and downstream consumers. Prior to this cybersecurity attack, SolarWinds boasted their robust and high-profile customer list on their website, a list which has subsequently been removed.

The SolarWinds cybersecurity attack was initially identified not by the organization itself but by one of its customers, FireEye, which just happens to specialize in cybersecurity. It is reported that a FireEye employee was prompted to reset their multifactor authentication settings, which prompted the employee to bring it to their team's attention. This subsequently led to FireEye investigating the incident and tracing it back to malicious software from SolarWinds, specifically their Orion software. The chief technology officer (CTO) of Mandiant, FireEye's incident response firm, is quoted as saying that the organization went through 50,000 lines of code to determine there was a backdoor in SolarWinds. Once FireEye identified the compromised software from SolarWinds, they contacted both the vendor and law enforcement to notify them of their findings.

While some details of the attack timeline vary depending on the source, there are some fundamental facts that have been provided by the same GAO report previously mentioned. The timeline can be viewed from both the private sector activity and public sector engagement once federal law enforcement became aware and federal agencies such as the FBI and Cybersecurity Infrastructure Security Agency (CISA) became involved.

From a timeline perspective, it is said that in September 2019 the SolarWinds internal systems were initially compromised. That said, SolarWinds CEO Sudhakar Ramakrishna stated at the RSA Conference in 2021 (`www.cyberscoop.com/solarwinds-ceo-reveals-much-earlier-hack-timeline-regrets-company-blaming-intern`) that initial reconnaissance activities can now be traced back to as early as January 2019. Around the same time of the initial system compromise in September 2019, the malicious actor also injected test code into the SolarWinds environment to validate they had indeed compromised the systems and could carry out their intended activities.

The malicious actors used malware dubbed "Sunspot" to compromise the SolarWinds software development process and build systems. They then injected a backdoor now called "Sunburst" into the Orion product from SolarWinds around February 2020. In March 2020, a hotfix was made available to customers and subsequently downloaded by 18,000 of the SolarWinds customer base. In June 2020, the threat actor removed the malware it had placed on the SolarWinds build machines. It was not until December 2020 that SolarWinds was notified of Sunburst. SolarWinds then filed an 8-K report (`http://sec.report/Document/0001628280-20-017451`) with the Securities and Exchange Commission (SEC), which provided insight into the situation to the extent that SolarWinds knew at the time.

On December 15, 2020, SolarWinds issued a software fix to address the impacted Orion products. This, of course, presented an interesting conundrum, given that the previous software updates from the vendor are what contained the malicious software and affected customers to begin with. CISA issued an alert (AA20-352A; `http://cisa.gov/uscert/ncas/alerts/aa20-352a`) on December 17, 2020, warning of an advanced persistent threat (APT) compromising government agencies, critical infrastructure, and the private sector as well. This alert identified that the compromise of a dynamic link library (DLL) in five different versions had been affected. The alert also specifically called out the threat actors' patience, complexity, and the overall elevated level of tradecraft associated with the attack. Additional findings related to Sunspot were found in January 2021 as well.

Cybersecurity company CrowdStrike published a detailed technical analysis (`http://crowdstrike.com/blog/sunspot-malware-technical-analysis`) of the SolarWinds cyberattack. It found that the malicious actor used the malware known as Sunspot to compromise the SolarWinds build process and to insert their Sunburst backdoor into the SolarWinds Orion IT management product. Sunspot worked by monitoring processes involved in compiling the Orion product and replaced one of the original source files with the Sunburst backdoor code. This backdoor then facilitated the creation of a reverse shell for the malicious actor to access the compromised victim's infrastructure who ran the impacted versions of SolarWinds' Orion.

There is much more that could be written about the SolarWinds cyberattack and its associated malware and backdoors, an example of one of the largest and most sophisticated software supply chain attacks to date. Several federal and commercial technology leaders have called the SolarWinds cyberattack a wake-up call and emphasized the need for increased rigor around how the industry secures the software supply chain.

Part of what made the SolarWinds cyberattack so nefarious was that the malicious actors took advantage of a long-standing best practice in cybersecurity, which is to ensure that you patch your software when updates are made available from vendors. In this case, the update was poisoned, so those following that best practice and updating/patching in a timely fashion were potentially impacted. By compromising the build process, the malicious actors were also able to pass the compromised software off as being signed and legitimate.

Since the fallout of the SolarWinds incident, the firm has made substantial investments in its software build processes and capabilities. Some reports and comments, such as by SolarWinds CISO Tim Brown, have claimed that their revised "Secure by Design" initiative will cost as much as $20 million annually (`http://cybersecuritydive.com/news/solarwinds-1-year-later-cyber-attack-orion/610990`). SolarWinds has participated in webcasts titled "Securing the Software Development Build Environment" (`http://cybersecuritydive.com/news/solarwinds-software-build-reproducible-cyberattack-code/596850`), where they discuss their Secure by Design approach, which includes using reproducible builds to weed out disparities in binary code. This involves changes with how the organization manages versioning and dependencies and consists of having multiple environments that a malicious actor would need to compromise to successfully compromise the organization's code. Reproducible builds (`http://reproducible-builds.org`) are cited in frameworks such as SLSA, specifically in their highest level of maturity and rigor, SLSA Level 4 (`http://slsa.dev/spec/faq`). We'll discuss reproducible builds in the following sections, but it is worth stressing that it is a mature implementation likely to be adopted by major software producers initially and, as noted by the SolarWinds CISO, not a cheap or light undertaking.

Landmark Case 2: Log4j

While the SolarWinds cyberattack was specific to a software vendor, the Log4j incident is much different in the sense that it targeted a widely used piece of open source software (OSS). The Log4j incident began receiving public attention on December 9, 2021, when security researchers discovered a flaw in the popular software library Log4j. Log4j is a Java-based logging utility that is part of the Apache Logging Services, a project of the Apache Software Foundation. Log4j, at the time, was primarily used for logging information related to debugging and other activities to help developers. At the time of the incident, Log4j was estimated to be present in over 100 million environments and applications.

On December 10, 2021, NIST's National Vulnerability Database (NVD) categorized the Log4j vulnerability as a 10.0 on their Common Vulnerability Scoring System (CVSS) and associated it with Common Vulnerability and Exposures (CVE) CVE-2021-44228. There were also subsequent CVEs published associated with Log4j that included not just remote code execution vulnerabilities, but denial-of-service CVEs as well.

Soon after the publication of the zero-day vulnerability, the Computer Emergency Response Team (CERT) of New Zealand warned that it was already being exploited in the wild (`http://cert.govt.nz/it-specialists/advisories/log4j-rce-0-day-actively-exploited`). Following this, the CISA issued an emergency directive (`http://cisa.gov/news/2021/12/17/cisa-issues-emergency-directive-requiring-federal-agencies-mitigate-apache-log4j`) requiring federal agencies to mitigate Apache Log4j vulnerabilities. Soon after, on December 22, 2021, the CISA, FBI, NSA, and international partners issued a joint advisory (`http://cisa.gov/news/2021/12/22/cisa-fbi-nsa-and-international-partners-issue-advisory-mitigate-apache-log4j`) to mitigate the Apache Log4j vulnerability. This joint advisory was issued in response to the active worldwide exploitation of the Log4j vulnerabilities. CISA Director Jen Easterly called the Log4j vulnerability a severe and ongoing threat to organizations and governments around the world, and partner nation leaders echoed similar sentiments. You can view the Log4j incident timeline in Figure 1.6 (`http://unit42.paloaltonetworks.com/apache-log4j-vulnerability-cve-2021-44228`).

Unlike SolarWinds, which affected a specific product family from a specific vendor, Log4j's impact was much more diverse and distributed. Log4j was in use across everything from developer tooling, cloud service offerings, and security vendor products. As we will discuss in the cloud-focused chapter of the book, the largest cloud service providers (CSPs), such as Amazon Web Services (AWS), Microsoft Azure, and Google Cloud, all issued guidance around Log4j because it was used in many of their cloud service offerings at the time of the incident. This, of course, can have a downstream impact on not just customers directly consuming the cloud services, but also on other organizations building on top

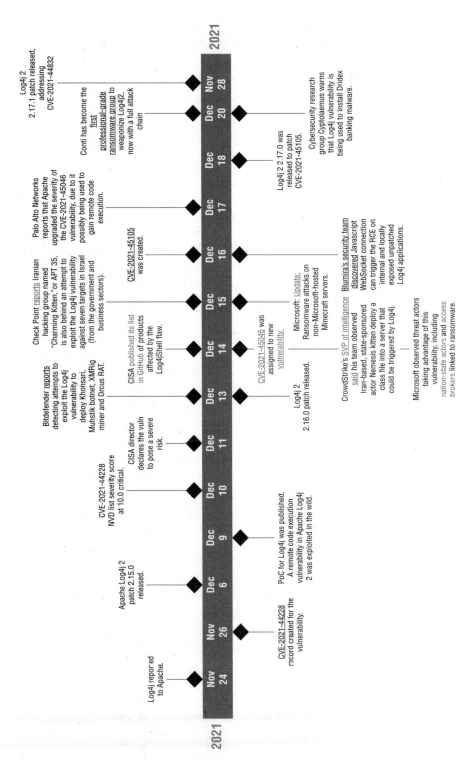

Figure 1.6

of the CSP's infrastructure and services which emphasized not only the impact of a vulnerable software component but also the cascading impact it can have due to service providers in the software supply chain.

In addition to the insight provided from GAO and others, the Cybersecurity Safety Review Board (CSRB) took aim at Log4j as their first cyber incident to investigate and report on (`http://cisa.gov/sites/default/files/publications/CSRB-Report-on-Log4-July-11-2022_508.pdf`). The CSRB was established pursuant to the cybersecurity Executive Order (EO) "Improving the Nation's Cybersecurity" (`http://cisa.gov/sites/default/files/publications/Cyber%20Safety%20Review%20Board%20Charter_508%20Compliant.pdf`). The CSRB was also established to be similar to the National Transportation Safety Board (NTSB) in the sense that its goal is to review major cyber events and make concrete recommendations to drive improvements across both the public and private sectors. The board's makeup consists of both public and private sector leaders of varying unique expertise. Their first report, which, as noted earlier, focused on Log4j, makes significant mention of the need for software transparency, inventory, and governance, with software bills of materials (SBOMs) a core component of that pursuit. The report calls for organizations to make use of SBOMs to improve accurate IT asset and application inventory, and for organizations such as the Office of Management and Budget (OMB), Office of the National Cyber Director (ONCD), and CISA to provide guidance for effectively using SBOMs as the ecosystem matures. The report mentions SBOM 18 times, calling for both adoption and increased investment in the area of SBOM and software transparency for public and private sector organizations.

CSRB's Log4j report is comprehensive and breaks their recommendations into four categories. Those include addressing the continued risks of Log4j, driving existing best practices for security hygiene, building a better software ecosystem, and making future investments. The report acknowledges that organizations will be wrestling with Log4j vulnerabilities for years to come and should continue to report and observe for Log4j exploitation. The report calls for organizations to invest in their capability to identify vulnerable systems, establish vulnerability response programs, and continue to develop accurate IT and application inventories, which is where SBOMs play a part in the context of software components and OSS consumption. Organizations with robust inventories of software components in their enterprise will be better positioned to respond to the next Log4j-type incident knowing if and where their organization is vulnerable. The report calls on OSS developers to participate in community-based security initiatives and to invest in training developers in secure software development, which is a key recommendation in the OpenSSF OSS Security Mobilization Plan, which we will discuss later in this book. It also calls for improvements in SBOM tooling and adoption and investments in OSS maintenance support for critical services. Lastly, the report also calls for making investments in key areas such as baseline requirements for software transparency for federal government vendors, exploring a cyber safety reporting system (CSRS), and studying incentive structures to build secure software. All these recommendations align with recommendations made by other leading organizations in both the public and private sector, such as NIST, the Linux Foundation, OpenSSF, and many others.

In a nod to the pervasiveness of the threat of vulnerable compromised OSS components, such as Log4j in this case, the FBI and CISA issued a Joint Cybersecurity Advisory as late as November 2022 announcing that a U.S. Federal Civilian Executive Branch (FCEB) agency had experienced an Iranian government-sponsored attack. The malicious actors exploited a Log4Shell vulnerability in an unpatched VMware Horizon server, installing cryptomining software and even moving laterally to a domain controller (DC) and compromising credentials to implement reverse proxies to maintain persistence in the environment (www .cisa.gov/uscert/sites/default/files/publications/aa22-320a_joint_ csa_iranian_government-sponsored_apt_actors_compromise_federal%20 network_deploy_crypto%20miner_credential_harvester.pdf).

Landmark Case 3: Kaseya

Another very prominent software supply chain attack worth discussing is the Kaseya ransomware attack. Kaseya (http://kaseya.com) is a unified IT management and security software firm that looks specifically to help managed service providers (MSPs) and IT teams. Their solutions are designed to help teams improve in the areas of IT security, efficiency, and service delivery.

The Kaseya ransomware attack occurred in July 2021 and is estimated to have impacted 2,000 organizations. It has been attributed to the REvil ransomware group, a Russian-speaking group of malicious actors, primarily. Individuals with the REvil group have been tied to attacks such as Kaseya but also other attacks against U.S.-based businesses and even government entities.

Kaseya offers both on-premises and software-as-a-service (SaaS)-based software solutions to customers. On July 2, 2021, the organization's incident response (IR) team detected a potential security incident with their remote management software named Kaseya VSA. The initial investigation warranted enough concern that the organization advised all their on-premises customers to shut down VSA servers until further notice, and they shut down their own SaaS-based offering as well (http://helpdesk.kaseya.com/hc/en-gb/articles/4403440684689). Kaseya advised customers that the shutdown was critical because the attackers were removing administrative access from VSA during their initial attacks.

Kaseya then engaged the external authorities and expertise of the FBI and CISA to collaborate on the IR activities. Kaseya quickly provided tools to help organizations determine if they were impacted by trying to detect the compromise. While organizations like CISA and the FBI were engaging with Kaseya, they also started to provide guidance to potentially impacted customers (`http://cisa.gov/uscert/ncas/current-activity/2021/07/04/cisa-fbi-guidance-msps-and-their-customers-affected-kaseya-vsa`). Their guidance included activities such as using the provided detection tool from Kaseya, bolstering authentication processes, and minimizing networking communications to known trusted IP addresses.

In the meantime, Kaseya began testing patches to resolve the issues and putting other mitigating security controls in place. They also published guidance for customers to try to prepare them for the upcoming patch activities (`http://helpdesk.kaseya.com/hc/en-gb/articles/4403709150993`).

During this process on July 8, 2021, the White House made official statements attributing the attack to Russia. U.S. government leadership echoed statements promising to hold Russia accountable for the attack. While Kaseya was diligent in their efforts to resolve the issue for customers, both on-premises and in the cloud, claims began to surface that the executives at the organization had previously been warned about their software's flaws over a several-year window (`http://krebsonsecurity.com/2021/07/kaseya-left-customer-portal-vulnerable-to-2015-flaw-in-its-own-software`). What made the incident more interesting is that the CVE involved, CVE-2015-2862, belonged to Kaseya themselves.

While the attack itself was said to have only impacted 0.1 percent of the organization's over-40,000 customers, according to comments from the organization's CEO, Fred Voccola, that percentage still equated to between 800 and 1,500 small to mid-sized organizations that were affected through their MSPs who were using Kaseya software. This trickle-down cascading impact is a perfect example of the complexity of the modern software supply chain and how the impact on a single piece of software can affect thousands of downstream consumers. Most of these consumers have no insight into the software their MSP uses to deliver services to them because the software supply chain is opaque, particularly when dealing with external service providers such as MSPs and CSPs. Downstream consumers are only aware of the services or software they directly consume from their providers use in the process of delivery.

It is worth noting, going back to the comments made by the White House regarding holding those responsible accountable, that arrests have been made. The U.S. Department of Justice (DOJ) announced in November 2021 (`http://justice.gov/opa/pr/ukrainian-arrested-and-charged-ransomware-attack-kaseya`) that Russia's domestic security agency arrested 14 individuals associated with the REvil ransomware group. This also included seizing $6.1 million associated with the group's various ransomware exploits. The DOJ leadership also emphasized that they would continue to target individuals who are focusing on victims in the United States.

What Can We Learn from These Cases?

The most important takeaway from these cases is that focus on traditional "last-mile" defenses like hashing and code signing is simply not enough and may project a false sense of security. The most successful attacks happen upstream of these processes, and signing malicious code might create more harm than not signing it at all.

Second, just like traditional network defense, establishing baselines of what "normal" looks like creates a standard reference for anomaly detection. This includes both the production of many software bills of material artifacts, as well as metadata about those artifacts like hashes and code signing. Though not definitive (and this may seem to contradict the previous paragraph), these are still valid techniques, but they must be performed early in the process and be validated and revalidated at every step in the process.

In addition to these static artifacts, understanding code execution flows and network behaviors for software can be valuable in identifying malicious functionality. For instance, in the case of SolarWinds, it was a behavioral change, not necessarily anything identified in a code review, that illuminated the compromise.

Secure software development is a process with many stages and many opportunities for compromise. While the concepts of zero-trust architecture were designed for identity and resource access, such as application access control, the core tenets are no less applicable to secure software development. As a reminder of the core tenets of zero trust, these include:

- Users and identity
- Device
- Network and environment
- Application workloads
- Software supply chain
- Data

Secure software requires a multidisciplinary approach throughout the life cycle. And while a technique like a software bill of materials is one tool in the toolbelt, it would not have prevented sophisticated attacks such as SolarWinds. There is no "one size fits all" security widget that will address these issues, and it requires a transformative change in how we develop software today and how we manage trust at all phases of the software development process and across our software supply chain. Organizations shipping code are responsible for all the code they ship, not just the code they write, and this means that validation of upstream inputs are just as, if not more, important than software produced by their own development teams.

Summary

In this chapter we discussed the background of software supply chain threats and some of the relevant incentives for attackers. We also discussed the potential anatomy of a software supply chain attack. We covered the fundamentals of Threat Modeling and the role it can play in preventing software supply chain attacks. Lastly, we discussed some of the landmark software supply chain attacks that have impacted various entities such as proprietary software vendors, OSS components and managed service providers (MSP)s.

CHAPTER 2

Existing Approaches—Traditional Vendor Risk Management

Traditional approaches to vendor risk management have been historically used to understand secure software development practices for software and product suppliers. The idea is that asking the vendor to answer a set of questions about how they approach certain security controls may be the only way to determine whether they understand what they should be doing, if they have a documented process to do it, and if they are doing what they say. It is accomplished by asking for additional evidence, indicating what they are doing. But first, let's unpack this a bit and examine the efficacy of this approach.

Assessments

To begin, these assessments suffer from a major scalability challenge. How can the enterprise conduct hundreds, if not thousands, of these assessments each year to support their risk management program? The most common answer is to leverage a standard questionnaire that they can send to all their suppliers, asking them all the same questions in order to benchmark their suppliers against each other. But which questions are good ones to ask? How many questions are enough or too much? Are all the suppliers evaluated the same way? How can we gain the context needed to ask good questions? How can we process all the questionnaires effectively? This is definitely a lot of work! It is cumbersome for not only the software consumers but also the software providers, as they must field several requests from their consumers and customers, especially if they are a large organization working with many customers.

Second, once you have established a process and a means of execution, which might be performed in house or outsourced to an assessment provider, obtaining cooperation from a vendor can be quite tricky. Typically, this assessment work is most effectively performed just before a renewal or is based on contract provisions that require the vendor to comply. These assessments are expensive for them to perform as well, and they may not be incentivized to share freely. For instance, if your contract requires them to share the results of a vulnerability in their software but also requires that they fix these vulnerabilities quickly, you might be asking them to voluntarily engage in activities that are not in their best interest from a cost standpoint.

Lastly, what is considered to be acceptable evidence? A screenshot of that one instance when they performed the required activity? This is nothing but a snapshot-in-time of a specific configuration or activity, not an assurance of it occurring in an ongoing and consistent fashion. How about a log of activities? How can you be sure that log has not been fabricated, or that the screenshot is representative of a recurring process across their entire environment? Evidence of a policy is great, but how do you know if it's being consistently enforced? These assessments are frequently conducted by risk teams without collaboration from security practitioners who can help to validate these results or even understand what the company is being told about that supplier's practices. For these reasons, many security practitioners have panned the idea of traditional risk assessments as being low-value, compliance activities. Certainly, there are exceptions to this, but in many cases this traditional method of risk assessment is not sufficient for a holistic risk management approach without additional rigor.

It also presents challenges on the consumer side as well. If you're an enterprise consuming software and services from external vendors, your organization and team have only so much bandwidth to field so many assessments, associated artifacts, and engagements with the vendors in a given time frame (such as a month or a year). In our experience, teams are often adding exponential numbers of software, vendors, and services to a typical organization, which outweighs the team's ability to properly field or govern them. This often leads to what is referred to as *shadow IT*, or simply ungoverned software in enterprise environments. There are also challenges with standardized assessments in the traditional sense, due to factors such as the subjectivity of the professionals performing the assessment and their occasional lack of knowledge of the technology and software being assessed. This isn't to say professional assessment and insight isn't and won't always be valuable. But there are also innovations in software transparency, automation, visibility, and artifacts that can lead to higher assurances of the security of a specific software or the vendor and their associated practices that create it.

Typically, the traditional vendor assessment process is done via self-attestation or with a third-party assessment organization, each of which presents its own challenges and drawbacks. Self-attestation leaves it up to the vendor to attest to their compliance with specific requirements, which is slippery when revenue and contracts are involved and opens the door to their subjective interpretation, which, of course, tends to fall toward a positive interpretation when they are assessing themselves. One notable example is the Defense Industrial Base (DIB) in the Department of Defense (DoD), which requires contractors to self-attest to their compliance with NIST 800-171 requirements and controls. Several reports have revealed significant gaps in self-attested scores, which were inflated and drew a stark contrast to the scores when assessed by a third party. This self-attestation method has also been called into question as several U.S. federal defense contractors experienced security breaches that could have been prevented or at least mitigated if the security controls that were claimed to have been implemented were in place and operating as intended. This reality has led to the creation of the DoD's Cybersecurity Maturity Model Certification (CMMC) framework, which requires a third-party assessment of compliance.

On the other side of self-assessment is the use of third-party assessment organizations (3PAOs), who are independent third parties that perform initial and periodic assessments of an entity's compliance with a specific framework or set of requirements. One example is the U.S. federal government's Federal Risk and Authorization Management Program (FedRAMP), which helps authorize cloud service providers (CSPs) for use across the federal government. Although this approach provides a higher level of assurance than self-assessment, it is also very tedious, expensive, and time-consuming.

To put that in perspective, FedRAMP has existed for a decade, and there are fewer than 300 cloud service offerings authorized in the FedRAMP marketplace as of this writing, despite there being tens of thousands of cloud service offerings available for consumption in the commercial market. This paradigm leads to potentially higher levels of assurance at the expense of significantly decreased access to innovative solutions and providers due to the time and cost that the 3PAO approach imposes on vendors and the market, making it either too expensive and cumbersome for some smaller firms or not justifiable by others. These methods simply have scale challenges or can impose burdensome costs, particularly on smaller firms without the revenue and budget to support the assessment process and requirements.

This traditional questionnaire-based process is cumbersome, time-consuming, and expensive. Worse than that, it is also rife with risk, as consumers are gaining assurances from momentary evidence, based on subjective assessment and frequently self-attestation by the software or service provider who's incentivized to give a positive perception of their firm and products because revenue and contracts are often at stake. The traditional vendor risk management practice is typically driven by manual, paper-based activities that are subjective and tedious. With the shift toward software transparency, we are now seeing evidence-based assessments that can look at a vendor's software and its associated components to determine its risk posture, which is a more valid attestation of secure development practices than verbal communication and forms-based questionnaires. We are also seeing innovative solutions in the market, especially with the cloud and declarative infrastructure and applications that allow for near-real-time compliance assessments, utilizing APIs and automation that provide higher assurances of compliance while shifting away from the manual forms-based process that has plagued the industry for decades. That said, we also recognize that not all security controls can be automated or are technical in nature, and they will always require professional insight and assessment accompanied by human interaction.

SDL Assessments

Software development life cycle (SDL) assessments can be a more focused approach to understanding the supplier's processes. In addition, the framework may be like a traditional vendor risk assessment, but these are typically more focused activities performed by a qualified application security consultant. Generally, these assessments are aligned with a documented process and may be informed by a defined SDL such as the Microsoft SDL. This allows the consultant to map the supplier's process to establish best practices in order to determine if the recommended activities are defined and understood, and most important, to verify that is implemented in a consistent way.

One issue, especially for large product suppliers, is that inconsistencies in process across product teams can be common. For instance, one large original equipment manufacturer (OEM) creates a different legal entity for every product line they bring to market, which has accounted for 10–20 different organizations where each entity had different processes and, due to different legal constructs, inconsistencies in contractual requirements for security provisions. If you were to assess the SDL of one of those 20 entities, it would be easy to apply the results of that assessment to every other product you bought from them. But doing so would be inaccurate and may drive wrong assumptions and harmful risk decisions.

This is one of the values of using frameworks such as Supply Chain Levels for Software Artifacts (SLSA), which we'll describe later in this book. SLSA takes a very SDL-like view of the threat landscape to identify where the likely weak points are—the interaction points—the external trust points that must be validated, as they have the potential to negatively impact your SDL.

Application Security Maturity Models

Like SDL assessments, looking at models such as the Building Security in Maturity Model (BSIMM) or the Software Assurance Maturity Model (SAMM) can be very effective ways to document the maturity of a supplier's software program. The SDL is part of this, of course, but it might be helpful to look at one of these models, such as the OWASP SAMM, also known as OpenSAMM in prior versions (`https://owasp.org/www-project-samm`).

BSIMM is also widely used, but as it is a proprietary model, we prefer to examine open-source approaches. SAMM defines the domains shown in Figure 2.1.

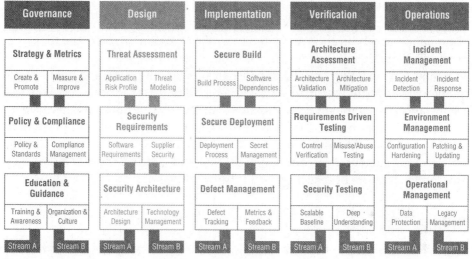

Figure 2.1

Source: OWASP SAMM v2 Model (`https://owasp.org/www-project-samm`), CC BY 4.0

SAMM defines five business functions, as depicted in Figure 2.1: Governance, Design, Implementation, Verification, and Operations. Within those business functions there are three security practices. Each security practice involves two streams of activities that complement and build on one another. Because SAMM is an open model, it can be used internally to assess an organization or be used externally by a third party. It is worth noting that the NIST Secure Software Development Framework (SSDF) guidance—which we discuss in Chapter 7, "Existing and Emerging Commercial Guidance," and is required of software vendors selling to the U.S. government—makes frequent use of SAMM, cross-referencing it in the SSDF practices and associated tasks.

Like all OWASP projects, SAMM is a community-driven effort and aims to be measurable, actionable, and versatile. Unlike BSIMM, SAMM is prescriptive, meaning that it prescribes specific actions and practices organizations can take to improve their software assurance. SAMM is, as the name states, a maturity model. It ranges from levels 1 to 3 across the security practices it specifies, with an implicit starting point of 0. While SAMM is a maturity model, it does not state that all organizations must achieve the highest level of maturity across all practices. Maturity requirements and goals depend on the organization's resources, compliance requirements, resources, and mission sets. Let's dive into some of the business functions and associated security practices within SAMM.

Governance

The first business function is Governance, which is focused on the processes and activities related to how an organization manages their software development activities. The practices involved include Strategy and Metrics, Policy and Compliance, and Education and Guidance. This function involves creating and promoting strategies and metrics, and then measuring and improving them over time. On the Policy and Compliance front, it involves creating policies and standards, and then managing their implementation and adherence across the organization. Underneath Education and Guidance, you have streams such as Training and Awareness and Organization and Culture. Training and Awareness focuses on organizations improving knowledge about software security with their various stakeholders, and Organization and Culture is oriented around promoting a culture of security within the organization.

Design

The second business function is Design, which focuses on processes and activities for how organizations create and design software. The security practices include Threat Assessment, Security Requirements, and Security Architecture. Threat Assessment focuses on streams such as application risk profiling and threat modeling. As part of profiling, an organization determines which applications pose serious threats to the organization if compromised, and threat modeling, as we have discussed elsewhere, is helping teams understand what is being built, what can go wrong, and how to mitigate those risks. Security Requirements involves requirements for how software is built and protected, as well as the requirements for relevant supplier organizations that may be involved in the development context of an organization's applications, such as outsourced developers. Security Architecture deals with the various components and technologies involved in the architecture design of a firm's software. It includes the architecture design to ensure secure design as well as technology management, which involves understanding the risks associated with the various technologies, frameworks, tools, and integrations that the applications use.

Implementation

The third business function is Implementation, which involves how an organization builds and deploys software components and may include defects as well. The security practices involved are as follows:

- Secure Build, which is using consistently repeatable build processes and accounting of dependencies
- Secure Deployment, which increases the security of software deployments to production
- Defect Management, which involves managing security defects of deployed software

The streams within the secure build practice are build process and software dependencies. The build process ensures that you are deploying predictable, repeatable secure build processes. Software dependencies focus on external libraries and ensures that their security posture matches the organizational requirements and risk tolerance. The secure deployment security practice focuses on the final stages of delivering software to production environments and ensuring its integrity and security during that process. The streams associated with this practice are the deployment process and secrets management. The deployment process ensures that organizations have a repeatable and consistent deployment process to push software artifacts to production as well as the requisite test environments.

Secrets management is focused on the proper handling of sensitive data, such as credentials, API keys, and other secrets, which can be abused by malicious actors to compromise environments and systems involved in software development. The last security practice in this business function is Defect Management, which focuses on collecting, recording, and analyzing software security defects to make data-driven decisions. The streams involved include defect tracking and metrics, in addition to feedback. Both involve managing the collection and follow-up of defects, as well as driving the improvement of security through these activities.

Verification

The Verification business function involves the processes and activities for how organizations check and test artifacts throughout software development. The security practices associated with verification are Architecture Assessment, Requirements-Driven Testing, and Security Testing. Architecture Assessment validates the security and compliance for the software and supporting architecture, whereas requirements and security testing are based on items such as user stories to detect and resolve the security issues through automation.

Architecture Assessment has streams involved that include both validation and mitigation, which means validating the provision of security objectives and requirements in the supporting architecture and mitigating the identified threats in the existing architecture. The testing streams under these practices ensure that organizations are performing activities such as misuse/abuse testing to use methods like fuzzing, which is a software testing method that can inject invalid or malformed inputs to reveal software defects or to identify functionality that can be abused to attack an application. Security Testing involves both a broad baseline of automated testing and a deep understanding that involves manual testing for high-risk components and complex attack vectors that automated testing cannot complete.

Operations

The Operations business function ensures the confidentiality, integrity, and availability (CIA) of applications and that their associated data is maintained throughout their life cycles, including in runtime environments. Security practices include Incident Management, Environment Management, and Operational Management. Going further, streams encompass various areas, such as incident detection and response, as well as configuration hardening and patching. Lastly, Operational Management ensures that data protection occurs throughout the life cycle of creation, handling, storage, and processing, and that legacy management to ensure end-of-life services and software is no longer actively deployed or supported. This reduces an organization's attack surface and removes potentially vulnerable components from its systems and applications.

By utilizing SAMM and covering the various business functions, security practices, and streams, organizations can gain more assurance for their application security maturity—the same goes for their software consumers.

Application Security Assurance

Traditionally, application security practices have focused on the concept of application testing, which we refer to here as application security assurance. This is where application security moves beyond softer topics, such as governance and process, and seeks to answer the question regarding the technical risk of the application. There are five primary approaches with several techniques used that we cover here:

- Static application security testing (SAST)
- Dynamic application security testing (DAST)
- Interactive application security testing (IAST)
- Mobile application security testing (MAST)
- Software composition analysis (SCA)

Static Application Security Testing

The concept of performing a code review, which may be familiar to those engaged in application security practices, is a static, point-in-time view of the source used for the application or software component in question. Frequently, exhaustive static application security testing (SAST) is performed at certain milestones such as a major release or architectural change, while the code review performed on an ongoing basis is limited to the new code written or updated in the code base.

SAST can be performed using manual or automated means, and large software projects can suffer from scalability issues, especially for manual review. It can also become quite confusing for the tester, as some application frameworks may reuse filenames in different paths of the application. Even for manual code review, frequently testers will follow a prioritization process looking for known vulnerable functions or high-trust areas of the application, such as authentication and access, password management, data encryption, and more. The challenge here is that often-important functions such as input validation routines may not always be captured in these reviews, and the results are highly subject to the skill of the tester and the time scoped for the test.

Likewise, automated testing can help with completeness of the test and handling such a large scope with speed, but out of all the testing methods we discuss, SAST suffers from the highest false positive rates. Even the best SAST tools are typically in the 5 percent or higher false positive range, which does not sound like much until you realize that a large application will identify thousands of bugs. That said, innovations are possible, leveraging technologies such as machine learning (ML), which can build on prior audit activities and lead to higher fidelity findings. (A false positive occurs when a finding is identified based on the ruleset, despite the finding not actually posing a risk to the system. These can lead to wasted time by teams analyzing findings from the rulesets that didn't pose actual risks to the systems but that were triggered based on the tooling and rules being used.) This, too, is a common criticism of the software bill of materials (SBOM) as a means of vulnerability detection. False positives create noise, damage the credibility of the application security program, and may create conditions that delay software releases or reprioritize security efforts in the wrong areas for no perceptible value. This cognitive drain can be demoralizing to a team and may impede software delivery velocity.

Regardless of the issues presented, SAST remains a highly used and valuable means of identifying software defects, security, and quality alike at the source-code level. It is also one of the best ways to help developers understand where they are writing insecure code. Many modern integrated development environments (IDEs) such as Eclipse and others have plug-ins for SAST tools that provide instant developer feedback when they are using insecure conventions or otherwise making questionable code quality choices. Additionally, many secure coding training platforms use insecure code snippet examples to train developers to write more secure code.

One of the most useful ways to leverage SAST within your software transparency efforts, though, is to help validate and improve your SBOMs and identify where large libraries are used, but only a subset of functionality is required. It is quite common that a library with 100 or more functions is imported, but fewer than 10 are ever called by your software, which creates a scenario also prone to false positives since the SBOM may identify vulnerabilities that are impossible to exploit. If you could strip out the unnecessary code, it would reduce a lot of the noise. Just do not forget to rename your library when you have made modifications, because SBOM tools will erroneously identify things based on library name and version.

Dynamic Application Security Testing

While SAST looks at applications inside out via their source code, dynamic application security testing (DAST) tests from the outside in, via HTTP and other web-based protocols. It should also be noted that DAST is typically constrained to web applications and often cannot be used on desktop, mobile, or other application types that do not listen and respond to HTTP. This testing class is focused on interacting directly with a running application or component of that application such as an API or listening service. The challenge here, of course, is that DAST cannot be performed until the application is in a state where it is operational enough for testing, and hence, happens much later in the process than SAST. A key advantage is that it has much lower false positive rates but consequently much higher false negative rates. (A false negative is when the test misses a valid security concern, which is also undesirable.)

Typically, the way this works is a scanner is configured to interact with the application programmatically, for instance, via a scripted browser emulation interface such as Selenium WebDriver. The scanner first navigates the web application, identifying all the paths other than those the tester removes from scope, following any links on those pages, and ignoring other web domains that are out of scope for testing. This also often can be referred to as a *web crawler* or *spider*. If authentication is required, this can be configured as well as how to handle specific web forms in the application.

After the spider is completed, the DAST tool builds a list of available paths for testing and uses a preconfigured list of tests to search for defects such as SQL injection, cross-site scripting, and more. Once it identifies the potential risk and captures the evidence that leads the tool to suspect the issue is valid, it returns those results to the tester in the form of a scanner report. Automated DAST testing typically requires little testing skill and interaction, but it does provide good visibility into how the application works. In some cases, this visibility may be very useful when constructing web application firewall rules and understanding the application's attack surface.

More sophisticated DAST scenarios usually involve the concept of interception proxies, which is where the tester configures a web proxy in their browser that intercepts their HTTP requests and responses to manipulate them to abuse the application. While this is typically a manual effort, starting with the application sitemap provides the tester with their scope for testing, and most of these tools do provide some level of automation natively or through plug-ins such as used by the Burp Suite or Zed Attack Proxy family of tools.

HYBRID ANALYSIS MAPPING (HAM)

Some techniques have emerged using the best of both worlds in SAST and DAST and have combined these results for a hybrid static-dynamic testing result. The idea is that SAST performs the best coverage of the software and identifies potential issues, and then DAST runs, exhaustively scanning the application's attack surface, looking for vulnerabilities that correlate to SAST findings. This is highly effective for prioritizing vulnerabilities with the greatest degree of confidence, but the SAST findings that are left over from this matching still must be validated.

As it applies to the topic of software supply chain security, it is advisable to return to the threat models for your application and consider how it might be abused. For instance, if your application is calling an external script, could a domain takeover of that external domain inject malicious code into your user's session? Interception proxies provide excellent capabilities for manipulating and redirecting traffic in such a way as to model these scenarios. What if the application performs component updates? The scenarios here are endless, and by empowering your testing teams with flexible tools to be creative and embrace their evil side, you can expand your understanding of potential risks.

Another point worth emphasizing when it comes to DAST is the potential ability to identify third-party client-side dependencies and their known vulnerabilities. One example is a web application where the library is included in the application using a script tag and not via a package manager such as npm. Most SBOM tooling would miss this insight and context, whereas DAST tooling may be able to identify it.

Interactive Application Security Testing

Another form of testing, interactive application security testing (IAST), uses application instrumentation within the runtime or uses a software development kit (SDK) to direct itself into the running application to follow code flows, to see how data moves throughout the application, and as claimed by IAST vendors, to produce a much more real-world view of how the application is functioning that is much more accurate than those produced by other testing methods. In some cases, using IAST is as simple as installing a software agent on the application server hosting the application, but it is not usually supported for all languages and frameworks.

This technology is also at the core of a new breed of protection mechanisms known as runtime application self-protection (RASP), which has emerged in the last decade as an alternative or at least a complementary approach to web application firewalls (WAFs). Because RASP understands what is happening inside the application, it will not be fooled by WAF bypass-style attacks or signature mutations the way a WAF can. However, because it does not see the native web traffic, RASP cannot mitigate the noisier attacks before they impact the web application.

In fact, research by IAST vendors such as Contrast Security has shown that much of the software we think creates risk for us is never called by our code. Most open-source components may only use 10–20 percent of their functionality. Additionally, as the topic of SaaSBOM (a BOM that captures services), APIs, data flows, and so forth, IAST may be one of the most viable ways to capture this information. This is an area unsupported by SBOM tool vendors at this time, but it will be interesting to see the role that IAST plays as the software transparency market matures over the next few years.

Mobile Application Security Testing

With the proliferation of mobile devices and their associated applications, another form of testing has become common in the industry. This is referred to as mobile application security testing (MAST). MAST involves using static and dynamic testing methods to identify security vulnerabilities and flaws associated with mobile applications, platforms, and devices such as Android and iOS. This testing can help identify dangerous functionality, excessive permissions, and vulnerabilities that can be exploited on mobile devices by malicious actors. With the evolution of the concept of an SBOM, we are now seeing innovative solutions in the mobile devices space for SBOMs, such as NowSecure, which can generate SBOMs from running applications, including their application library dependencies, OS-level dependencies, and services the application is communicating with (www.nowsecure.com/press-releases/nowsecure-announces-the-worlds-first-dynamic-software-bill-of-materials-sbom-for-mobile-apps).

Software Composition Analysis

Another common application assurance methodology and tooling category is software composition analysis (SCA). In short, SCA helps identify open-source software (OSS) and associated dependencies in a codebase. Organizations have begun making extensive use of OSS components and libraries. SCA can help evaluate the security, license compliance, and code quality of an application. Some SCA tools provide support for producing an SBOM to help provide a detailed inventory of the components and dependencies that make up the application. As we will discuss in Chapter 10, "Practical Guidance for Suppliers," understanding what OSS components are in an application or product and the related licensing and vulnerability information is critical. Industry practitioners often also recommend using SCA tooling earlier in the SDLC to identify and mitigate vulnerabilities during software development to prevent passing these vulnerabilities downstream to application users or needing to rectify them later in the SDLC, when it may be more costly and disruptive to do so. We will touch on this in Chapter 6, "Cloud and Containerization," when we discuss the push for DevSecOps.

Hashing and Code Signing

The use of cryptographic verification has roots going back decades, through algorithms such as MD5 and SHA-256 to construct a one-way hash. The idea is that because this is not a reversible encryption, it cannot be manipulated, and because a hash should theoretically be unique, it can be used to represent the integrity of a file. If an attacker modified the software and the resultant hash of that file that you calculate does not match the hash that the software supplier provided, you are safe. But what if the attacker also replaced that hash when they replaced the software? Is it calculated or stored out of band in any way? If the answer is no, it may be difficult to be sure that the hash is legitimate. Furthermore, tools such as monomorph (`https://github.com/DavidBuchanan314/monomorph`) allow for the creation of what is known as a *hash collision*, where two different files can derive the same hash, invalidating its uniqueness. Therefore, MD5 has not been considered forensically sound for quite some time. Stronger hashing mechanisms such as SHA-256 and others are better, but they still suffer from trust issues.

Additionally, the process of calculating the hash separately is not very operationally efficient. Consider the following eight-step process:

1. Identify the file to be downloaded.
2. Download the file.
3. Identify where the hash is stored.
4. Download the hash file.
5. Determine the hashing method.
6. Download and install the hash calculation tool if not already installed.
7. Run the file through the hashing tool.
8. Compare the output with the hash of the file.

Alternatively, some tools exist that make this process easier, but you still need the origin files to process. Some vendors have started performing hash validation inside their software update mechanisms, but it's hard to know what they are doing here and if it is effective.

Hashing, though, is useful for more than validating the integrity of a download. It is useful to ensure the validity of elements in a software bill of materials, to look up component hashes in malware databases, and to understand if the attestation you are looking at actually matches the attestation you think you are. Many reverse engineering tools will even create hashes of blocks of code or function-level hashing to uniquely identify functions, referred to as function IDs (FIDs) in some tools.

Hashes, however, can be extremely fragile because two exact files can match in every way and result in a different hash, depending on how that hash was generated or when that hash was generated in the process.

Some typical scenarios include hashing a component as part of the build, as opposed to the component as represented in source code. Optimizations in code such as stripping symbols or special characters may result in software that is functionally identical but that hashes differently. Even hashes created on Windows versus Linux can vary, depending on how you are handling end-of-line characters in the creation of the hash.

One technique that has emerged in forensic science is that of hash similarity, or the use of a distance algorithm for hashing. Hash functions such as ssdeep and TLSH (`https://tlsh.org`) provide a means for identifying when two hashes are extremely similar and can be useful when trying to identify unique software components that are not necessarily identical but close enough to allow you to draw comparisons.

Similar to the idea of hashing is that of code signing, which is a technique where code or file objects can be cryptographically signed by a trusted entity to verify that they produced that artifact. This is done using public key cryptography, where the signer uses a private key proving their identity. Anyone can use the public key to validate the signature.

This is a very robust mechanism until you realize that anyone can obtain a code-signing certificate and if the verifier isn't also validating that the entity who signed the file is the same entity they were expecting to see, it may result in a false sense of security. In the context of public key cryptography, if a certificate authority is compromised, it could invalidate a signature or trust in the certificates issued. Lastly, we have seen several scenarios where signing crypto material has been stolen from legitimate software and embedded in malicious files, or where entities have been compromised and their private keys stolen. However, this risk can be mitigated to some extent if the use of a Time Stamp Authority (TSA) is required.

One technique that has emerged and that shows promise is chaining attestations by using signing. For instance, a large SBOM may require input from multiple stakeholders, or we may wish to link a build attestation with an SBOM. By signing these attestations, we create mechanisms where automated verification and linkage of multiple attestations can be performed, without a single entity needing to know all aspects of the SBOM.

One of the most recent innovative developments in the signing space is an effort known as Sigstore, which will be discussed in depth in subsequent chapters.

Summary

Throughout this chapter, we have discussed some of the historical context related to traditional vendor risk assessments, first- versus third-party attestation challenges, and application maturity models. We also discussed some of the common tooling and methodologies associated with application assurance and security measures to identify and facilitate mitigating vulnerabilities and flaws in applications. In the next chapter, we will do a deep dive into some of the industry approaches to vulnerability scoring, databases, and emerging improvements upon traditional vulnerability prioritizing methodologies.

Vulnerability Databases and Scoring Methodologies

One critical aspect of the conversation about application security and vulnerability management is the method by which vulnerabilities are categorized and scored. This is an important aspect of the push for software transparency and, more important, software security. Without understanding what software vulnerabilities are present and the way those vulnerabilities are scored, it is difficult for organizations to prioritize vulnerabilities for remediation. Software producers can prioritize vulnerabilities for remediation to reduce risk to their customers and inform their customers about the severity and exploitability of vulnerabilities in their products. Software consumers can understand the inherent risk of the software they are using and make risk-informed decisions about its consumption and use. So, first let's look at some of the common terms associated with software vulnerabilities.

Common Vulnerabilities and Exposures

Common Vulnerabilities and Exposures (CVE) is oriented around a program with the goal of identifying, defining, and cataloging publicly disclosed cybersecurity vulnerabilities impacting software or hardware. As an organization, CVE involves participation from international researchers and organizations who serve as partners to help discover and publish vulnerabilities, including descriptions of the vulnerabilities in a standardized format.

Origins of the CVE Program and concept can be traced back to a MITRE white paper in January 1999 titled "Towards a Common Enumeration of Vulnerabilities" by David Mann and Steven Christey (`https://cve.mitre.org/docs/docs-2000/cerias.html`). This white paper laid out the cybersecurity landscape at the time, which included several disparate vulnerability databases with unique formats, criteria, and taxonomies. The white paper's authors explained how this impacted interoperability and the sharing of vulnerability information. Among the roadblocks to interoperability, they cited inconsistent naming conventions, managing of similar information from diverse sources, and complexity of mapping between databases.

To facilitate interoperability between security software tools, the CVE was proposed as a standardized list to help enumerate all known vulnerabilities, assign standard unique names to vulnerabilities, and be open and shareable without restrictions.

This effort has grown to be an industry staple for over 20 years, with over 200 organizations from over 35 countries participating, and over 200,000 vulnerabilities represented by the CVE system. Participating organizations are referred to as CVE Numbering Authorities (CNAs; `www.cve.org/PartnerInformation/ListofPartners`). Examples of CNAs are software vendors, open-source software projects, bug-bounty service providers, and researchers. They are authorized by the CVE Program to assign unique CVE IDs to vulnerabilities and publish CVE records to the CVE list. Organizations can request to become a CNA but must meet specific requirements such as having a public vulnerability disclosure policy, having a public source for vulnerability disclosures, and agreeing to the CVE Terms of Use (`www.cve.org/Legal/TermsOfUse`).

In Chapter 1, "Background on Software Supply Chain Threats," we discussed the National Vulnerability Database (NVD), and although there is close collaboration between the NVD and CVE, they are distinct efforts. CVE originated with MITRE and is now a collaborative community-driven effort. The NVD, on the other hand, was launched by the National Institute of Standards and Technology (NIST). Both programs are sponsored by the U.S. Department of Homeland Security and the Cybersecurity Infrastructure Security Agency (CISA) and are available for free public use. Whereas CVE manifests as a set of records for vulnerabilities, including identification numbers, descriptions, and public references, the NVD is a database that synchronizes with the CVE list so that there's parity between disclosed CVEs and the NVD records. The NVD provides additional information such as remediations, severity scores, and impact ratings. The NVD also makes the CVEs searchable with advanced metadata and fields.

CVE consists of several working groups with distinct focus areas , including automation, strategic planning, coordination, and quality. These working groups strive to improve the overall CVE Program and enhance its value and quality for the community. In addition to working groups, CVE has a CVE Program Board to ensure the program meets the needs of the global cybersecurity and technology community (www.cve.org/Resources/Roles/Board/General/Board-Charter.pdf). This board oversees the program, steers its strategic direction, and evangelizes it in the community.

Some fundamental terms to understand as they relate to the CVE Program include the following:

- Vulnerabilities
- CVE identifier
- Scope
- CVE list
- CVE identifiers
- Scope CVE record

CVE defines vulnerabilities as flaws in software, firmware, or hardware that result from weaknesses that can be exploited and that have a negative impact on the confidentiality, integrity, and availability (CIA) triad of impacted components. CVE identifiers (CVE IDs) are unique alphanumeric identifiers assigned by the CVE Program to specific vulnerabilities that enable automation and common discussion of the vulnerabilities by multiple parties. Scopes are sets of hardware or software for which organizations within the CVE Program have distinct responsibility. The CVE list is the overarching catalog of CVE records that are identified by or reported to the CVE Program. A CVE record provides descriptive data about a vulnerability associated with a CVE ID and is provided by CNAs. CVE records can be reserved, published, or rejected. *Reserved* is the initial state when reserved by a CNA, *published* is when the CNA populated the data to become a CVE record, and *rejected* is when a CVE ID and record should no longer be used but remains on the CVE list for future reference of invalid CVE records.

CVE records undergo a defined life cycle as well. This life cycle includes the stages of discover, report, request, reserve, submit, and publish (see Figure 3.1). Initially, an individual organization discovers a new vulnerability, reports it to the CVE Program or participant, and requests a CVE ID that gets reserved while the CVE Program participant submits the associated details. Finally, that CVE record is published for public downloading and viewing to begin appropriate response activities, if warranted.

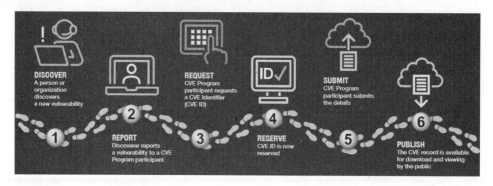

Figure 3.1
Source: The MITRE Corporation. `www.cve.org/About/Process`, last accessed March 27, 2023

The CVE Program and the list of CVE records has grown linearly since the program's inception. Looking at the published CVE Record Metrics (`www.cve.org/About/Metrics`), annual CVE records by quarter have grown from the hundreds to over 6,000 per quarter as of this writing. This is due to the growing popularity of the program, an increase in security researchers, an uptick in involvement by software vendors, and the overarching growth and visibility of cybersecurity.

National Vulnerability Database

Vulnerabilities help inform activities to drive down risk for both software producers and consumers, and provide broad industry knowledge of the vulnerabilities present in the ecosystem. While there are several vulnerability databases in the industry, one of the most notable examples, as mentioned in the previous section, is NIST's National Vulnerability Database (NVD; `https://nvd.nist.gov`). NVD is a comprehensive cybersecurity vulnerability database that integrates all publicly available U.S. government vulnerability resources and provides references to industry resources.

The NVD was officially formed in 2005 (`https://nvd.nist.gov/general/brief-history`). The origins of the NVD trace all the way back to 1999, with NVD's predecessor: the Internet Category of Attack Toolkit (ICAT). ICAT was developed as a database of attack scripts. ICAT originally involved students from the SANS Institute, who worked as analysts involved with the project. ICAT faced some funding challenges but was kept alive through efforts by SANS as well as employees of NIST. It grew to reach over 10,000 vulnerabilities before receiving some additional funding from the Department of Homeland Security (DHS) to create a vulnerability database that was rebranded as the NVD, as it's known today. As the project evolved, the NVD went on to adopt the popular vulnerability data and scoring still in use today, such as the Common Vulnerability Scoring System (CVSS) and Common Platform Enumeration (CPE; `https://nvd.nist.gov/products/cpe`).

As of this writing, the NVD contains over 200,000 vulnerabilities, and that number continues to grow as new vulnerabilities emerge. The NVD is used by professionals around the world interested in vulnerability data, as well vendors looking to correlate vulnerability findings and their details.

NVD facilitates this process by analyzing CVEs that have been published in the CVE Dictionary. By referencing the CVE Dictionary and performing additional analysis, the NVD staff produce important metadata about vulnerabilities, including CVSS scores, Common Weakness Enumeration (CWE) types, and applicability statements in the form of CPEs. It's worth noting that the NVD staff does not perform the vulnerability testing and uses insights and information from vendors and third-party security researchers to aid in the creation of the attributes. As current information emerges, the NVD often revises the metadata, such as the CVSS scores and CWE information.

NVD integrates information from the CVE Program, which is a dictionary of vulnerabilities that we'll discuss in the section "CPE," later in this chapter. The NVD assesses newly published CVEs after they are integrated into the NVD with a rigorous analysis process, which includes reviewing reference material for the CVE that encompasses publicly available information on the Internet. CVEs are assigned one or more CWE identifiers to help categorize the vulnerability, and the vulnerability is also assigned exploitability and impact metrics through the CVSS. Applicability statements are given through CPEs to ensure that specific versions of software, hardware, or systems are identified through these applicability statements. This helps organizations take the appropriate action, depending on whether the vulnerability impacts the specific hardware and software they are using. Once this initial analysis and assessment is performed, any assigned metadata such as CWEs, CVSSs, and CPEs are reviewed as a quality assurance method by a senior analyst before it is published on the NVD website and associated data feeds.

NVD offers a rich set of data feeds (`https://nvd.nist.gov/vuln/data-feeds`) and APIs (`https://nvd.nist.gov/developers/start-here`) for organizations and individuals to consume published vulnerability data. APIs allow interested parties to programmatically consume the vulnerability information in a much more automated and scalable manner than manually reviewing the data feeds. The NVD APIs, which are frequently updated and searchable, include other benefits, such as data matching, and they are often used by security product vendors to provide vulnerability data as part of their product offering.

Software Identity Formats

One fundamental aspect of the push for software supply chain security and software transparency is the need for effective ways of identifying software components, including having sufficient information to uniquely identify each software component. This need is far from a trivial problem, though, as the software landscape consists of thousands of different software vendors, sectors, and communities. The National Telecommunications and Information Administration (NTIA) focuses on this problem in their "Software Identification Challenges and Guidance" white paper (www.ntia.gov/files/ntia/publications/ntia_sbom_software_identity-2021mar30.pdf), which was produced through the NTIA multistakeholder process. NTIA notes that there's a need to functionally identify software components in the short term but also to rationalize multiple existing identification systems in the future. Doing so would ease some of the challenges and help the industry rally around a unified solution. To rein in some of the confusion surrounding software component identification, NTIA recommended using existing identification systems when possible, but noted that it isn't always possible, leading some to use a "best-effort" identification approach.

Despite the broad push for software bill of materials (SBOM) adoption and integration by software producers and consumers across the industry, there currently isn't an authoritative source when it comes to SBOM component identification. Software suppliers often define and identify software components based on the needs of their organization and associated activities. The problem can be further exacerbated by the fact that component identification isn't a static event and can change due to factors such as forking and adoption of projects and organizational acquisitions, among other examples.

All that said, there are some primary software identification standards that are recognized within the industry and by NTIA, such as CPEs, Software Identification Tags (SWIDs), and Package URLs (PURLs) which we will take a quick look at next.

CPE

The Common Platform Enumeration (CPE) is a structured naming scheme used to describe and identify classes of applications, operating systems, and hardware devices across enterprise IT assets. Originally released in August 2011 by NIST (www.govinfo.gov/content/pkg/GOVPUB-C13-5d78ccf04a5285bc768fb03ea45dd6bb/pdf/GOVPUB-C13-5d78ccf04a5285bc768fb03ea45dd6bb.pdf), CPE has gone through several iterations, with the latest version 2.3 as of this writing (https://cpe.mitre.org/specification). CPE addresses the need to refer to IT products and platforms in a standardized fashion, while also being machine readable for processing and automation. NIST maintains a CPE Dictionary (`https://csrc .nist.gov/Projects/Security-Content-Automation-Protocol/Specifications/ cpe/dictionary`), which serves as an agreed-upon list of CPE names. It is available in XML format and for public consumption and use.

The latest CPE specification, 2.3, breaks the CPE standard into a suite of separate specifications in a stack, which includes the following:

- Name
- Name matching
- Dictionary
- Applicability language

The *name* is the foundation of the CPE specification and is used to define standardized methods for assigning names to IT product classes. *Name matching* is used to define a method for conducting a one-to-one comparison of a source CPE name to a target CPE name. It determines whether common relations exist between two entities. IT asset management tools, for example, can gather information about software installed on a system and identify specific software installed or present. The *dictionary* defines a standardized method to create and manage CPE dictionaries, which are repositories of CPE names and their associated metadata. The last specification in the stack is *applicability language*, which defines a standardized way to describe IT platforms by forming complex logical expressions of the constituent CPE names and references. One example the CPE specification provides would be an operating system such as Windows XP, which is running Microsoft Office 2007, and a specific configuration on the OS, such as an active wireless network card.

Software Identification Tagging

Software Identification (SWID) tagging is a format recognized by the International Organization for Standardization and is a structured metadata format for describing a software product (`https://csrc.nist.gov/projects/software-identification-swid/guidelines`). SWID uses data elements to identify software products, as well as product versions, organizations, or individuals who had a role in the production and distribution of the product and the artifacts that a software product is composed of. Some software asset management and security processes use SWID as part of activities such as vulnerability assessment for software assets, missing patches, or specific configuration management assessments. It can also be used as part of verifying software integrity or as part of security operational activities.

NIST describes using SWID tags at length in their publication NISTIR 8060, "Guidelines for the Creation of Interoperable Software Identification (SWID) Tags" (`https://nvlpubs.nist.gov/nistpubs/ir/2016/NIST.IR.8060.pdf`).

NTIA also discusses SWID in their publication "Survey of Existing SBOM Formats and Standards" (`www.ntia.gov/files/ntia/publications/sbom_formats_survey-version-2021.pdf`). SWID tags are used by various standard bodies, such as the Trusted Computing Group (TCG) and the Internet Engineering Task Force (IETF). As a standard, SWID helps define the life cycle of a software product. SWID uses four types of tags:

- Primary
- Patch
- Corpus
- Supplemental

A *primary* tag is used to identify and describe a software product installed on a computing device, whereas a *patch* tag represents an incremental change being made to the installed software product. *Corpus* tags represent the installable software products in preinstallation states, such as metadata about installation packages or a software update. *Supplemental* tags can be used to add information to any referenced SWID tag. They can be used by software management tools to add metadata without altering the other tag formats. To visualize the life cycle functionality of SWID tags, see Figure 3.2, which shows an example from the NTIA publication mentioned earlier.

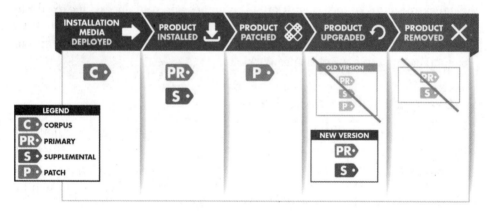

Figure 3.2
Source: NTIA SBOM Formats Survey, U.S. Department of Commerce, Public domain

While we included SWID in our discussion of SBOM formats, SWID has not been given the same focus as other primary SBOM formats, such as SPDX and CycloneDX, due to primarily being focused on software identification as its primary use case and lacking some of the rich context that the other formats provide. However, it should be noted that CycloneDX natively supports SWID for software identification.

PURL

Package URL (PURL; `https://archive.fosdem.org/2018/schedule/event/purl/` `attachments/slides/2298/export/events/attachments/purl/slides/2298/` `meet_purl_FOSDEM_2018_narrow.pdf`) helps address an issue that relates to software package naming conventions and protocols. Modern software development involves consuming and producing a significant number of software packages like NPM and Rubygems. However, each package manager and ecosystem uses diverse naming conventions and methods when it comes to the identification, location, and provisioning of software packages.

To address this challenge, nexB (`www.nexb.com`)—who offers ScanCode and VulnerableCode, software composition analysis (SCA), and free and open-source software (FOSS) security scanning tools—developed the PURL specification (`https://github.com/package-url/purl-spec`). The goal of the PURL project is to standardize approaches to identify and locate software packages across the package managers, tools, and the broader software ecosystem. PURL consists of six data elements:

- Scheme
- Type
- Namespace/name
- Version
- Qualifiers
- Subpath

Some of the elements are optional, whereas others are required. This culminates in a URL string such as `pkg:bitbucket/birkenfeld/pygments-main@244fd47e07d1014f0aed9c`. *Scheme* is the URL scheme with the constant value of `pkg`. *Type* is a required element that indicates the package type, such as `maven` or `NPM`. *Namespace*, such as `Maven` and `Docker`, is an optional element. *Name* is a required field showing the name of the package; *version* is an optional data element. *Qualifiers* provide additional context such as the operating system, architecture, or distribution, and *subpaths* can identify additional subpaths within a package; both elements are also optional.

PURL was originally presented at events like FOSDEM 2018. Since its inception, it's now considered by many to be a de facto standard used for package URLs by projects such as the leading SBOM formats CycloneDX and SPDX, the OSS Index, and other organizations around the world.

Members of the Open Worldwide Application Security Project (OWASP), the Linux Foundation, and Oracle, among others, have also begun efforts to get the NVD to adopt PURL to improve automation and component identification for vulnerability management (`https://owasp.org/blog/2022/09/13/sbom-forum-recommends-improvements-to-nvd.html`). A group known as the SBOM Forum,

led by supply chain consultant and blogger Tom Alrich (`http://tomalrichblog`
`.blogspot.com`), released a paper titled "A Proposal to Operationalize Component Identification for Vulnerability Management" (`https://owasp.org/`
`assets/files/posts/A%20Proposal%20to%20Operationalize%20Component%20`
`Identification%20for%20Vulnerability%20Management.pdf`). In the paper,
the authors point out the naming problem, which is that open-source products
or components have varying names across package managers and registries.
The case is made that to be more effective at vulnerability identification and
remediation, organizations need a standardized naming convention for software components.

NVD currently uses CPE names for software products; however, CPE naming conventions present a variety of challenges that hinder automation efforts
tied to software security. CPEs within the NVD primarily identify software and
hardware components by vendor, product, and version strings. The adoption
of PURL by the NVD has the potential to alleviate some of the challenges associated with CPE use and to facilitate improved software identification as well
as to aid efforts related to SBOM adoption and automation.

Sonatype OSS Index

As OSS adoption has continued to grow and increasingly contribute to significant
portions of modern applications and products, there has been more demand to
understand the risk associated with OSS components. The Sonatype OSS Index
has emerged as one reputable source to aid with this issue. This index provides
a free catalog of millions of OSS components as well as scanning tools that can
be used by organizations to identify vulnerabilities with OSS components and
the associated risk, and to drive down risk to organizations. The OSS Index
also provides remediation recommendations and, much like the NVD, has a
robust API for scanning and querying as part of integration. One key distinction
between the NVD and the OSS Index is the use of PURL rather than CPE. The
NVD uses CPE for uniquely identifying vulnerable products affected by vulnerabilities, whereas the OSS Index uses the PURL specification to describe the
coordinates of components or packages.

In addition to being able to search for OSS components and find any information
related to their vulnerabilities, the OSS Index supports scanning projects for OSS
vulnerabilities and integration with modern continuous integration/continuous
delivery (CI/CD) toolchains through the indexes' representational state transfer
(REST) application programming interface (API). As part of the broader push
to "shift security left," moving security earlier in the software development life
cycle (SDLC), this toolchain and build-time integration facilitates identifying

vulnerabilities in OSS components prior to deploying code to a production runtime environment. The OSS Index API integration is used by many popular scanning tools for various programming languages, such as the Java Maven plug-in, Rust Cargo Pants, OWASP Dependency-Check, and Python's ossaudit, among several others. It is worth noting that while the OSS Index is free for community use, it also doesn't include any specially curated intelligence or insight from experts. Sonatype, however, does offer other service offerings to provide additional intelligence, manage libraries, and provide automation capabilities.

Open Source Vulnerability Database

In 2021, Google Security launched (https://security.googleblog.com/2021/02/launching-osv-better-vulnerability.html) the Open Source Vulnerabilities (OSV) Project (https://osv.dev) with the aim of "improving vulnerability triage for developers and consumers of open-source software." The project evolved out of earlier efforts by Google Security dubbed "Know, Prevent, Fix" (https://opensource.googleblog.com/2021/02/know-prevent-fix-framework-for-shifting-discussion-around-vulnerabilities-in-open-source.html). OSV strives to provide data on where vulnerabilities are introduced and where they are fixed so that software consumers can understand how they are impacted and how to mitigate any risk. OSV includes goals to minimize the required work by maintainers to publish vulnerabilities and improve the accuracy of vulnerability queries for downstream consumers. OSV automates triage workflows for open-source package consumers through a robust API and querying vulnerability data. It also improves the overhead associated with software maintainers trying to provide accurate lists of affected versions across commits and branches that might impact downstream consumers.

The Google Security team has published blogs demonstrating how OSV connects SBOMs to vulnerabilities due to OSV's ability to describe vulnerabilities in a format specifically designed for mapping to open-source package versions and commit hashes. It also aggregates information from a variety of sources, such as the GitHub Advisory Database (GHSA) and Global Security Database (GSD). There is even an OSS tool dubbed *spdx-to-osv* (https://github.com/spdx/spdx-to-osv) that creates an OSS vulnerability JavaScript Object Notation (JSON) file from information listed in a Software Package Data Exchange (SPDX) document.

OSV isn't just a database available at OSV.dev; it's also a schema and OSV format. OSV points out that there are many vulnerability databases but no standardized interchange format (https://ossf.github.io/osv-schema).

If organizations are looking to have widespread vulnerability database coverage, they must wrestle with the reality that each database has its own unique format and schema. This fact hinders the adoption of multiple databases for software consumers and stymies publishing to multiple databases for software producers. OSV aims to provide a format that all vulnerability databases can rally around and allow broader interoperability among them, as well as ease the burden for software consumers, producers, and security researchers looking to use multiple vulnerability databases. OSV operates in a JSON-based encoding format with various field details such as ID, published, withdrawn, related, summary, and severity, among several others, including subfields.

Global Security Database

Despite the wide adoption of the CVE Program, many have pointed out issues with the program, its approach, and its inability to keep pace with the dynamic technological landscape. With the emergence of cloud computing, groups such as the Cloud Security Alliance (CSA; `https://cloudsecurityalliance.org`) have emerged as reputable industry leaders for guidance and research in the modern era of cloud-driven IT. Among notable efforts of CSA is the creation of the Global Security Database (GSD), which paints itself as a modern approach to a modern problem, claiming CVE is an antiquated approach that has not kept pace with the modern complicated IT landscape. The effort has been spearheaded by Josh Bressers and Kurt Seifried, both of whom have extensive experience and expertise in vulnerability identification and governance both at Red Hat, and in Kurt's case, even serving on the CVE board.

In their CSA blog post titled "Why We Created the Global Security Database" (`https://cloudsecurityalliance.org/blog/2022/02/22/why-we-created-the-global-security-database`), Kurt lays out several reasons for the creation of the GSD and why other programs like CVE have fallen short. The blog traces back the origins of vulnerability identification, predating CVE to the program known as BugTraq IDs, which required interested parties to subscribe and read available vulnerability information. He describes the growth of the CVE Program that initially was only a thousand or so findings per year, peaking at 8,000 CVEs before beginning to decline in 2011. The article also demonstrates the growth of CNAs, as we discussed earlier. However, despite the growth of CNAs, Kurt points out that nearly 25 percent of CNAs have been inactive for at least a year. In 2017, the number of CVEs published and assigned peaked, and aside from a spike in 2020, CVE assignment activity has remained flat, as you can see in Figure 3.3.

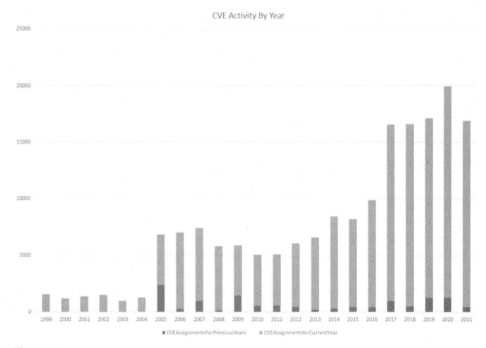

Figure 3.3
Source: "Why We Started the Global Security Database" (https://cloudsecurityalliance.org/
blog/2022/02/22/why-we-created-the-global-security-database). Cloud Security
Alliance, last accessed March 27, 2023

The article describes earlier efforts Josh and Kurt were involved with, such as the Distributed Weakness Filing project, and discusses how even the Linux kernel got involved with the effort. The Linux project declined to work with the CVE Program, which is discussed at length by Greg Kroah-Hartman in the talk titled "Kernel Recipes 2019—CVEs are dead, long live the CVE!" (www.youtube .com/watch?app=desktop&v=HeeoTE9jLjM). In that video, Greg points out that the CVE Program doesn't work well with the Linux kernel due to the number of fixes applied and backported to users through a myriad of methods. Greg explains how the average "request to fix" timeline for Linux CVEs is 100 days, indicating a lack of concern for Linux kernel CVEs, and at a broader level, how the Linux project moves too fast for the rigidly governed CVE process.

The GSD announcement describes how services have "eaten the world," and modern software and applications are overwhelmingly delivered *as-a-service*, which is hard to argue given the proliferation of cloud computing in its various models, but most notably for applications like software-as-a-service (SaaS). The authors explain how the CVE Program lacks a coherent approach when it comes to covering as-a-service applications. The "eaten the world" comment is in reference to the previous mantra that software has eaten the world, but now much of the world's software is delivered as-a-service.

Among other changes cited by the authors and GSD leads is the rampant growth of packages like Python (200,000) or NPM (1.3 million). There's also a perception that the CVE Program lacks transparency, community access, engagement, and a lack of data as it relates to vendors using OSS packages, using Log4j as an example.

If you're interested in getting involved in the open and community-driven GSD effort, you can find out more on the GSD home page (`https://globalsecuritydatabase.org`) or communication channels such as Slack or the Mailing-list (`https://groups.google.com/a/groups.cloudsecurityalliance.org/g/gsd?pli=1`).

Common Vulnerability Scoring System

While the CVE Program provides a way to identify and record vulnerabilities and the NVD enriches CVEs and presents them in a robust database, the Common Vulnerability Scoring System (CVSS) assesses the severity of security vulnerabilities and assigns severity scores. CVSS strives to capture technical characteristics of software, hardware, and firmware vulnerabilities. It offers an industry standardized way of scoring the severity of vulnerabilities that is both platform and vendor agnostic and that is entirely transparent with regard to the characteristics and methodology from which a score is derived.

The CVSS originated out of research by the National Infrastructure Advisory Council (NIAC) in the early 2000s, with CVSS version 1 originating in early 2005. While NIAC's research led to the creation of CVSS, in 2005 NIAC selected the Forum of Incident Response and Security Teams (FIRST) to lead and manage the CVSS initiative in the future. FIRST is a U.S.-based nonprofit organization that aids computer security incident response teams with resources, such as CVSS. While CVSS is owned and operated by FIRST, other organizations can use or implement CVSS if they adhere to the FIRST CVSS specification guidance. CVSS has gone through several iterations with the original CVSS in early 2005, CVSS v2 in 2007, and CVSS v3 in 2015. CVSS, as of this writing, is on v3.1 specification. CVSS consists of three core metrics groups, as shown in Figure 3.4.

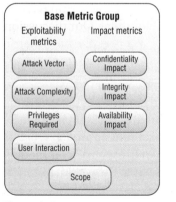

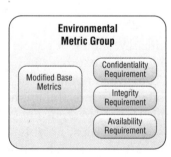

Figure 3.4

Source: Forum of Incident Response and Security Teams, CVSS v3.1 Specification Document (`www.first.org/cvss/specification-document`), last accessed March 27, 2023

As mentioned, CVSS consists of three metrics groups: base, temporal, and environmental. The severity of a vulnerability based on intrinsic characteristics that remain constant assumes worst-case scenarios, regardless of the deployed environment. Temporal, on the other hand, adjusts the base score, accounting for factors that change over time, including the actual availability of an exploit. Environmental metrics adjust both the base and temporal severity scores based on specifics of the computing environment, including the presence of mitigations to reduce risk. The base score is assigned by the organization that owns the product or by third parties, such as security researchers. These are the scores/metrics that are published, as they remain constant upon assignment. Because the publishing party will not have the full context of the hosting or operating environment as well as potential mitigating controls in place, it is up to CVSS consumers to adjust scores through temporal and environmental scores, if desired. Mature organizations that make informed adjustments based on these factors are better able to prioritize vulnerability management activities based on more accurate risk calculations that account for their specific environment and controls involved.

Diving a little deeper into each metric group, the base metric group involves intrinsic characteristics over time that are consistent unless new information emerges, regardless of the environment in which the group exists. The Base Metric group involves both exploitability metrics and impact. Exploitability metrics include things such as the attack vector or complexity as well as the privileges required. These metrics revolve around a vulnerable component and the ease with which it can be exploited. On the other side of exploitability are the impact metrics, using the traditional cybersecurity CIA triad. This deals with the consequences of the vulnerability being exploited and the impact it would have on the vulnerable component.

Base Metrics

Base metrics make assumptions, such as the knowledge of the attacker as it relates to the system as well as its defense mechanisms. As of this writing, CVSS 3.1 is the existing version, and CVSS 4.0 is under development. Our discussion will be from the perspective of CVSS 3.1. As mentioned earlier, the base metric includes exploitability- and impact-specific metrics as well. Within the exploitability metrics, you have factors such as attack vector and complexity, privileges required, user interaction, and scope.

The attack vector metric seeks to provide context about the methods of exploitation that are possible by a malicious actor. Factors such as the physical proximity required for exploitation influence the scoring for this metric, due to the reality that the number of malicious actors with physical proximity to a vulnerable component will most likely be lower than the number of those with logical access, except in rare circumstances. The attack vector metric includes values such as network, adjacent, local, or physical. From a network perspective, the attack vector could be bound to a local network, remote exploitability, or potentially to the entire Internet. Adjacent, on the other hand, would be bound to a specific physical or logical scope, such as sharing a Bluetooth network/range or being on the same local subnet. Local involves factors such as accessing the system's keyboard or console but could also include remote SSH access. Local may also require user interaction such as through phishing attacks and social engineering. Lastly, the physical metric value would mean the malicious actor needs physical access to the vulnerable component to take advantage of the vulnerability.

Although the attack vector metric is based on the available paths and methods an attacker has available to them, attack complexity involves conditions beyond the malicious actor's control and could include examples such as specific configurations being present on the vulnerable component. Attack complexity is categorized as either low or high. Low would be a situation that allows the malicious actor's repeatable success of exploiting the vulnerable component, whereas high would be more nuanced and require the malicious actor to gather knowledge, prepare a target environment, or inject themselves in the network path such as with an on-path style attack.

The privileges required metric describes the level of privileges an attacker must possess to successfully exploit a vulnerability. Situations where no privileges are required would generate the highest base score metric, whereas the score would be lower, for example, if exploitation required the malicious actor to have administrative levels of access. Privileges required values are

- None: Requires no access to systems or components
- Low: Requires basic user capabilities
- High: Requires administrative levels of access to a vulnerable component to exploit it

The user interaction metric describes the level of involvement that a human user, other than the malicious actor, must conduct to allow for a successful compromise. Some vulnerabilities can be successfully executed without any involvement from anyone other than the malicious actor, whereas others require involvement from additional users. This metric is straightforward, with either none or required the possible value.

The last exploitability metric is scope, which describes the potential for exploitation of a vulnerable component to extend beyond its own security scope and impact other resources and components. This metric requires an understanding of the extent to which a vulnerable component can impact other resources under its authority, and more fundamentally, what components are under its authority to begin with. Two metric values exist, unchanged or changed, representing the extent to which exploitation could impact components managed by another security authority.

Within base metrics, there are also the impact metrics, represented by the traditional CIA triad. CVSS recommends that analysts keep their impact projections reasonably aligned with realistic impacts a malicious actor could have. If you're familiar with NIST Risk Management Framework guidance for CIA, you will notice a similarity. The CIA metric values are none, low, or high. None means no impact to CIA, Low means some loss of CIA, and High means a total loss of CIA and the most devastating potential impact possible in the given scenario related to exploitation of the vulnerability.

Temporal Metrics

As mentioned previously, temporal metrics can change over time due to such factors as an active exploit driving up a score or an available patch driving a CVSS score down. Keep in mind that these factors are related to the industry and are not specific to the user's environment or specific mitigations an organization may have put in place. Temporal metrics include exploit code maturity, remediation level, and report confidence.

Exploit code maturity is based on the current state of the relevant exploit techniques and the availability of code to exploit the vulnerability. This is often referred to as "in-the-wild" exploitation, and a notable example is CISA's "Known Exploited Vulnerabilities Catalog" (www.cisa.gov/known-exploited-vulnerabilities-catalog), which is updated regularly with vulnerabilities that are known to be actively exploited and which require federal agencies to patch known exploitable vulnerabilities. This list already includes hundreds of vulnerabilities and a wide variety of both software and hardware exploits that may apply to many organizations. This list is updated regularly as new vulnerabilities that are known to be actively exploited are discovered and confirmed. Exploitability code maturity metrics include unproven, proof-of-concept (PoC), functional, high, and not defined. These metrics represent everything from an exploit code not being available or theoretical, all the way to being fully functional and autonomous and requiring no manual trigger.

The remediation level metric helps drive vulnerability prioritization efforts and involves possibilities such as workarounds through the official fixes available. The potential metric values include unavailable, workaround, temporary fix, and official fix. Fixing the vulnerability may be possible, or unofficial workarounds may be required until an official fix is published, verified, and vetted for consumption and implementation.

The last temporal metric, report confidence, deals with the actual confidence in the reporting of the vulnerability and its associated technical details. Initial reports, for example, may be from unverified sources but may mature to be validated by vendors or reputable security researchers. Potential metric values include unknown, reasonable, and confirmed, representing the increasing confidence in the reported vulnerability and details. These factors can influence the scoring of the vulnerability overall.

Environmental Metrics

For organization-specific context, this is where the environmental metric comes into play. It will look different for every software consumer, because every environment is unique and has a range of factors that could impact the environmental score, such as their technology stack, architecture, and specific mitigating controls.

Environmental metrics facilitate organizations adjusting base scores due to factors specific to their operating environment. The modifications revolve around the CIA triad and allow analysts to assign values aligned with the role each CIA aspect plays in the organization's business functions or mission. Modified base metrics are the result of overriding base metrics due to the specifics of that user's environment. It is worth noting that these modifications require a detailed understanding of base and temporal metric factors to make an accurate modification that doesn't downplay the risk a vulnerability presents to an organization.

CVSS Rating Scale

CVSS uses a qualitative severity rating scale, ranging from 0.0 to 10.0, as shown in Figure 3.5.

RATING	CVSS SCORE
None	0.0
Low	0.1 – 3.9
Medium	4.0 – 6.9
High	7.0 – 8.9
Critical	9.0 – 10.0

Figure 3.5

All the various CVSS scoring metrics and methods produce what is known as a *vector string*, which the CVSS specification defines as a "specifically formatted text string that contains each value assigned to each metric and should always be displayed with the vulnerability score." Vector strings are composed of metric groups, metric names, possible values, and whether they are mandatory. This culminates in a vector string that would be presented as "Attack Vector: Network, Attack Complexity: Low, Privileges Required: High, User Interaction: None, Scope: Unchanged, Confidentiality: Low, Integrity: Low, Availability: None."

Calculating the metrics requires a detailed understanding of the possible fields, values, and other factors. We strongly recommend that you visit the CVSS v3.1 Specification to learn more about the equations and guidance (www.first.org/cvss/v3.1/specification-document).

Critiques

Despite its widespread use and adoption, CVSS isn't without its critics either. Security researcher and author Walter Haydock in his "Deploying Securely" blog (`www.blog.deploy-securely.com`) takes aim at CVSS in his article "CVSS: An (Inappropriate) Industry Standard for Assessing Risk" (`www.blog.deploy-securely.com/p/cvss-an-inappropriate-industry-standard`). In the article, Walter makes the case that CVSS isn't appropriate for assessing cybersecurity risk. He cites several articles from industry leaders who demonstrate why CVSS alone shouldn't be used for risk assessment, despite it being used by the industry for exactly that purpose (`https://pt-br.tenable.com/blog/why-you-need-to-stop-using-cvss-for-vulnerability-prioritization`). As pointed out by Walter's article as well as others, CVSS is often used to help organizations prioritize vulnerabilities for mitigation or remediation, based on assessing the ease of exploitation and level of impact if it occurs. Research by organizations such as Tenable points out that over 50 percent of vulnerabilities scored as high or critical by CVSS, regardless of whether they are ever likely to be exploited (`https://pt-br.tenable.com/research`). It is demonstrated that 75 percent of all vulnerabilities rated as high or critical never actually have an exploit published and associated with them, but security teams prioritize these vulnerabilities nonetheless. This means that organizations are wasting limited time and resources prioritizing vulnerabilities that are unlikely, if ever, to be exploited, rather than addressing vulnerabilities with active exploits. Organizations are potentially missing a large amount of risk due to not addressing vulnerabilities rated between 4 and 6 with active exploits by taking the blanket approach of chasing high- and critical-scored vulnerabilities per CVSS. This is understandable, since organizations are often dealing with hundreds or thousands of assets, all of which often have many vulnerabilities associated with them. It is difficult to track down and perform granular vulnerability management efforts when you're drowning in a sea of vulnerability data, let alone get a clear picture of the assets that belong to your organization and pose a risk. For an even further deep dive on CVSS, check out the NIST Published Internal Report 8409 "Measuring the Common Vulnerability Scoring System Base Score Equation" (`https://nvlpubs.nist.gov/nistpubs/ir/2022/NIST.IR.8409.pdf`).

Exploit Prediction Scoring System

Building on the critiques of CVSS, some have called for using the Exploit Prediction Scoring System (EPSS) or combining both CVSS and EPSS to make vulnerability metrics more actionable and efficient. Like CVSS, EPSS is governed by FIRST. EPSS prides itself on being an open and data-driven effort that aims to estimate the probability that a software vulnerability will be exploited in the wild. CVSS focuses on the innate characteristics of vulnerabilities, culminating in a severity score. That said, just the severity score alone doesn't indicate a likelihood of exploitation, which is critical information for vulnerability management professionals who need to prioritize their vulnerability remediation and mitigation efforts to maximize their impact on reducing organizational risk. EPSS has a special interest group (SIG) open to the public for those interested in participating in the effort. EPSS is volunteer driven and led by researchers, security practitioners, academics, and government personnel, but FIRST does own the rights to update the model and the associated guidance as the organization sees fit, despite this industry collaborative approach. Currently, the group boasts chairs and creators from organizations such as RAND, Cyentia, Virginia Tech, and Kenna Security, among others. EPSS has several papers that dive into related topics such as attack prediction, vulnerability modeling and disclosure, and software exploitation (`www.first.org/epss/papers`).

EPSS Model

EPSS aims to help security practitioners and their organizations improve vulnerability prioritization efforts. An exponential number of vulnerabilities are being identified in today's digital landscape, and that number is only growing due to factors such as increased digitization of systems and society, increased scrutiny of digital products, and improved research and reporting capabilities. EPSS points out that organizations can only fix between 5 and 20 percent of vulnerabilities monthly. There is also the reality that fewer than 10 percent of vulnerabilities that are published are ever known to be exploited in the wild. Longstanding workforce issues are at play, such as the annual (ISC)^2 Cybersecurity Workforce Study (`www.isc2.org/News-and-Events/Press-Room/Posts/2021/10/26/ISC2-Cybersecurity-Workforce-Study-Sheds-New-Light-on-Global-Talent-Demand`), which shows shortages exceeding two million cybersecurity professionals globally (see Figure 3.6).

Figure 3.6
Source: EPSS Model (`www.first.org/epss/model`), last accessed March 27, 2023

These factors warrant organizations having a coherent and effective approach to prioritizing vulnerabilities that pose the highest risk to avoid wasting limited resources and time. The EPSS model provides support by creating probability scores that a vulnerability will be exploited in the next 30 days, and the scores range between 0 and 1, or 0 percent and 100 percent. To provide these scores and projections, EPSS uses data from various sources such as the MITRE CVE list, data about CVEs such as days since publication, and observations from exploitation-in-the-wild activity from security vendors like AlienVault and Fortinet.

The EPSS team publishes data to support their approach of using not just CVSS scores but also EPSS scoring data to yield more effective vulnerability remediation efforts. For example, many organizations mandate that vulnerabilities with a specific CVSS score or higher, such as 7 or above, must be remediated. But this approach prioritizes vulnerability remediation based on only the CVSS score, not whether or not the vulnerability is known to be exploited. Coupling EPSS with CVSS is more effective because then organizations prioritize vulnerabilities not merely based on their severity rating but also if they are known to be actively exploited, letting organizations address CVEs that pose the greatest risk to them.

EPSS focuses on two core metrics: efficiency and coverage. The efficiency metric looks at how adept organizations are at using resources to resolve the percentage of remediated vulnerabilities. EPSS points out that it is more efficient for most of an organization's resources to be spent remediating mostly known-exploited vulnerabilities as opposed to random vulnerabilities based on only CVSS severity scores. The coverage metric looks at the percentage of exploited vulnerabilities that were remediated.

To show the efficiency in their proposed approach, EPSS conducted a study in 2021 using CVSS v3 base scores: EPSS v1 and EPSS v2 data. They considered a 30-day period to determine the total number of CVEs, the number of remediated CVEs, and the number of exploited CVEs. As you can see in Figure 3.6, a couple of things jump out. Initially, the reality is that the majority of CVEs simply aren't remediated. Second, the number of exploited CVEs that are remediated is just a subset of the total remediated CVEs. This means that organizations don't remediate most CVEs, and among those they do, many aren't actively known to be exploited and potentially don't pose the greatest risk. It also demonstrates that the EPSS v2 further improves the efficiency of vulnerability remediation efforts by maximizing the percentage of exploited vulnerabilities that are remediated. When organizations have resource challenges with cybersecurity practitioners, it is crucial to maximize their return on investment by having the resources focus on the vulnerabilities that pose the greatest risk to the organization. EPSS is trying to help organizations make more efficient use of their limited resources and improve their effectiveness of driving down organizational risk.

EPSS Critiques

Much like CVSS, EPSS isn't without critiques from industry and academia. An article titled "Probably Don't Rely on EPSS Yet" (`https://insights.sei.cmu.edu/blog/probably-dont-rely-on-epss-yet`) comes from the blog of Carnegie Mellon University's Software Engineering Institute (SEI). SEI originally published a paper titled "Towards Improving CVSS," which laid out some sharp criticisms of CVSS, from which EPSS originated shortly after the publication (`https://resources.sei.cmu.edu/library/asset-view.cfm?assetid=538368`).

Some of the primary criticisms leveled by the article include EPSS's opacity as well as issues with its data and outputs. The article discusses how it isn't clear how the development processes, governance, or intended audience of EPSS are dictated. The article points out that EPSS relies on preexisting CVE IDs, meaning that EPSS wouldn't be helpful for entities such as software suppliers, incident response teams, or bug-bounty groups due to the reality that many vulnerabilities these groups deal with don't have CVE IDs yet and may never receive them. There is the issue that EPSS wouldn't be helpful when dealing with zero-day vulnerabilities, given that they gain visibility as exploitation is underway already, despite the lack of a known correlating CVE ID.

The article's author also raises concerns about the openness and transparency of EPSS. Although EPSS dubs itself an open and data-driven effort—and even has a SIG, as mentioned earlier—EPSS and its governing organization, FIRST, still retain the right to change the site and model at any time, without explanation. There is also the reality that even SIG members have no access to the code or data that is used in the underlying EPSS model. The SIG itself has no oversight or governance of the model, and the process by which the model is updated or modified isn't transparent to SIG members, let alone the public. The article points out that the EPSS model and data could also be pulled back from public contribution and use, given it is governed and managed by FIRST.

The article demonstrates that EPSS focuses on the probability that a vulnerability will be exploited in the next 30 days. But a few fundamental things are required for that to be projected. These include an existing CVE ID in the NVD with an associated CVSS v3 vector value, an intrusion detection system (IDS) signature tied to an active attempted exploit of the CVE ID, contribution from AlienVault or Fortinet (who provide data to EPSS), and lastly the model itself tied to the next 30 days. As the author points out, only 10 percent of vulnerabilities with CVE IDs have accompanying IDS signatures, meaning that 90 percent of vulnerabilities with CVE IDs may go undetected for exploitation. This also creates a dependency on Fortinet and AlienVault with regard to IDS sensors and associated data and could be mitigated by further involvement from the broader security vendor community.

CISA's Take

As the conversation around vulnerability prioritization and management has heated up, organizations such as CISA have weighed in on the topic. In an article published in November 2022 titled "Transforming the Vulnerability Management Landscape" (`www.cisa.gov/blog/2022/11/10/transforming-vulnerability-management-landscape`), CISA Executive Assistant Director Eric Goldstein discusses the complexity of the modern digital landscape and the accelerating pace of vulnerabilities.

According to the article, CISA outlines three critical steps to advance the vulnerability management ecosystem:

1. Expanding the use of the Common Security Advisory Framework (CSAF) for automated machine-readable security advisories

2. Bolstering adoption of the Vulnerability Exploitability eXchange (VEX), which helps software consumers understand when specific products are impacted by exploitable vulnerabilities

3. Helping organizations prioritize vulnerability management resources using things such as the Stakeholder-Specific Vulnerability Categorization (SSCV) and CISA's Known Exploited Vulnerabilities (KEV).

We will discuss each of these steps in a bit more depth in this section.

Common Security Advisory Framework

First on the CISA list is the use of CSAF for automating machine-readable security advisories. As CISA points out, every time a new vulnerability is discovered and disclosed, software vendors must evaluate their product offerings and validate whether it is applicable, and if it is, decide what must be done to remediate it and then communicate this information to their customer base. While vendors are doing this, so are malicious actors, seeking to actively exploit the vulnerability either before the vendor can fix it directly, say in the context of SaaS, or issue a patch and then have it applied by end users, in the context of traditional on-premises software. With the accelerating pace of vulnerability discovery and disclosures as they relate to CVEs, there is a critical need to automate and expedite this activity to get this information out to software consumers—and that's where machine readability and automation comes into play.

CSAF is led by the OASIS Common Security Advisory Framework (CSAF) Technical Committee. OASIS is a nonprofit consortium that helps create and evangelize various best practices and standards. OASIS provides some excellent resources for those wanting to learn more about CSAF, including their "What Is a Common Security Advisory Framework (CSAF)?" video (`www.youtube.com/watch?app=desktop&v=vQ_xY3lmZOc`) or the incredibly comprehensive CSAF 2.0 Specification (`https://docs.oasis-open.org/csaf/csaf/v2.0/csaf-v2.0.html`).

As defined by the specification, "CSAF supports the creation, update, and interoperable exchange of security advisories as structured information on products, vulnerabilities and the status of impact and remediation among interested parties." These advisories are available in JSON format.

Traditionally, security advisories are published as static documents like PDF files and websites and are intended for human consumption. The challenge with this is the accelerating pace of vulnerability discovery and disclosure coupled with the race to remediate them before exploitation by malicious actors, making the need for machines and automation critical. There are several parallels to this situation and other areas of cybersecurity, which are increasingly adopting machine-readable artifacts, such as governance risk and compliance (GRC) tools with Open Security Controls Assessment Language (OSCAL) and traditional IT with the advent of infrastructure-as-code and compliance-as-code. The modern technological landscape simply moves too fast for humans to serve as a medium.

CSAF is also striving to offer a robust set of tooling (`https://oasis-open.github.io/csaf-documentation`) such as CSAF Parser, Visualizer, Trusted Provider, and Aggregator, just to name a subset of the portfolio. It is worth noting that as of this writing these tools are still under development and may lack some capabilities, such as CSAF Parser not supporting CSAF 2.0 yet. Each of these tools is accompanied by a GitHub repository, documentation, and codebase to help organizations and adopters make better use of CSAF and operationalize it as part of their cybersecurity and vulnerability management activities, both as a software consumer or producer.

CSAF schema documents primarily involve three classes of information:

- The frame, aggregation, and reference information for the document
- Product information considered relevant by the CSAF advisory creator
- Vulnerability information in relation to the product(s) being discussed

CSAF also natively supports referencing schemas for industry-standardized things such as platform data and vulnerability classification and scoring. Examples are CPE, CVSS, and CWE, each of which has a schema for use.

With this basic overview, it is easy to see how CSAF can help usher in an age of machine-readable security advisories that can be automated and help expedite the creation, distribution, and ingestion of security advisories to benefit both software providers and consumers and empower fast decisions about cybersecurity risk in the software ecosystem. To learn more, you can review the robust specification itself or watch some of the CSAF videos available for review (`https://oasis-open.github.io/csaf-documentation`).

Vulnerability Exploitability eXchange

Building on the conversation around CSAF, CISA's second critical step is the widespread adoption of VEX. We discuss VEX in Chapter 4, "Rise of Software

Bill of Materials," so we will keep it brief here. At a high level, VEX allows software vendors to assert whether specific vulnerabilities affect a product as well as if they do *not* affect a product. The reality is that organizations face a shortage of cybersecurity talent, and VEX allows organizations to prioritize spending their time and resources on vulnerabilities that pose risk to them rather than vulnerabilities that may not be exploitable and pose no risk. VEX documents are shaping up be a close companion of SBOMs to provide clarity about the exploitability of vulnerabilities contained within SBOMs for software products and could be produced both with and outside of SBOMs. And new vulnerabilities may emerge despite the lack of a new software release due to vulnerabilities being regularly discovered and disclosed, allowing VEX to have a different cadence than SBOMs in some cases.

The industry continues to see innovations in not just the SBOM but also the VEX space in terms of specifications and tooling. For example, in early 2023 software supply chain leader Chainguard announced that, through a partnership with others such as HPE and TestifySec, they have created the OpenVEX specification. OpenVEX was designed to be minimal, compliant, interoperable, and embeddable. More can be found at the OpenVEX GitHub repository (`https://github.com/openvex/spec`).

Stakeholder-Specific Vulnerability Categorization and Known Exploited Vulnerabilities

An ongoing need in the industry is the need to help organizations prioritize vulnerabilities that pose the greatest risk.

CISA has curated and published a KEV catalog and has mandated through a binding operational directive (BOD) (`www.cisa.gov/binding-operational-directive-22-01`) that federal agencies remediate KEVs. CISA recommends that commercial organizations do the same if they are impacted by these KEVs. The catalog is published as a web page but also as a CSV or JSON file. Organizations and individuals can also subscribe to the KEV catalog update bulletin, which delivers email notifications when new KEVs are added to the catalog.

The criteria for a vulnerability to make it into the KEV catalog include the following:

- It must have a CVE ID assigned.
- It is actively being exploited in the wild based on reliable evidence.
- There is clear remediation guidance for the vulnerability, such as vendor-provided patches or updates.

As we discussed earlier, the CVE Program is sponsored by CISA but is run by MITRE, which is a federally funded research and development center (FFRDC). The purpose of the CVE Program is to identify, define, and catalog publicly disclosed vulnerabilities. CVE IDs are assigned by CVE Numbering Authorities and have three potential statuses: reserved, published, or rejected.

CISA's KEV catalog does not use exploitability itself as a criterion for inclusion in the catalog. Instead, there must be reliable evidence that the vulnerability either has attempted or successful exploitation. For example, there may be evidence that a malicious actor tried to execute code on a target but failed or merely did so on a *honeypot system*, a mechanism aimed at exposing malicious activity through observation. Unlike attempted exploitation, successful exploitation means that a malicious actor successfully exploited vulnerable code on a target system, thus allowing them to perform unauthorized actions of some sort on the system or network. CISA is careful to point out that PoC exploits do not make it to the KEV catalog, given that while a researcher may have shown something *could* be exploited, there's no evidence that it has been or even was attempted to be exploited in the wild.

The third criterion for KEV catalog inclusion is clear remediation guidance. This means that there are clear actions organizations can take to remediate the risk of the KEV. These could be actions such as applying vendor updates or, in potentially dire situations, removing the impacted product from the network entirely if there's no update available or if the product is end-of-life and is simply no longer being updated or supported. CISA also acknowledges that in the absence of relevant updates and patches, organizations often will seek to implement either mitigations (to prevent a vulnerability from being exploited) or workarounds, which are manual changes to protect a vulnerable system from exploitation until patches are available.

Building on the guidance for using the KEV, CISA is striving to help organizations prioritize vulnerability management resources using Stakeholder-Specific Vulnerability Categorization (SSVC). SSVC was created through collaboration by CISA and Carnegie Mellon University's SEI. SEI, no stranger to critiquing the sole use of sources such as CVSS, in 2018 released their somewhat damning white paper titled "Towards Improving CVSS," where they point out several of the shortcomings of the widely used CVSS for vulnerability prioritization (`https://resources.sei.cmu.edu/library/asset-view.cfm?assetid=538368`). One irony worth mentioning as well is that despite this advocacy of frameworks such as SSVC, federal organizations like CISA still enforce the use of CVSS, despite actively partnering with organizations such as SEI who have pointed out its shortfalls and deficiencies (`www.blog.deploy-securely.com/p/revealing-the-governments-approach`).

As described in the CISA's SSVC guide, SSCV is a customized decision tree model designed to assist in prioritizing a vulnerability response for the U.S. government and associated entities, but it can be used by others as well. SSVC includes four possible decisions, as depicted in Figure 3.7.

Track	The vulnerability does not require action at this time. The organization would continue to track the vulnerability and reassess it if new information becomes available. CISA recommends remediating **Track** vulnerabilities *within* standard update timelines.
Track*	The vulnerability contains specific characteristics that may require closer monitoring for changes. CISA recommends remediating **Track*** vulnerabilities *within* standard update timelines.
Attend	The vulnerability requires attention from the organization's internal, supervisory-level individuals. Necessary actions may include requesting assistance or information about the vulnerability and may involve publishing a notification, either internally and/or externally, about the vulnerability. CISA recommends remediating **Attend** vulnerabilities *sooner than* standard update timelines.
Act	The vulnerability requires attention from the organization's internal, supervisory-level and leadership-level individuals. Necessary actions include requesting assistance or information about the vulnerability, as well as publishing a notification either internally and/or externally. Typically, internal groups would meet to determine the overall response and then execute agreed upon actions. CISA recommends remediating **Act** vulnerabilities as *soon as possible.*

Figure 3.7

The guidance recommends that organizations understand the vulnerability's scope, since that will impact the decision tree as well—for example, whether a vulnerability is pervasive across an entire enterprise or part of a critical system.

When using SSVC and walking through the decision tree, organizations should consider several factors. These include factors such as the state of exploitation, using sources such as the National Vulnerability Database (NVD) or Information Sharing and Analysis Centers (ISACs). These sources usually provide insight into whether a vulnerability has no evidence of exploitation, has a PoC, or is actively being exploited in the wild.

Next, organizations need to understand the technical impact of exploiting a vulnerability. Parallels here can be drawn to CVSS's base-score concept of severity. Potential values include partial, where a malicious actor has limited control or impact on a system, and total, meaning they have total control over the behavior of the software or system to which the vulnerability pertains.

Another key consideration is whether the exploitation is automatable. It is far easier for malicious actors to scale their nefarious activities with exploits that can be automated than with those that require manual intervention and implementation. The decision value here is a simple yes or no. If the answer is yes, then the malicious actor can automate steps 1–4 of the Lockheed Martin Cyber Kill Chain (`www.lockheedmartin.com/en-us/capabilities/cyber/cyber-kill-chain.html`): reconnaissance, weaponization, delivery, and exploitation. The guidance mentions that in addition to automation, vulnerability chaining must be considered, as it is potentially required or possible to chain several vulnerabilities or weaknesses together to have a successful exploitation.

Moving on from the technical impact, there is the consideration of mission prevalence, which is the impact on mission-essential functions (MEFs) or relevant entities. The SSVC guidance defines these as functions that are "directly related to accomplishing the organization's mission as set forth in its statutory or executive charter." Organizations identify MEFs through exercises such as business continuity planning (BCP). Decision values include minimal, support, or essential. Essential would be where a vulnerable component directly provides capabilities to at least one MEF or entity and an exploit would lead to mission failure. Support, on the other hand, means the vulnerable component supports MEFs but does not support them directly. Lastly, minimal is a situation where neither essential nor support applies.

Next in the decision tree is public well-being impact, or the extent to which a vulnerable component or system impacts humans. SSVC uses the Centers for Disease Control and Prevention's (CDC's) definition of well-being: the physical, social, emotional, and psychological health of humans. Decisions here are broken out across the impact, which can be material or irreversible, as well as the type of harm, which can run the range from physical to psychological or even financial.

Lastly is the consideration of mitigation status, which measures the degree of difficulty of mitigating the vulnerability in a timely manner. The factors to consider include

- Whether mitigations are publicly available
- The difficulty of making the required system change
- Whether a fix exists or a workaround is required

The guidance stresses that the value of the mitigation should not change the priority of the SSVC decision, but SSVC should be actively tracked and considered. Figure 3.8 is an example of the decision tree, but it can be represented in table format as well.

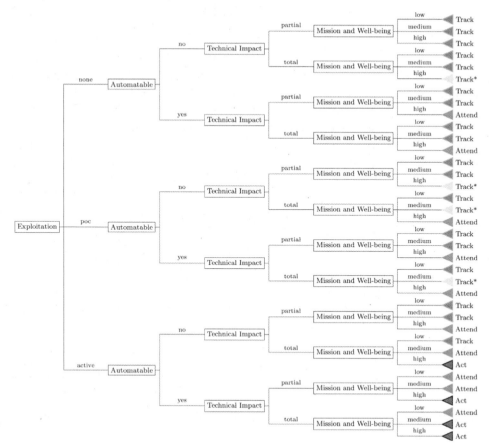

Figure 3.8

Moving Forward

The CISA guidance prioritizes steps such as automating security advisories with CSAF and informing software consumers of the impact of vulnerability exploitability with resources such as VEX. However, it is also clear that subjective cybersecurity expertise is required, especially in complex decision trees. Automation plays a pivotal role in reducing cognitive load on organizations and cybersecurity teams, but a need still exists for cybersecurity and software expertise to understand the broader enterprise and system context that vulnerabilities pose and how to prioritize organizational resources to address them.

Summary

In this chapter, we took a look at industry vulnerability databases and scoring methodologies. This included traditional vulnerability databases and their potential limitations as well as emerging databases across the vulnerability ecosystem. We also examined common software identity formats and the challenges they pose and solutions that are being proposed to alleviate some of those challenges. We also explored how vulnerabilities are categorized, scored, and communicated. In the next chapter, we will be taking a look at the rise of the software bill of materials (SBOM) and companion artifacts such as VEX.

Rise of Software Bill of Materials

This chapter discusses the origins of the SBOM concept, including early failures and successes and the U.S. federal and industry organizations who have contributed to its maturity. We'll also dive into some of the details of SBOM formats, specific fields, and the emergence of the Vulnerability Exploitability eXchange (VEX).

SBOM in Regulations: Failures and Successes

While there may be a flurry of SBOM momentum under way in the industry, it has been an effort over several years to get to this point, which has taken the involvement of a variety of government and industry organizations. Most notably, recent SBOM momentum occurred with the National Telecommunications and Information Administration (NTIA).

That said, while NTIA and events such as Log4j and SolarWinds may have played a critical role in recent momentum around SBOM, early events involving vulnerabilities associated with Apache Struts 2 and OpenSSLled to the introduction of legislation such as the Cyber Supply Chain Management and Transparency Act of 2014 (www.congress.gov/bill/113th-congress/house-bill/5793/text).

The bill focuses on the integrity of software, firmware, and products developed for or purchased by the U.S. Government that use third-party and OSS code and calls for a component list, or bill of materials, to be in software, firmware, or product contracts for the Federal Government. One early pioneer who was heavily involved in this effort is industry leader Joshua Corman, who has worked for various industry-leading private sector firms, and CISA, and who founded "I am The Cavalry," which focuses on the intersection of digital security, public safety, and human life.

The Cyber Supply Chain Management and Transparency Act of 2014 never fully materialized, partially due to industry's resistance to the calls for increased transparency of software components in their products. However, it does show that while SBOM may be heavily discussed at the time of this writing, it is a topic that has been discussed and desired for nearly a decade.

Other notable examples include the Health Care Industry Cybersecurity Task Force report in June 2017, which calls for manufacturers and developers to create a "bill of materials" to describe components in medical devices (`www.phe.gov/Preparedness/planning/CyberTF/Documents/report2017.pdf`).

NTIA: Evangelizing the Need for SBOM

Recent software bill of materials (SBOM) efforts in the federal space were championed by the NTIA. Since as early as 2018, the NTIA has been working to promote software component transparency. In July 2018, the NTIA held meetings (`http://ntia.doc.gov/federal-register-notice/2018/notice-071918-meeting-multistakeholder-process-promoting-software`) with multiple stakeholders to discuss the topic of software component transparency, challenges, and potential solutions.

Those early meetings involved Dr. Allan Friedman, who served at NTIA at that time as the Director of Cybersecurity Initiatives. Friedman has been a prominent figure throughout the industry conversation around SBOMs and software transparency since early on, along with Josh Corman, as mentioned above, and he now serves as a senior adviser and strategist at the Cybersecurity and Infrastructure Security Agency (CISA), still helping lead the software transparency and SBOM push.

The NTIA recognizes that modern software is created with many components and libraries from both the open source and commercial industry alike (`http://ntia.gov/blog/2018/ntia-launches-initiative-improve-software-component-transparency`). It also acknowledges that creating and maintaining an inventory of these components and their associated vulnerabilities is incredibly challenging. The organization, along with its multistakeholder community, has sought to understand improved approaches to software component inventory, practices, and the associated policies and market challenges that are relevant.

Throughout its efforts, NTIA has produced a robust set of documents and guidance (found at `http://ntia.gov/SBOM`) relating to software transparency and SBOMs. These include introducing SBOM to those who are unfamiliar, improving the understanding of SBOMs, SBOM implementation, and their accompanying technical resources.

Building on the Cybersecurity Executive Order (EO), Section 4, "Enhancing Software Supply Chain Security," sub-section (F) tasked the NTIA with publishing the minimum elements for an SBOM 60 days after the date of the Cybersecurity EO's publication. The NTIA subsequently published "The Minimum Elements for a Software Bill of Materials (SBOM)" (`http://ntia.doc.gov/files/ntia/publications/sbom_minimum_elements_report.pdf`) in July 2021. This guidance established the minimum elements required, defined the scope of how to think about the minimum elements, and described SBOM use cases for software supply chain transparency. The NTIA's guidance makes the case that system sharing and the tracking of component metadata help support software supply chain transparency.

In this section, we will break down the minimum elements guidance from the NTIA. Their guidance includes and details three categories of elements:

■ Data fields

■ Automation support

■ Practices and processes

The NTIA's guidance points out that each piece of software can be represented as a hierarchical tree that can consist of both components and subcomponents. These include third-party components that originate from another source, as well as first-party components that are freestanding and trackable as an independent unit of software themselves. The first of the three categories of elements, data fields, contain the baseline information about each component that should be tracked and maintained. The primary purpose of these data fields is to enable organizations to track these components across the software supply chain. The NTIA defines a baseline collection of data fields, which includes the fields shown in Table 4.1.

Table 4.1: The baseline collection of data fields

FIELD	DESCRIPTION
Supplier Name	The name of an entity that creates, defines, and identifies components
Component Name	Designation assigned to a unit of software defined by the original supplier
Version of the Component	Identifier used by the supplier to specify a change in software from a previously identified version

Continues

Table 4.1 (*continued*)

FIELD	DESCRIPTION
Other Unique Identifiers	Other identifiers that are used to identify a component or serve as a lookup key for relevant databases
Dependency Relationship	Characterizing the relationship that an upstream component X is included in software Y
Author of SBOM Data	The name of the entity that creates the SBOM data for this component
Timestamp	Record of the date and time of the SBOM data assembly

Source: `ntia.doc.gov/files/ntia/publications/sbom_minimum_elements_report .pdf`. `U.S Department of Commerce, Public domain`

Organizations can use these data fields to map components with other sources of data, a process known as *enrichment*. As evident from Table 4.1, the intent is to provide baseline information such as the supplier of the component, the component's name, and its version, and then tie the component to relevant upstream components. This is often referred to as a *dependency relationship*, because most software includes third-party code, leading to a dependency relationship of first-party and third-party code to make components and applications. It is worth noting that the NTIA's guidance discusses some challenges, such as disparate approaches to versioning among vendors and software suppliers.

Moving beyond data fields, another core component as identified by NTIA for SBOMs is the need for automation support. Skeptics of SBOM proliferation and adoption have pointed out the need for robust tooling and automation to empower SBOM adoption to be accurate and successful at magnitude of scale. The support for automation will enable organizations to integrate SBOMs into their existing vulnerability management, supply chain risk management, and cybersecurity programs. The NTIA SBOM guidance discusses the three primary SBOM formats, which will be covered in section "SBOM Formats."

Lastly, the NTIA SBOM guidance covers practices and processes, which focus on the mechanics of SBOM use for organizational operations and adoption. The primary practices and processes discussed include the following:

- Frequency
- Depth
- Known unknowns
- Distribution and delivery
- Access control
- Accommodation of mistakes

Frequency is related to how often a new SBOM is created. The NTIA's guidance stresses that new SBOMs *must* be created with *every* new build or release of software. There is also a need to create a new SBOM if a software supplier learns additional details about components, including correcting previously communicated errors.

Depth is how far down a dependency tree the SBOM should go. The NTIA guidance states that an SBOM should contain at a minimum all top-level components as well as list transitive dependencies. *Transitive dependencies* can be defined as components that are necessary for the software to run, compile, or be tested. While it isn't always practical or feasible to list all transitive dependencies, the guidance does state that enough information should be made available to seek the transitive dependencies out if necessary. In terms of depth, different organizations and industries might have differing requirements, even due to internal policies or regulatory requirements, and SBOM consumers will attempt to specify depth to their software products, particularly when dealing with proprietary software vendors where contracts and legal aspects are involved.

The concept of *known unknowns* revolves around the need for SBOM authors to be clear in their communications regarding further dependencies. There are cases where not all dependencies are known, and this is referred to as known unknowns in the guidance. SBOM authors can communicate that the data is known to be incomplete, which informs software consumers that there are potentially unaddressed and unknown risks in their software consumption.

Distribution and delivery deals with ensuring that the entities who are to be informed by the SBOMs have them in a timely fashion with the appropriate permissions and access control. This area of SBOM adoption is still evolving, and undoubtedly there will be several approaches used. The method of distribution and delivery will also vary depending on the nature of the software and systems involved, such as with embedded systems or online services, each of which are distributed and deployed differently for end consumers. For the U.S. government, the Cybersecurity EO states the requirement as "providing a purchaser a Software Bill of Materials (SBOM) for each product directly or by publishing it on a public website."

Access control is a critical part of SBOM adoption and use across the industry. As the practice of delivering SBOMs continues to be standardized among software producers, there will be different levels of tolerance with sharing the data. Some might wish to make the information open and public, including open source maintainers or even private software companies such as JupiterOne (`http://jupiterone.com`), who've posted their SBOM at `http://jupiterone.com/sbom`. However, some software vendors, particularly those who feel their SBOM is sensitive or who have specific needs from their customers, such as those in the defense or national security community, might want to provide this information only under specific terms and conditions and with specific access controls in place. This is an area of SBOM and software transparency that will continue to evolve and mature.

Lastly, the practice of *accommodation of mistakes* is cited in the guidance. In short, this means allowing for omissions or errors. The internal practice of software supply chain security is still maturing across the entire industry, and mistakes and oversights will certainly occur. It is a two-way street, with software producers able to provide additional insight or clarifications when appropriate, and software consumers understanding that everything may not be perfect initially. Through this mutual collaboration, the hygiene of the entire software supply chain can be improved.

The NTIA's contributions to the dialogue and adoption of SBOM go well beyond the Minimum Element's guidance, as previously mentioned, including dispelling myths (`http://ntia.gov/files/ntia/publications/sbom_myths_vs_facts_nov2021.pdf`), explainer videos, and common FAQs (`http://ntia.gov/files/ntia/publications/sbom_faq_-_20201116.pdf`). One of their most cited publications is the SBOM Framing document (`http://ntia.gov/files/ntia/publications/ntia_sbom_framing_2nd_edition_20211021.pdf`), which covers everything from the problem statement related to software transparency and system risk, to what an SBOM is, SBOM processes and use cases, and an overview of the multistakeholder process NTIA used to produce its guidance.

While the NTIA served as a fundamental catalyst to bolster the dialogue around SBOM adoption and, more broadly, software supply chain transparency, the effort has continued to evolve and is now supported by the CISA (`http://cisa.gov/sbom`). This is undoubtedly partially due to the move of Allan Friedman to CISA from the NTIA, given he has been one of the most vocal proponents for SBOM adoption and use. CISA is striving to advance the SBOM work beyond early efforts by the NTIA through their activities of community engagement, development, and progress, with the overarching goal of scaling and operationalizing SBOM in the industry.

CISA's most notable SBOM event and community engagement at the time of this writing was the SBOM-a-Rama, which took place in December 2021. It was a two-day event, with the first day focused on the current state of SBOM capabilities and the second day focused on making SBOM adoption and use more scalable and effective. Participants included a range of public and private sector leaders, such as Congressman James Langevin, longtime SBOM and software transparency evangelist Josh Corman, and representatives from industry organizations such as the Open Worldwide Application Security Project (OWASP), Linux Foundation, and many more.

Discussions included fundamental topics such as what an SBOM is and why it matters, leading SBOM formats such as SPDX and CycloneDX, and early proof of concept (PoC) efforts across the healthcare, energy, and automotive industries. Recordings and presentations from both event days are available at `http://cisa.gov/cisa-sbom-rama`. We will be diving into topics such as the leading SBOM formats in subsequent chapters as well.

Industry Efforts: National Labs

As part of the NTIA SBOM workshops, several PoC groups formed to address industry-specific needs. The Healthcare PoC has gone through at least three iterations, and an automotive PoC and several others have formed as well. Some of these are open to the public, yet some are by invite only. In many cases, even the public workgroups have restrictions on how solution providers can support these efforts. One PoC focused on energy use cases was established by Idaho National Labs (INL; `http://inl.gov/sbom-poc`) and was initially formed by Virginia Wright of INL and Tom Alrich, a noted supply chain and North American Electric Reliability Corporation Critical Infrastructure Protection (NERC CIP) compliance consultant and industry blogger, now seen by many as an SBOM expert. Tom's role has now been replaced by Allan Friedman, but this working group is noteworthy in its openness to education and discussion of issues pertinent to critical infrastructure.

The materials collated from the Energy PoC are some of the most well-preserved available for public consumption, second only to the official NTIA website (`www.ntia.gov/SBOM`). Full recordings are available for prior meetings as well as many other references, links, and subject matter pertinent to the SBOM topic. While the focus has been on energy use cases, the foundational educational aspect of this effort provides a rich starting point for anyone looking to gain familiarity on these topics.

The National Labs perform a valuable function from a research and thought leadership standpoint under the auspices of the Department of Energy (DoE), focusing on everything from climate change to advances in green energy to, yes, cybersecurity. For instance, a research initiative referred to as Blockchain for Optimized Security and Energy Management (`http://netl.doe.gov/BLOSEM`) focused on multiple use cases for blockchain technologies, many of which are focused on supply chain security. Some notable examples include the use of blockchain to identify when equipment delivered to the utility is the same equipment they were expecting to see, integrity checking for configurations and set point values, and, yes, secure distribution and blockchain interoperability for SBOMs and hardware bills of materials (HBOMs).

This effort is sponsored by the Grid Modernization Initiative, which is a DoE collaborative effort funded by the Office of Electricity Delivery and Energy Reliability and the Office of Energy Efficiency and Renewable Energy, and executed by the National Renewable Energy Lab (NREL) and the National Energy Technology Laboratory (NETL), which operate the program. There are many other industry partners including Pacific Northwest National Laboratory (PNNL) and others. PNNL is co-leading the development of use cases for blockchain, leveraging their expertise in cybersecurity for the grid as well as their experience running a pre-existing federally funded blockchain for electric power.

Additionally, through the Cyber Testing for Resilient Industrial Control Systems (CyTRICS) program (`http://cytrics.inl.gov`), significant effort has gone into determining how best to represent the components of a system, including both hardware and software. These efforts are somewhat closed-door and only available to product suppliers, but the ecosystem created here provides a foundational use case for the topic of SBOM as a system descriptor. Additionally, CyTRICS creates a common framework and repository for product security and supply chain information for critical infrastructure, and, though not transitioned yet for commercial use, is an example of how public-private collaboration creates opportunities for innovation in the topic of software transparency.

SBOM Formats

Among efforts to standardize and mature SBOM adoption are efforts to rally around a few primary SBOM formats. The three primary SBOM formats to date are software identification (SWID) tags, CycloneDX, and the Software Package Data Exchange (SPDX). Each of these three SBOM formats have pros, cons, and primary use cases. CycloneDX and SPDX are each backed by different organizations as well, with CycloneDX benefiting from support by OWASP and SPDX being championed by the Linux Foundation. As mentioned, much of the public dialogue around SBOMs over the last few years has been led by efforts such as NTIA and SBOM formats, and standards are no exception. NTIA published their SBOM Formats and Standards white paper (`http://ntia.gov/files/ntia/publications/ntia_sbom_formats_and_standards_whitepaper_-_version_20191025.pdf`), which identified the problems in software transparency and assessed available current formats for SBOMs. This white paper was published in 2019, and the conversation around these SBOM formats, particularly CycloneDX and SPDX, has only continued to evolve since then. While SWID was mentioned early in the conversation in sources such as NTIA's documentation as an SBOM format, it doesn't specifically meet the NTIA minimum elements for an SBOM, such as a timestamp of when the SBOM was produced, per the SWID specification. Furthermore, one organization that is moving toward wide-scale SBOM adoption, the U.S. Army, has specifically stated they will not use SBOMs in SWID format and will require either CycloneDX or SPDX (`https://sam.gov/opp/0b824ec63e2541e082c58c65b6e1702d/view`).

Some key areas that the group NTIA focused on was the need to document workable and actionable machine-readable formats, while also acknowledging that no single format will be required, and to usher in an ecosystem where various formats can exist in tandem. Each of the leading SBOM formats presents information in different representations and file formats. Table 4.2 is an example of each of the three formats using the NTIA SBOM Minimum Elements as a baseline.

Table 4.2: Three SBOM formats

ATTRIBUTE	SPDX	CYCLONEDX	SWID
Author Name	(2.8) Creator:	metadata/ authors/author	`<Entity> @role (tagCreator), @name`
Timestamp	(2.9) Created:	metadata/ timestamp	`<Meta>`
Supplier Name	(3.5) Package Supplier:	Supplier publisher	`<Entity> @role (softwareCreator/ publisher), @name`
Component Name	(3.1) PackageName:	name	`<softwareIdentity> @version`
Version String	(3.3) PackageVersion:	version	`<softwareIdentity> @version`
Component Hash	(3.10) Package Checksum: (3.9): Package VerificationCode:	Hash`"alg"`	`Payload>/../<File> @[hash-algorithm]: hash`
Unique Identifier	(2.5) SPDX Document Namespace: (3.2) SPDXID:	bom/ serialNumber component/ bom-ref	`<softwareIdentity> @taqgID`
Relationship	(7.1) Relationship: DESCRIBES: CONTAINS:	(Inherent in nested assembly/ subassembly and/or dependent graphs)	`<link> @rel, @href`

Source: `ntia.gov/files/ntia/publications/ntia_sbom_framing_2nd_edition_20211021.pdf`. U.S Department of Commerce, Public domain

Software Identification (SWID) Tags

SWID is used with software inventory and entitlements management in mind. It works by looking for SWID tags within software. The SWID tag format is defined by the International Organization for Standardization (ISO) and the International Electrotechnical Commission (IEC) standard ISO/IEC 19770-2, with the latest version being ISO/IEC 19770-2:2015 as of this writing.

SWID tag documents consist of structured sets of data elements used to identify software products, including the products version, organizations/individuals who participated in the production and distribution of the product, and the artifacts that the software product is composed of. They can also be used to establish relationships between various software products.

SWID is often used by tools such as software asset management (SAM) and security tooling to help automate some of the administrative overhead associated with software products throughout the SDLC.

The SWID specification encompasses several personas and stakeholders, such as tag producers, platform providers, software providers, tag tool providers, and tag consumers. Each of these stakeholders use SWID for their various use cases and tasks in the broader software ecosystem.

Despite being recognized in the early NTIA documentation as an SBOM format, the industry has rallied around CycloneDX and SPDX as the two leading SBOM formats. SWID is often considered more like CPE than an SBOM format.

CycloneDX

While SPDX is being championed by groups such as the Linux Foundation, CycloneDX (http://cyclonedx.org) is being led by longtime security community leader OWASP. CycloneDX is a self-defined "lightweight SBOM standard designed for use in application security contexts and supply chain component analysis" (see Figure 4.1). CycloneDX's core team involves Patrick Dwyer, Jeffry Hesse, and software supply chain leader and Dependency Track creator Steve Springett, who serves as the group's chair (http://dependencytrack.org). Aside from OWASP support, CycloneDX includes supporters from Lockheed Martin, Contrast Security, Sonatype, and others as well.

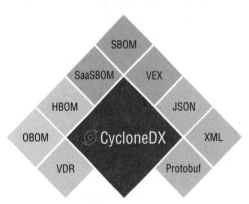

Figure 4.1

One thing that makes CycloneDX unique is that it was designed from the onset to be a BOM format and meets a variety of use cases, including software-as-a-service BOM (SaaSBOM). CycloneDX supports a myriad of use cases beyond software.

CycloneDX supports referencing components, services, and vulnerabilities in other systems and BOMs as well, in a nesting and hierarchical approach that aligns with the complexity of the modern software ecosystem when it comes to hardware, cloud, and SaaS. CycloneDX refers to this capability as a BOM-Link. It supports this capability in both JSON and XML formats. Users can reference the URL of the external BOM or even a BOM-Link URI, which uses serial numbers and versions for the external BOMs.

In addition, CycloneDX allows for a complete and accurate inventory of all first- and third-party components for risk identification. It allows this through a robust list of component types and classes, which extend beyond software and applications and get into devices and even services. It allows for the identification of vulnerabilities through three fields:

- CPE: A specification that can be used for vulnerabilities in operating systems, applications, and hardware devices
- SWID: A specification that can used for installed software
- PURL: A specification that can be used for software package metadata

CycloneDX provides support for the integrity verification of the components associated with the BOMs that it is used for through hash values and cryptography. Software signing is increasingly becoming a best practice in the push for maturing software supply chain security through projects such as Sigstore and its accompanying Cosign. CycloneDX supports enveloped signing for both Extensible Markup Language (XML) and JavaScript Object Notation (JSON), which is currently not supported by Cosign. CycloneDX also supports *provenance*, which is the ability to represent component authors and suppliers from which the component is obtained. Building on the concept of provenance, CycloneDX can support a component's pedigree by communicating component ancestors, descendants, and variants to describe the lineage of the component. For high-assurance software supply chain requirements, the implementation of provenance, pedigree, and digital signatures represents robust supply chain capabilities and is recommended by guidance such as NIST's Cybersecurity Supply Chain Risk Management (C-SCRM).

CycloneDX also provides support for the Vulnerability Exploitability eXchange (VEX), which provides insight into the exploitability of known vulnerabilities in software products and components and can be communicated by software producers. We will be diving much deeper into VEX in the section "Vulnerability Exploitability eXchange (VEX) and Vulnerability Disclosures."

Software Package Data Exchange (SPDX)

As a project, SPDX was formed with the purpose of creating a common data exchange format for information related to software packages for sharing and collection. SPDX supports the largest collection of file formats among the leading SBOM formats, including RDF, XLSX, SPDX, JSON, and YAML. SPDX also aims to be a dynamic specification by being able to describe a set of software packages, files, or snippets. Much like SWID, SPDX is also one of the three leading formats that has currently achieved ISO certification status (`http://linuxfoun dation.org/press/featured/spdx-becomes-internationally-recognized-standard-for-software-bill-of-materials`), meaning that it has met all the requirements for standardization and quality assurance as defined by ISO. This achievement was announced in September 2021 by the Linux Foundation. The announcement also highlighted SPDX's adoption by major corporations such as Intel, Microsoft, Siemens, Sony, and several others who all participate in the SPDX community.

The SPDX specification as of this writing is on version 2.3 (`http://spdx .github.io/spdx-spec`). To be considered a valid SPDX document, specific fields and sections must be present, which are defined in the SPDX specification itself.

SPDX documents can be composed of various fields and data, such as document creation information, package information, file information, snippet information, licensing information, relationships, and annotations. Document creation information is used for forward and backward compatibility when working with processing tools. Package information is used to describe different entities, such as products, containers, and components, among others, and can be used to group related items that share context. File information includes file metadata such as names, checksum licenses, and copyright information. Snippets are optional and are used primarily when data has been derived from a different original source or is tied to another license. SPDX also supports relationships for documents, packages, and files. Lastly, annotations allow a reviewer to include information from their review activities in an SPDX document.

SPDX also offers an "SPDX Lite" profile, which is a subset of the SPDX specification, with the goal of aligning with specific industries' workflows while balancing adherence to the overarching SPDX standard and specification. The Lite profile focuses on fields from the Document Creation and Package Information sections as well as accompanying basic information.

Vulnerability Exploitability eXchange (VEX) and Vulnerability Disclosures

The fallout of the SolarWinds cybersecurity incident (`http://cisa.gov/ news/2020/12/13/cisa-issues-emergency-directive-mitigate-compromise-solarwinds-orion-network`), coupled with the Cybersecurity EO, put the topic of software supply chain security, and by association, SBOM, center stage in the security dialogue. Coupled with the Log4j vulnerability (`http://cisa.gov/ sites/default/files/publications/CSRB-Report-on-Log4-July-11-2022_508 .pdf`) that left countless organizations scrambling to determine the impact, SBOM is now considered a critical component of modern cybersecurity vulnerability programs, with adoption poised to take off rapidly (`http://cisa.gov/sites/default/files/publications/VEX_Use_Cases_April2022.pdf`).

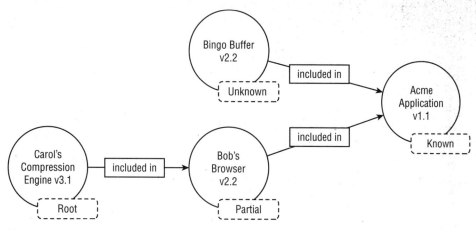

Figure 4.2

As shown in Figure 4.2 above, an SBOM tree can depict the upstream relationship assertions to demonstrate components and their relationships, including stating if the origins are unknown.

Among the most touted benefits of the use of SBOMs is the ability to identify potentially vulnerable components. Leading SBOM platforms and tools such as Dependency Track do this by tying vulnerabilities associated with components to the attention of those using the SBOM to analyze their software components. Dependency Track and other tools facilitate this process by querying sources such as the National Vulnerability Database (NVD; `http://nvd.nist.gov`), the Sonatype OSS Index (`http://ossindex.sonatype.org`), VulnDB (`http://vulndb.cyberriskanalytics.com`), or OSV (`http://osv.dev`). However, just because a vulnerability is associated with a component in software does not mean that the component is exploitable. This is where VEX comes into play.

VEX Enters the Conversation

As defined by NTIA's guidance (`http://ntia.gov/files/ntia/publications/vex_one-page_summary.pdf`), VEX's primary use case is

> **to provide users (e.g., operators, developers, and services providers) additional information on whether a product is impacted by a specific vulnerability in an included component and, if affected, whether there are actions recommended to remediate.**

This is a lengthy way of saying VEX adds context to vulnerabilities to inform risk management activities. Much like other leading SBOM and software supply chain transparency and security guidance, VEX was born out of the NTIA's Multistakeholder Process for Software Component Transparency. That said, it is worth noting that the guidance states that although VEX was developed for a specific SBOM use case, it is not limited to use with SBOMs or necessarily required either.

As mentioned elsewhere in this book, just because a vulnerability is present does not mean it is exploitable. This is critical information to know because vulnerability management programs and activities, along with organizations, are performing risk management. In cybersecurity risk management, organizations are looking to identify, analyze, evaluate, and address cybersecurity threats based on the organization's risk tolerance. This leads to the organization prioritizing risks based on the likelihood and severity of the risk materializing. Without knowing if a vulnerability is exploitable, it would be impossible to accurately project its likelihood.

VEX: Adding Context and Clarity

So, how exactly does VEX solve this challenge? It empowers software suppliers to issue a VEX, which is an assertion about the status of a vulnerability in a specific product. VEX supports the following four primary status options:

- Not Affected: No remediation is required regarding this vulnerability.
- Affected: Actions are recommended to remediate or address this vulnerability.
- Fixed: These product versions contain a fix for the vulnerability.
- Under Investigation: It is not yet known whether these product versions are affected by the vulnerability. An update will be provided in a later release.

With the SBOM itself as an example, we are seeing a push toward machine-readable artifacts and documentation, which enables better automation, accuracy, and speed. We are seeing similar trends in the realm of compliance, with NIST's Open Security Controls Assessment Language (OSCAL; http://pages .nist.gov/OSCAL), which brings traditional paper-based security controls and authorization documents into a machine-readable format.

VEX is doing something similar, avoiding the need to email security advisories or details about vulnerabilities and recommendations, and instead is bringing that information into a machine-readable format to foster automation and the use of modernized security tooling that moves at a pace much closer to the current threat landscape than humans and manual activities. As the push for software supply chain transparency and security evolves, it is not hard to imagine a world where enterprise software inventories are able to be visualized in dashboards and tooling, along with their associated vulnerabilities and the actual exploitability of the vulnerabilities, all empowered by SBOMs and accompanying VEX data. It's a stark contrast to the modern ecosystem where most organizations do not have accurate inventories of the software components they consume and have deployed, or the vulnerabilities associated with them. This is all despite the reality that modern software is overwhelmingly composed of open source software (OSS) components, with some estimates reaching as high as 80–90 percent.

The guidance also states that while VEXs can be authored by a software supplier, they can also be authored by third parties, leaving users in a position to determine how to use the data. This makes it easy to see scenarios where security researchers and vulnerability vendors might make attempts to produce VEXs for products as part of their own product offering.

VEX vs. VDR

In addition to VEX concepts, the topic of vulnerability advisories or vulnerability disclosure reports (VDRs) have added some confusion, but it's really a very simple topic. The VDR informs you when a vulnerability is present and can include both known and unknown vulnerabilities. In addition, the VDR provides additional metadata about the vulnerability, who discovered it, information about public exploits, along with additional information. The ISO 29147 Standard as well as NIST 800-161r1 documents outline the following elements of a VDR, as shown here:

Outline of VDR Elements

1. **General** Information about the advisory helpful for the target audience to understand if the advisory is applicable to them.

2. **Identifiers** These are unique identifiers for the advisory itself, such as a unique numbering scheme used by the vendor, or vulnerability identifiers such as a CVE, or product identifiers such as a CPE or PURL. In terms of correlation against an SBOM, this attribute may be one of the better attributes to connect attestations together.

3. **Date and Time** Date and time for the initial advisory as well as any updates. When comparing VDR timestamps to other attestations, it may be helpful to determine whether the VDR came before or after, and if it contains more updated information than other processed attestations about the product.

4. **Authenticity-Signed** While not included in the ISO standard, the need for signed attestations has been noted by NIST, and signing may be one of the best ways to link multiple attestations together with any level of trust.

5. **Title**   A brief title should be unique enough to clearly understand what the advisory covers, including product names and versions or CWE categories.

6. **Overview**   Expanding on the title, with enough detail to allow readers to understand the applicability of the advisory for their products

7. **Affected Products**   The products affected by the VDR should be clearly stated, and there should be sufficient information for the reader to understand whether their product is affected. This may include links to online scripts for testing, or specific metadata that can be used, such as a file hash, character string, or unique version indicator.

8. **Affected Components**   While not included in the ISO standard, it is spelled out in the NIST documentation, and this is ideally where we would capture information providing details at the component level that can be combined with an SBOM and used in much the same way as the Affected Product—for instance, a description of how the component needs to be implemented or used in order to be vulnerable. The presence of the vulnerable component alone may not be enough to satisfy vulnerable conditions.

9. **Intended Audience**   Who is the intended audience for the advisory? Developers? End users? While this is an optional field in a VDR, it can be used to convey additional context for its usage.

10. **Localization**   Advisories might be issued for specific regions and specific languages. This section allows for any region-specific information or context that needs to be conveyed, even if it is simply a translation.

11. **Description**   The description should convey additional information, such as the class of software weakness and under what conditions it can be exploited, and might include external references such as CWE classifiers.

12. **Impact**   This typically relates to technical impacts such as loss of confidentiality, integrity, or availability, like what might be found in a CVE or CVSS sub-score.

13. **Severity**   Use of standard severity scales such as CVSS, or vendor severity scales if used, to provide a quantifiable measure of the severity of the vulnerability. Regardless of how you feel about CVSS scoring, this is how the industry at large measures severity, and it's the indicator most likely to be used.

14. **Remediation**   The VDR should indicate how the vulnerability can be remediated, patched, or reconfigured, or at a minimum a workaround should be provided that allows for mitigation of risk for the vulnerability. In many cases, the initial VDR may not include remediation guidance but should be followed quickly with an update once more is known about how to reduce risk of exploitation.

15. **References** There may be many external references, to a CVE, a vendor knowledge base, product page, researcher blog, or other supporting information useful to reference within the VDR.

16. **Credit** Credit should be given to researchers and organizations involved in the detection, research, mitigation, and other phases of the vulnerability reporting life cycle. This is purely voluntary.

17. **Contact Information** Sufficient information for users of the product to contact the vendor for more information

18. **Revision History** It should be very clear if this is the original advisory or an update. If it's an update, version history should be maintained and be consistent with date and time information within the VDR.

19. **Terms of Use** Lastly, an advisory is a licensed article and should have copyright information and terms of use. For instance, in many cases it is only permissible for licensed product owners, or redistribution may be forbidden altogether.

You will notice, however, that while the VDR informs the user of an issue, it does not inform them of when something is *not* an issue. This is an important distinction, because, similar to a VDR, an analysis report for an SBOM may produce a significant number of false positives. By including VEX statements within an existing VDR format, such as how CycloneDX has constructed their data model for vulnerability reporting, there is a concise and consistent way to identify when vulnerabilities exist and to notify the user whether or not that vulnerability presents an issue.

There are many reasons why a vulnerability might not present an issue. Based on an industry report (`www.contrastsecurity.com/security-influencers/2021-state-of-open-source-security-report-findings`) by Contrast Security, 80 percent of open source components used in software are never actually called from the product's execution flow. By extension, we might assume that 80 percent of the subsequent vulnerabilities identified in the open source components might similarly present no risk because they are never used. This is certainly a hygiene problem, a likely code bloat and efficiency issue, and an increased attack surface most likely, but it might not represent a truly vulnerable software.

Second, many suppliers will "backport" security fixes where the code is remediated or another mitigation is inserted into the codebase to prevent exploitation, but the version number for the component is never updated. This means that any analysis against the NVD looking for specific versions to inform of a vulnerability might be instead looking at a different component. Currently, there is no concept within the NVD to uniquely identify a software file, only the Common Platform Enumeration (CPE), which is a description of the vendor, product, version, architecture, and similar metadata.

Lastly, configuration matters. In many instances, software is only vulnerable when configured in very specific ways, or perhaps when using a specific shared library that does not ship with the software by default. The VEX can provide additional context to inform the user when these scenarios are present and thus do not translate to an actual exploitable risk.

While contemplated as a machine-readable document, we think of the VEX as a much more dynamic attestation than an SBOM. While an SBOM is mostly a static document, tied to a specific software release, its vulnerability status can change over time as new vulnerabilities are discovered, found not to be exploitable, fixed through mitigations, and so on. We believe this might be more well suited to an application programming interface (API)-based distribution model where vulnerability status updates are not only machine readable but also continuously delivered through automation as new information is uncovered about the status of the vulnerability in question.

Moving Forward

As we have discussed, the SBOM initiative moved from NTIA to the Cybersecurity Infrastructure Security Agency (CISA), coinciding with the move of SBOM evangelist and leader Allan Friedman as well. Since that move, CISA published two additional VEX documents in 2022. One is the *VEX Use Case Document* and the other is the Vulnerability Exploitability eXchange (VEX) Status Justifications (http://cisa.gov/sites/default/files/publications/VEX_Status_Justification_Jun22.pdf).

The VEX Use Case document provides minimum data elements of a VEX document, much like NTIA defined the Minimum Elements (refer to Table 4.1) for an SBOM (as tied to the Cyber EO). In this guidance, it states that a VEX document must include the VEX metadata, product details, vulnerability details, and product status. These product status details include status information about the vulnerability in a product and can be Not Affected, Affected, Fixed, or Under Investigation.

The VEX Status Justification subsequently focuses on the requirement for VEX documents to contain a justification statement on why the VEX document creator chose to assert that the product's status is Not Affected, if they indeed did make that choice. This allows suppliers to provide justifications for why a product is not affected by a vulnerability. Options include the component or vulnerable code not being present, the vulnerable code not being able to be controlled by an adversary, or the code not being in the execution path, and lastly, the existence of inline mitigations already being in place in the product.

VEX represents a key next step in assisting SBOMs to become actionable by providing contextual insights and assertions from product vendors about the exploitability of vulnerabilities present in their products. By using both the minimum elements as defined for VEX documents and their associated Not Affected justification fields if applicable, software producers are able to empower software consumers to make risk-informed decisions to drive their vulnerability management activities as part of broader cybersecurity programs.

Using SBOM with Other Attestations

An SBOM is just a type of attestation; it is a document that contains evidence about the claims made within it. It is reinforced by the quality and veracity of the crypto-validation that can be attached to these claims. It is for this reason that the concepts of linking SBOMs together through digital signing becomes feasible and allows for incomplete SBOMs to still provide value, as they can be combined with other SBOMs where each additional attestation adds assurance information to the first SBOM. We want, however, to explore some other types of attestations that can likewise be included with the SBOM to build the evidence package.

Source Authenticity

Source authenticity is a concept that is heavily focused on in the NERC CIP compliance requirements for CIP 010 and 013, where the idea is that you can validate the file itself using a file hash or code-signing material, but what is equally important is validating trust in the provenance of the file. It seeks to answer questions like where did the file come from? Is it a trusted entity? Is it the same entity we think it is? Has that entity become compromised or modified in some unexpected way?

Some of the common ways solution providers have begun to tackle this is by looking at the Transport Layer Security (TLS) certificate information associated with the web domain where the software file is retrieved, and ensuring that the certificate is valid, but also ensuring that the certificate is trusted. Does it have a reasonable expiration? Has it changed recently in unusual ways? Does the name of the company match what is expected? Perhaps yesterday it was Microsoft Corp., but today it is Microsoft, Inc. That might be something to investigate. Most importantly, creating a baseline of normal and identifying anomalies helps organizations identify the authenticity of a source or attempts to compromise it.

DNS information is something else that might need verification. Has the domain changed to a new set of IP addresses or geolocated to a different part of the world? This becomes difficult to explore with a high degree of confidence with content delivery networks (CDNs) that may serve traffic from various parts of the world based on Internet health or requester location. Some have even suggested that Internet routing hijacks, such as the BGP hijacks that have happened over the years, could be used to serve malicious files. This, too, becomes exceedingly difficult to validate, but the scenarios become quite interesting to threat-model.

By performing checks against these criteria and producing an attestation file that can be cryptographically bound to the SBOM being produced, we can further enrich the provenance data already contained within the SBOM.

Build Attestations

Attestations about the build environment are also quite useful in enhancing the assurance for the software artifact. These can include information about the build system itself or even validation of processes or controls used within the build activities.

Consider that in the Supply Chain Levels for Software Artifacts (SLSA) framework, one of the attack targets is the build system. If an attacker can compromise the build system, how can you trust anything built on that server? Ideally, the build server is properly segmented from production and hardened appropriately as an extremely sensitive asset. Validating that the server is compliant with hardening guidance such as Security Technical Implementation Guides (STIGs), which are security templates that provide additional assurances that the build server is less likely to be a source of intrusion. There are some supply chain vendors such as TestifySec that use these attestations as part of their automation and can even apply build policies that require a passing STIG check for the build to succeed.

Likewise, you might have processes that you have put into place such as needing multiple developers to agree to a code check-in before a build can proceed. These build attestations can capture any number of security requirements needed from upstream processes to use as security gates for the build process, as well as the attestations that can be used to validate a high assurance software build. One example of tooling to support this is the OSS project "Witness," which helps create attestations and enforce policies to ensure the integrity of the software supply chain. (`www.testifysec.com/blog/attestations-with-witness`).

Dependency Management and Verification

As the consumption of pieces of software components from external sources continues to increase among developers, the need to manage those libraries, packages, components, or dependencies, as they are often referred to, increases. As we have discussed, dependencies are often integrated to save developers and organizations time and resources and to expedite time-to-market/-mission and to accelerate innovation. There is the unavoidable reality that the more dependencies you use, the more you must manage.

Dependencies are discussed typically in two contexts, which are either direct or transitive dependencies. Direct dependencies, as the name infers, are components that your application directly references and uses. Transitive dependencies are components that your dependencies themselves use, creating a dependency *upon* dependencies situation. Both types of dependencies have their associated risks and considerations. While the benefits are plentiful, as the number of dependencies, either direct or transitive, rise, so do the potential risks. These include licensing concerns, of course, but from the security perspective, they also include the potential for vulnerabilities, malicious code, and attack vectors.

This is pointed out by reports such as "The State of Dependency Management" from Endor Labs. The report found that 95 percent of vulnerabilities are found in transitive dependencies, which increases the difficulty for developers to assess and resolve. This was coupled with the finding that 50 percent of the most popular packages didn't have a release in 2022, and 30 percent had their most recent release prior to 2018, leading to old and potentially vulnerable code (www.endor labs.com/blog/introducing-the-state-of-dependency-management-report).

There are also challenges with the administrative overhead associated with the use of many dependencies. The development community itself uses the endearing term "dependency hell," due to the frustration associated with installing software packages that have dependencies on other specific versions of software packages. The problem occurs due to situations where several packages have dependencies on the same shared components but have differing versions or compatibility issues.

Each dependency or component comes with its various concerns. These include the library being abandoned and not maintained, poorly written code, no documentation, and of course, vulnerable code that may or may not be remediated by the maintainers, should they still exist or be active participants in the projects currently.

That said, there are several best practices organizations can take to mitigate some of the challenges and risks associated with dependency management. These recommendations include prioritizing which dependencies must be updated before others, using factors such as criticality to the project or security risks. Another recommendation, which, of course, is often easier said than done, is to minimize unused dependencies through removal entirely, keeping only the dependencies needed from the code. Failing to do so leads to bloated code, an increased attack surface, and administrative overhead challenges. You can also automate software dependency updates in many cases, which minimizes the magnitude of the manual toil associated with dependency management. One of the most popular examples in this case is Dependabot, which helps automate dependency updates for various programming languages such as Ruby,

JavaScript, Python, and several others. Dependabot is supported by the largest continuous integration platforms such as GitHub and GitLab.

In addition to automation, organizations should establish a software dependency management policy. The establishment of dependency management guidelines for the organization's developers can ensure that a standardized approach is followed across the organization and that governance can be implemented, as cited in frameworks such as Microsoft's S2C2F or NIST's software supply chain guidance, which we cover in Chapter 6, "Cloud and Containerization." Having standardized policy and processes in place helps with monitoring for security issues, improving application performance, and ensuring licensing compliance.

Software dependencies aren't going anywhere, and the wide-scale reuse of packages, libraries, and components is only accelerating across the industry. This inevitably leads to the need for proper software dependency management and verification processes. Failing to implement a structured approach will leave security risks unaddressed, thus creating a burden on development teams that could impede delivery and leave the door open for licensing violations.

Sigstore

A fundamental aspect of software supply chain security involves the need for integrity, transparency, and assurance. This is where Sigstore comes into place. As mentioned throughout this book, we have seen tremendous focus on the software supply chain, following notable incidents such as SolarWinds and Log4j in particular. There was the Cybersecurity EO and updated guidance from NIST in their Cybersecurity Supply Chain Risk Management (C-SCRM) 800-161 document as well as from the CISA. We have also seen a focus from the White House, which hosted a Software Supply Chain Security Summit in early 2022. Coming out of that summit, the Linux Foundation and OpenSSF have published the OSS Security Mobilization Plan, which has a task focused on using digital signatures to enhance trust in the software supply chain. That task focuses heavily on the adoption and evolution of a technology called Sigstore.

Sigstore is a standard for signing, verifying, and protecting software. As we have discussed, software use is ubiquitous across every industry vertical and business category. However, while the way we use software has and is changing the world, the methods of ensuring that the software we consume from across the ecosystem has the level of integrity often required is lacking. The software supply chain often lacks the use of digital signatures, and when it does not, it typically uses traditional digital signing techniques that can be challenging to automate, scale, and audit.

Sigstore was initially released in March 2021 through collaboration by Red Hat and Google and as a project with the Linux Foundation, and aimed to solve issues around where software comes from or how it was built. Sigstore specifically seeks to improve the software supply chain integrity and verification activities.

As Sigstore co-creator Dan Lorenc has stated, Sigstore is "a free signing service for software developers that improves the security of the software supply chain by enabling the easy adoption of cryptographic software signing backed by transparency log technologies." As Sigstore project founder Luke Hinds from Red Hat wrote in the blog "Introducing Sigstore" (`https://next.redhat.com/2021/03/09/introducing-sigstore-software-signing-for-the-masses`), the project set out with some true assumptions, such as very few projects implementing code signing and the reality that key management is a difficult activity. From there, the group asked themselves a series of "what if" questions, such as "What if keys didn't require revocation or storage?" and "What if all signing events were publicly available on a secure medium?"

Adoption

Sigstore continues to see increased industry adoption and interest since its launch. Despite being released as recently as early 2021, Sigstore has already received the attention of some of the largest OSS projects, one of which is the Kubernetes project. Kubernetes is the largest and most widely adopted container orchestration platform in the market. It announced that it was standardizing on Sigstore, using it with their 1.24 release (`https://blog.sigstore.dev/kubernetes-signals-massive-adoption-of-sigstore-for-protecting-open-source-ecosystem-73a6757da73`). This allows Kubernetes's consumers to ensure the distribution they're using is what is intended for consumption. Adding to that endorsement, as previously mentioned, the OSS Security Mobilization Plan by OpenSSF has a section dedicated to digital signatures that heavily focuses on the adoption and use of Sigstore as a solution to software supply chain integrity gaps. In early 2022, Sonatype announced that Maven Central would be adopting Sigstore as a solution to address provenance concerns in the software supply chain (`https://blog.sonatype.com/maven-central-and-sigstore`).

Sigstore Components

So, what is Sigstore exactly, how does it work, and why does it matter? Sigstore was set up to help address some of the existing gaps in the OSS supply chain and how we handle integrity, digital signatures, and verification of the authenticity of OSS components. This is critical since it's estimated that 90 percent of IT leaders are using OSS (see `www.soocial.com/open-source-adoption-statistics`), organizations are prioritizing hiring OSS talent, and we have seen several notable software supply chain incidents. Sigstore brings together several OSS tools, such as Fulcio, Cosign, and Rekor, to assist with digital signing, verification, and checks of code provenance. *Code provenance* is the ability to have a chain of custody showing where code originated and from whom. The Uber Privacy and Security team have published an excellent blog discussing how they approach the path to code provenance at `https://medium.com/uber-security-privacy/code-provenance-application-security-77ebfa4b6bc5`.

Unpacking some of the core Sigstore components, let's start with Fulcio (`https://github.com/sigstore/fulcio`). Fulcio is a root certificate authority (CA) that focuses on code signing. It is free and issues certifications tied to OpenID Connect (OIDC) and often uses existing identifiers with which developers are already associated. With the rapid adoption and growth of cloud-native architectures and deployment of containers, signing containers has become a key security best practice (`www.csoonline.com/article/3656702/managing-container-vulnerability-risks-tools-and-best-practices.html`). Key management is a cumbersome activity that is often offered as a managed service in the cloud space by CSPs or third-party providers. Sigstore helps mitigate some of that complexity by the way in which it supports Cosign and alleviates some of the key management challenges by using "keyless signing" or using ephemeral or temporary keys (`www.chainguard.dev/unchained/zero-friction-keyless-signing-with-kubernetes#:~:text=Keyless%20enables%20this%20signing%20process,Let's%20Encrypt%20did%20for%20TLS`). Despite the use of ephemeral keys, you can still have assurances of the validity of signatures through Fulcio's timestamping service (`www.chainguard.dev/unchained/busting-5-sigstore-myths`).

This is where Cosign comes in, as it supports various signing options and can seamlessly support generating keypairs and signing container artifacts for storage in a container registry. It empowers cloud-native environments to validate the container against a public key and ensures the container is signed by a trusted source. Digitally signing image artifacts during build time and validating those signatures is a key security best practice highlighted in the Cloud Native Computing Foundation (CNCF) Cloud Native Security white paper (`https://github.com/cncf/tag-security/blob/main/security-whitepaper/v2/CNCF_cloud-native-security-whitepaper-May2022-v2.pdf`).

Next up is Rekor (`https://docs.sigstore.dev/rekor/overview`), which is an immutable and tamper-resistant ledger created as part of software maintenance and build activities. It empowers software consumers to examine the metadata and make risk-informed decisions about the software they are consuming and the activities involved throughout its life cycle. Going back to our previous point on software provenance, developers can use Rekor to contribute to the provenance of software via the transparency log.

Another notable callout is the emerging guidance, such as Supply Chain Levels for Software Artifacts (SLSA; `https://slsa.dev/spec/v0.1/levels`) and the NIST Secure Software Development Framework (SSDF) (`https://csrc.nist.gov/publications/detail/sp/800-218/final`). SLSA level 3 emphasizes the need for auditing the source and integrity of software provenance, which Sigstore supports, as previously discussed. Specific practices called out in SSDF also point to the need for providing provenance and verification mechanisms. This is significant because the federal government is moving toward requiring software producers selling to the government to attest with practices outlined in SSDF (`www.nextgov.com/cybersecurity/2022/02/nist-suggests-agencies-accept-word-software-producers-executive-order/361644`). By adopting Sigstore, you can position your organization to align with the emerging standards and best practices discussed here and mitigate critical software supply chain risks that could lead to a security incident and the associated impact.

Commit Signing

In the context of modern source code management, Git is often the de facto system of choice. Git allows for various entities, such as the author who did the work and the committer, to commit proposed changes. Typically, these entities are usually the same individual, but not always. That said, in many cases it can be simple to impersonate another committer by setting usernames or emails and so on. For this reason, it is becoming a best practice, particularly in sensitive environments, to sign Git commits, which ensures that you can prove you are the author of a specific piece of code as well as its metadata, such as timestamps. Signed commits, while not a cure, can mitigate some potential risks, such as former employees seeking to introduce malicious code by impersonating a coworker or creating malicious pull-requests under an assumed identity that has a good reputation.

Signed commits don't stop malicious actors from impersonating others, because they can still try to assume the identity, but without the digital signature it will quickly raise the eyebrows of those who are paying enough attention.

Git often uses methods such as the GNU Privacy Guard (GPG) to facilitate signing commits. GPG works in the context of Git by allowing you to upload a public key to popular Git platforms like GitHub and GitLab, and then use your private key to sign your commits. GitHub offers documentation explaining how to manage commit signatures and signing commits (`https://docs.github.com/en/authentication/managing-commit-signature-verification/signing-commits`).

SBOM Critiques and Concerns

We would be remiss if we didn't also cover some of the most prevalent critiques, concerns, and challenges of SBOM adoption across the industry as well.

One of the most consolidated sources of those concerns comes in an SBOM FAQ published by NTIA (`www.ntia.doc.gov/files/ntia/`

`publications/sbom_faq_-_fork_for_october_22_meeting.pdf`), in its "Common Misconceptions & Concerns" section, but such concerns have been raised elsewhere by others in the industry through various outlets.

Let's look at the common misconceptions and concerns laid out in the NTIA document and then from some others as well.

Visibility for the Attacker

One concern around SBOMs is that they may serve as a "roadmap to the attacker," as they're often referred to. This can be painted more broadly as the security through obscurity debate, which has raged on in the cybersecurity industry for some time, with valid points coming from both sides. Security through obscurity is often summarized as secrecy being the main method of providing security to a system or component, rather than specific security controls and sound security engineering. Our personal experience can be summarized nicely by longtime industry thought leader Daniel Miessler, who breaks down good obscurity versus bad obscurity, stating, "the key determination for whether obscurity is good or bad reduces to whether it's being used a layer on top of good security, or as a replacement for it. The former is good. The latter is bad." (`https://danielmiessler.com/study/security-by-obscurity`).

The point Miessler is making is that secrecy can certainly be beneficial in some scenarios, but it isn't a replacement for sound security engineering. That said, others in the industry have made the case that SBOMs can be used to do things such as attack APIs, as in Dan Epp's blog on the topic, "Can SBOM Help You Attack APIs?" (`https://danaepp.com/can-sbom-help-you-attack-apis`). But even that article points out that SBOMs help defenders understand *if* they are vulnerable and *where*, which outweighs concerns on the offensive side, as attackers inevitably seek to find those weaknesses, even in the absence of SBOMs.

To answer this question of an SBOM being a "roadmap to the attacker," NTIA points out that malicious actors don't need SBOMs given that foreknowledge is not a prerequisite for attacks. NTIA also states that malicious actors already have the tooling to identify software components and aren't bound from doing so, unlike law-abiding ethical users of software. NTIA states that SBOMs will "level the playing field," giving defenders a level of insight and transparency that malicious actors already have. Malicious actors are able to use binary analysis tooling to understand software composition and component makeup. This isn't debated; however, having an SBOM puts software consumers in a much better position to understand both the initial risk associated with software use as well as new and emerging vulnerabilities associated with software components in the software they consume. If anything, an SBOM helps to level a currently lopsided playing field where malicious actors have visibility where defenders currently do not.

Intellectual Property

Another common concern discussed around SBOMs is that of intellectual property and source code. NTIA pushes back on this point, stating that SBOMs do not require organizations to disclose source code and that source code can be shared at the software provider's discretion, if at all. SBOMs are focused on software components used to build a piece of software, not disclosing the source code itself. Software components represent some of the picture, but not a full roadmap to how the code necessarily operates. NTIA's guidance states that there's a significant difference between knowing third-party ingredients and the entire recipe for execution when it comes to software, not to mention third-party components are not intellectual property of the software vendors using them, but instead belong to the upstream entities who created the components and who are bound by any appropriate licenses assigned to them upon creation. It is worth pointing out as well that although there is a push for increased SBOM adoption, all relevant sources recommend properly safeguarding the SBOMs themselves, aligning with the longstanding security best practice of least permissive access control and need-to-know. Sources such as OMB's 22-18 memo, which calls for federal agencies potentially to require artifacts such as SBOMs from software vendors, also call for agencies to securely store these artifacts if they are not posted publicly by the vendor.

Tooling and Operationalization

Among the most valid concerns around widespread SBOM adoption is a lack of widely available tooling for the facilitation of creating, distributing, ingesting, enriching, analyzing, and operationalizing SBOMs. Many now agree that there are ample tools to aid in creating SBOMs, and we have touched on several of them throughout this book. However, as of this writing, tools to handle additional activities such as distribution, ingestion, enrichment, and analysis are still maturing. As we've mentioned, efforts are underway to innovate in this space by such organizations as the Department of Homeland Security (DHS) and the Cybersecurity Infrastructure Security Agency (CISA), as well as in the commercial space where we've seen a slew of commercial companies making research and development (R&D) investments and products to fill this void. Notable examples include companies such as Chainguard, founded by former Google engineers, which raised $50 million in 2022. Other notable examples include companies such as Endor Labs, TestifySec, and several others, including industry leaders such as Google, who are making innovative software supply chain-focused managed service offerings to help organizations manage their OSS ingestion and use. Once again, citing the U.S. federal space, OMB's 22-18 memo also calls for the government to "establish a centralized repository for software attestations and artifacts," which would include SBOMs.

While the concerns around SBOM, such as visibility for the attacker, intellectual property, and immaturity of tools and capabilities, may be valid, it is overwhelmingly agreed on as an industry, as evidenced by major commitments from leading commercial and government organizations, that the push for transparency and its benefits outweigh the concerns. This isn't to say that the concerns are entirely devoid of merit and shouldn't be addressed, but that continuing on the path of an opaque software ecosystem and lack of visibility into underlying software components and their associated risks and vulnerabilities isn't tenable any longer.

Summary

In this chapter we covered the rise of SBOM and its early efforts from agencies such as NTIA to its transition currently to CISA from the U.S. Federal perspective. We discussed the various SBOM formats and also the emergence of the VEX concept to help reduce some of the noise produced by vulnerabilities from SBOMs. We also discussed some common SBOM critiques and concerns and areas that will continue to evolve as the adoption and implementation of SBOMs grows in the industry.

Challenges in Software Transparency

Early in the discussion in the National Telecommunications and Information Administration (NTIA) software bill of materials (SBOM) initiatives, the topic of SBOMs for devices arose as a complicated factor. Currently, the consensus is that SBOM is such a new concept for many organizations that complicating the discussion is undesirable. After all, isn't device software and firmware just software?

Firmware and Embedded Software

We'll break up this category into a few discussion areas: firmware as an operating system, firmware for embedded devices, and the topic of how SBOMs are used in certain device-specific scenarios such as medical devices.

Linux Firmware

Firmware as an operating system, especially as it relates to Linux firmware, is the most easily understood, but it's important to note that these are very complex SBOMs. Linux is essentially thousands of software products cobbled together to form an operating system. As such, it may be challenging to obtain the level of clarity needed to gain transparency into that software. But this is one of the easier problems to solve in this space. Many of the tools we see for Linux tend to do little more than run a Red Hat Package Manager (RPM) command, unless the image is processed by large-scale reverse engineering processes or SBOMs are produced on a per-software-object level as part of the build process. The reality is that there's so much fragmentation in the way Linux OSs are built that relying on a single entity to produce high-fidelity visibility can be a challenge.

Real-Time Operating System Firmware

Real-time operating system (RTOS) firmware tends to be a bit more challenging, as RTOS in the traditional sense does not actually have a filesystem. In many cases, the RTOS resembles a binary more than a Linux style of firmware image. For the RTOS author, this is a solvable issue, and we have seen public SBOMs from VxWorks in the past. However, for legacy or proprietary RTOSs—such as those produced for some industrial control systems that don't use popular RTOSs like QNX or VxWorks—this issue tends to be a bit of a blind spot. Reverse engineering may be the only viable approach for legacy software or when suppliers can't provide the visibility required.

Embedded Systems

Embedded firmware tends to be highly optimized code with a small footprint. This might be the code that operates on a system on a chip (SoC), or a system BIOS, and in many instances is represented as such low-level code that it becomes challenging for humans to understand the analysis of that firmware. Additionally, because so many strings and symbols are stripped out of the code to optimize and reduce the memory footprint of the firmware, traditional methods for identification of software components can be quite difficult. When combined with high-security zones such as a trusted execution environment (TEE), much of this code runs in a protected area that not only adds security but also creates abstractions that may complicate your understanding of how the software functions and where it runs. This can be especially true when trying to understand the exploitability of software components or how an adversary may, or may not, influence the execution of software.

Device-Specific SBOM

When considering how SBOMs are used in heavily regulated environments, most notably medical devices, it's important to note that certification is designated at the device level. The U.S. Food and Drug Administration (FDA) may certify an insulin pump as a device, and the SBOM for medical devices frequently only goes one level deep. This typically looks more like a software inventory than a full SBOM. As these devices are heavily regulated and changes happen infrequently, the SBOM and resulting analysis tends to be a bit more static. But what should be concerning to most is that the functionality of these devices may sometimes be less reliant on the code running on the device than the cloud infrastructure and other external dependencies that impact them. This is true for many Internet of Things (IoT) devices, where external application programming interfaces (APIs), support infrastructure located in scary parts of the world, or other external dependencies create significant risk. Although these devices appear as very static and mature technological footprints, this variability in inputs and trust relationships creates a blind spot for software transparency and supply chain use cases. There are also challenges associated with the fact that different devices receive updates. Some may receive updates over the air, over the network, or even via USB thumb drives. This could lead to a situation where identical device model numbers may have different SBOMs at any given point in time.

Open Source Software and Proprietary Code

In the world of software, there are two primary forms of code—open source software (OSS) and proprietary software—which complicates the discussion of software transparency in software supply chains. OSS is distinctly different in that anyone can see, use, and contribute to OSS code. Although there are some scenarios for what is known as "source-available" proprietary software (where the source may be viewed or even modified without being considered open source), proprietary code often isn't open for everyone to see, use, or contribute to, and it is often controlled by software and technology vendors or organizations developing software for their various business purposes, whether internal or external. This ability for anyone to use OSS code includes proprietary software producers, and that is exactly what they often do. Some estimates project that 97 percent of all software contains at least some OSS code (www.synopsys .com/content/dam/synopsys/sig-assets/reports/rep-ossra-2022.pdf). Not only is OSS contained in nearly all codebases, but it can often make up nearly 80 percent of the codebase.

In the conversation of software, the term *digital commons* is often used and is a subset of the commonly used term *commons*. Commons are said to be social institutions that help govern the production of resources and collective action (https://policyreview.info/concepts/digital-commons). In this context, digital commons is a subset of the commons, where the resources involve data and information, along with the culture and knowledge involved in the digital domain. Code typically becomes OSS when software developers apply existing OSS licenses granting other users some rights that copyright laws grant exclusively to them, such as the ability to edit and redistribute the code. Once this occurs, everyone with digital access to the project can copy, use, change, and propose contributions to the project and code.

Software products are often tied to several types of software licenses that help govern their use through terms, support agreements, restrictions, and costs. Not only does the software license define definitions for the distribution and use of software, but it also typically lays out the rights of end users for things such as installation, warranties, and liabilities. In the discussion of OSS and proprietary software, OSS software licenses typically give the user the ability to modify and reuse the source code, along with actual access to the source code itself. Proprietary software licenses, however, generally do not provide the ability to modify and reuse the code and, of course, do not provide direct access to the source code itself. Situations exist where software is not covered by a license and is considered either public domain software or private unlicensed software, such as business applications that may still warrant copyright protection. Failing to comply with software licensing requirements can have ramifications, such as allowing the copyright holder to sue or the offender to even face an injunction.

Common software license types include the following:

Permissive   These licenses contain minimal restrictions on how the software can be modified or distributed but may require attribution in copyright information of subsequent distributions. Common examples include Apache, BSD, and MIT licenses.

Weak Copyleft   Often called the GNU Lesser General Public License (www.gnu.org/licenses/lgpl-3.0.en.html), it allows linking to OSS libraries with minimal obligation, and the entire work is about to be distributed under subsequent license types, even proprietary, with minimal requirements.

Public Domain License   Everyone is free to use and modify the software without any restrictions; this license type is not common.

Copyleft   Copyleft licenses are also known as *reciprocal licenses* and can be more commercially restrictive than some other license types. Copyleft allows developers to modify the license code and incorporate it into other projects, or even modify proprietary code and distribute it, but that must be done under the same license. The original software and modifications are included in the new project, making this license less appealing for developers with commercial interests.

Commercial/Proprietary   These license types are used to restrict the ability to copy, modify, and distribute the code. Considered among the most restrictive software license types, commercial/proprietary licenses prevent unauthorized use of the software and are the most protective of commercial interests.

Licensing considerations aside, the use of OSS is pervasive, even as mentioned previously, in proprietary software and products. This is for obvious reasons, such as saving development time, leveraging existing work, minimizing cost, and expediting time to market. The use of OSS code frees up developers and teams to focus on more value-added activities, such as developing custom code or functionality and focusing on mission and business objectives. As mentioned in this book's Introduction, OSS code is prevalent in nearly every environment, including critical infrastructure sectors such as energy, finance, communications, health care, and the defense industrial base. While on the surface the prevalence of OSS may make sense, given the innovative and community emphasis it brings, it brings challenges as well. Studies have found that 88 percent of codebases include OSS components that have had no new development in over two years, 81 percent contain at least one vulnerability, and nearly 90 percent contain OSS that isn't on the latest version.

This means that out-of-date, poorly maintained, and vulnerable OSS exists across nearly *all* aspects of society, including critical infrastructure sectors.

On the proprietary side, challenges exist that are unique. While OSS often has Common Vulnerabilities and Exposures (CVEs) assigned to it in sources such as the National Vulnerability Database (NVD) and it can be searched and scanned with tools such as vulnerability scanners to identify known vulnerabilities, proprietary code can be a bit more difficult and can require other techniques to identify vulnerabilities. Also, source code for proprietary software is generally not disclosed, making assessment and analysis not quite straightforward. The push for SBOMs will create a situation where software producers and vendors will begin providing SBOMs that shine a light on the OSS components in their products, along with the vulnerabilities associated with those OSS components.

Distinct differences exist between OSS and proprietary software when it comes to vulnerability disclosure and remediation. On the proprietary side, vendors generally have contractual documents and agreements that allow them to inform software users of potential impacts from vulnerabilities and risks. The same isn't true when it comes to OSS. Because OSS is generally open for everyone to access, use, reuse, and modify, it is much more difficult for a centralized notification or mechanism to notify everyone impacted by a vulnerability in an OSS project or component. This is further exacerbated by the integration of OSS components into other projects and code as dependencies. This makes it critical for software consumers to thoroughly understand the software they have in their environment and to be cognizant of any notifications, vulnerabilities, and risks associated with those software components.

Often the case is made that OSS can be more secure than proprietary software because the code is accessible and visible to everyone for review and analysis. A common adage in the OSS community referred to as Linus's Law asserts that "given enough eyeballs, all bugs are shallow." This seems intuitive, given that if there are enough software developers and security experts looking at code, the chance of bugs and vulnerabilities likely decreases. Although this may be true of wildly popular OSS projects such as Linux and Kubernetes, the adage doesn't hold up across the broader OSS ecosystem. There are millions of OSS projects, and while some may have robust thriving ecosystems of maintainers and contributors, others are often maintained by a small group or even a single individual. Some studies show that almost a quarter of OSS projects have a single contributor (`https://dl.acm.org/doi/abs/10.1145/3510003.3510216`), and even more surprising, almost 95 percent of projects have fewer than 10 developers contributing the bulk of the code (`www.synopsys.com/content/dam/synopsys/sig-assets/reports/rep-ossra-2022.pdf`). It is worth noting that proprietary software vendors have resource constraints as well, meaning that companies also do not have infinite development resources and often have to prioritize revenue-generating features and product enhancements over security activities. It's a simple reality that resource constraints radiate risk, and this should be a consideration for all software consumers, whether they're consuming OSS or proprietary code. The antiquated model of security by obscurity has also largely fallen to the wayside, with many experts agreeing that obscurity benefits the adversary far more than the broader community. With that said, it doesn't stop some organizations from trying to hide behind obscurity, either due to genuinely believing it leads to better security outcomes or because of fears of exposing inefficiencies and gaps that they are aware of but are reluctant to disclose.

Another distinct difference between OSS code and proprietary code is that because of the way OSS functions, with anyone able to consume and use it, open disclosure is the only effective way to notify potentially impacted consumers and parties. There's no unified list of everyone using an OSS component, so open disclosure allows consumers to act, but it also requires that OSS consumers be cognizant of these disclosures, and most important, understand their OSS consumption in order to be able to do anything to address the risk. On the proprietary side, organizations can notify their customers and consumers because there is typically an exchange of agreements, such as contracts, service-level agreements, and so on.

While OSS has led to a thriving ecosystem of innovative software solutions that save organizations time, resources, and strife, it has also led to a complex modern software supply chain with exponential dependencies. Studies show that the average application and project have nearly 70 dependencies based on the programming language used, and the average application also has at least five critical vulnerabilities. Many software consumers are unaware of the full extent of their dependencies and, by extension, the vulnerabilities associated with those dependencies. These studies show that despite the pervasive use of OSS, half of the organizations surveyed have no security policy in place that governs the use of OSS. Organizations such as the National Institute of Standards and Technologies (NIST) recommend best practices, such as establishing policies governing the use of OSS and going beyond that to establish internal repositories of known trusted OSS components for developers to use, versus allowing the unconstrained use of external OSS components.

User Software

The concept of user software as opposed to device firmware, or enterprise-grade products that are used to manage networks and security, frequently brings with it a much different perspective. Largely panned as not being critical, and hence not worthy of our attention, user software and common utilities are frequently the subject of attacks against our users. When you consider that any software runs with the user's permission and many organizations still permit their users to run with local administrator privileges, it becomes clear that software itself does not need to be designed for administrative functions to become capable of administrator utility.

As part of the Executive Order 14028, one of the many deliverables for NIST was a definition of critical software. This was designed to ensure that these new SBOM requirements would be limited in scope to only the most critical applications. This makes a lot of sense on the surface, until you start to realize that software itself is not critical, but how it is used can be. NIST defined critical software as software that

- Is designed to run with elevated privilege or manage privileges

- Has direct or privileged access to networking or computing resources

- Is designed to control access to data or operational technology

- performs a function critical to trust (www.nist.gov/itl/executive-order-improving-nations-cybersecurity/critical-software-definition-faqs#Ref_FAQ3)

- Operates outside of normal trust boundaries with privileged access

User software such as Adobe Reader or Notepad++ don't really meet any of these criteria, but when you consider potential threat scenarios such as users finding themselves frequently parsing and viewing external documents of questionable trust, this has the potential to introduce risk or serve as an attack vector. Adobe, in particular, is no stranger to compromise in phishing scenarios, and it might not fit the bill for critical software but provides no less credible a pathway for attack.

Quite possibly the biggest challenge for all this user software is the sheer scope and scalability required in addressing the challenge. In the vulnerability incident response following the Log4j vulnerability disclosure in December 2021, one of this book's authors was sent a list of over one million CPEs, or unique product versions, and was asked the question "How many of these are vulnerable to log4shell?" This agency understood that it did not matter what the software was used for—any instance where such a vulnerability could be so trivially exploited, as seen by the log4shell exploits, could be easily expanded into much more critical targets.

This is the perfect example of how supply chain attacks allow attackers to move beyond the perimeter in interesting ways. These are not direct attacks, and by trusting our internal users and not properly validating their actions, overly permissive access characteristics, and so on, even the most innocuous software creates a gateway for compromise. How can we address these challenges of scale? It will likely take time to standardize on much of the guidance presented in this book before we get there. We hope that at some point these software supply chain best practices all become so commonplace that it isn't much different than food inspectors ensuring that all food in the grocery store is safe for consumption, but we also understand that from a practical perspective we have quite a ways to go as an industry and society.

Legacy Software

If we look at all the great projects coming out of the open-source ecosystem to address supply chain concerns, including modern application development frameworks and tools, it paints a particularly rosy picture of where we are going. But what does this mean for legacy software?

Especially in critical infrastructure or defense—where the useful life of a system is frequently 20–30 years or longer—and in cases where no package managers were used in the production of software, source code is no longer available, the original developers have since retired, or, worse, left this Earth, we have a different set of problems to understand. In some cases, software has fallen out of support or perhaps sees periodic custom patches applied. In these scenarios, frequently reverse engineering may be the only viable option for determining the composition of the software. But let's examine another challenge here with regard to proprietary software that becomes even more interesting as we address legacy software.

Once upon a time, almost all software was proprietary. It was commonly shared with academia and for other information-sharing reasons, but by and large when we think about the current definition of OSS, it has only been in the last 25 years or so that this became a structured concept with defined licenses. There are some exceptions, such as glibc, the GNU C library, and GNU Compiler Collection (GCC), with the C compiler going back to 1987. But when comparing software built over 30 years ago to software built today, we see that far more components are recognizable and understood in modern software.

Why is the concept of open source so important? Because most application security tools today do not take into account what goes into the production of proprietary software. The vast majority of SBOM tools on the market today will only inform you if your software is vulnerable based on the known open-source components. This is a huge blind spot for legacy software with few, or no, open-source components. In fact, many of these same SBOM tools are only useful when a package manager is used in the construction of your software. While Linux has used package management for over 20 years, modern languages such as Python and Node.js have been using the current iteration of tools for only 10 years or so. Modern SBOM tools are developed against what is used today, not what was used decades ago and is still pervasive in many environments. For instance, the package installer pip was introduced in Python 2.7.9 in 2014.

If source code is not available, then static analysis tools cannot evaluate it. If there is no runtime to instrument, it becomes challenging to validate using modern interactive application security testing (IAST) tools. And without researcher access to source, most certainly there are no public CVEs to understand when that proprietary code is terribly vulnerable. In fact, understanding how the software is built is almost certainly a black box in many instances, with the only saving grace being if the software is vulnerable and it's not a new risk. The downside is that this is some of the most critical software on the planet, running missile silos, nuclear reactors, water treatment plants, and the like.

Secure Transport

At the core of supply chain risk management is the concept of trust or the verification of trust. It's trust in the source or the provenance of the software. Trust that it does not contain components or libraries that exceed our desired risk tolerance. Trust that it arrived to us unchanged. Trust that we are about to install the product we are intending to install.

Secure transport mechanisms can come in a few different flavors, but we are talking about Transport Layer Security (TLS), the successor to Secure Sockets Layer (SSL). TLS is tasked with the job of moving bits from point A to point B and doing so with a high degree of trust to ensure that the contents remain confidential and that their integrity hasn't been compromised—trust that the endpoints sharing information are the ones we think they are, and that the bits and bytes have arrived unaltered. While TLS is also used for encryption and safeguarding the confidentiality of our data stream, this makes the job of transparency harder. However, it does make manipulating that data stream much harder as well. This is one of the areas where a conscious trade-off between transparency and security is established. You can no longer see what's happening, but if you trust the source and the data did not change—could not change then you trust what arrives at the destination.

Unfortunately, at the root of these trust decisions is the certificate authority (CA) infrastructure. This mechanism establishes a web of trust that operates the Internet. It's a fairly centralized ecosystem in that a compromise of the CA may result in a compromise of certificates they issued for TLS, or even code signing, for that matter. Yet a CA creates a reasonable assurance that the difficulty required in carrying out these attacks is sufficient for most organizations' threat models, and therefore decisions based on TLS are deemed safe.

As alluded to earlier, adversaries will commonly abuse encrypted channels to hide their own malicious traffic. But due to the very nature of modern TLS protocols, especially those using concepts such as Perfect Forward Secrecy, breaking and reestablishing encrypted transport becomes difficult, if not impossible, and similarly so for the defender. But it narrows the realm of possibilities for compromise to point A and point B and eliminates the 30 or so network hops in the middle as a point of compromise.

Similarly, we need to be able to trust the attestations that we use for risk decision-making. How do we know that the SBOM or build attestation is legitimate? The use of transparency logs and blockchain-enabled ledgers provides transparency and trust on one end of the transaction, point A, and in some implementations, perhaps end to end. But how do we know that data that transits the network remains unchanged? Thankfully, utilizing TLS tunneling helps answer these questions as well.

But what if software and attestations are not secured this way? Does that mean they are insecure? Even many modern Linux distributions do not secure repository traffic this way and instead rely on GNU Privacy Guard (GPG)-level signing to ensure software integrity. You will need to determine your own risk appetite here, but suffice it to say, if you require software transport over TLS for all software, even in the year 2023, you will be eliminating a lot of enterprise software from use.

Until the use of TLS becomes more ubiquitous, we think this is probably a "nice to have" for all but the most critical software. That said, despite some of the challenges associated with implementing TLS, momentum around movements such as Zero Trust are advocating end-to-end encryption as a best practice and implementation that organizations should be applying.

Going further, organizations are increasingly striving to adopt mutual TLS (mTLS), which uses the same protocols as TLS but occurs in a two-way verification instead of unidirectional. This way, the identities of both the server and client are verified before connections are established and data exchanges occur.

Summary

In summary, although there is a tremendous amount of momentum behind the push for software transparency, there are also several issues that still need to be resolved, and doing so may be challenging. We discussed some of them in this chapter, such as embedded and legacy software, OSS and its various licensing types, and the need for security of data in transit. That said, each of these respective areas also have their share of innovation and solutions being developed within the community and by vendors working in the ecosystem. Continuing to address these challenges will help close the gap for software transparency regardless of where the software resides. In the following chapter we will discuss the role that technologies such as cloud, containers and Kubernetes play in the software supply chain and transparency discussions and some of their associated challenges as well.

Cloud and Containerization

While pursuing software bills of materials (SBOMs) and software transparency in traditional, on-premises infrastructure is challenging, the challenge is significantly different when dealing with cloud services and cloud-native architectures. In this chapter, we will discuss some of the metrics surrounding the growth of cloud and containerization, as well as software transparency and supply chain security concerns in the context of cloud computing.

When discussing technology, it often helps to have a shared lexicon. With that said, the most used definition of cloud computing comes from NIST 800-145 (`https://nvlpubs.nist.gov/nistpubs/Legacy/SP/nistspecialpublication800-145.pdf`), which states:

> **Cloud computing is a model for enabling ubiquitous, convenient, on-demand network access to a shared pool of configurable computing resources (e.g., networks, servers, storage, applications, and services) that can be rapidly provisioned and released with minimal management effort or service provider interaction. This cloud model is composed of five essential characteristics, three service models, and four deployment models.**

Expanding further, those characteristics include on-demand self-service, broad network access, resource pooling, rapid elasticity, and measured service. Cloud also comes with three service models: Infrastructure-as-a-Service (IaaS),

Platform-as-a-Service (PaaS), and Software-as-a-Service (SaaS). Each of these service models has its own unique shared responsibility models and associated implications for how software makes it to the downstream consumer. Cloud computing has four primary deployment models: private, community, public, and hybrid cloud, each of which has implications for topics such as multitenancy and security.

Each of these unique models associated with cloud computing still involves software in some shape and requires downstream consumers to have a level of assurance regarding the security of the services and associated software they are consuming.

Shared Responsibility Model

No conversation about security and risk in the cloud would be complete without coverage of the shared responsibility model (SRM). Many business leaders still ask, "Is the cloud secure?," which is the wrong question to ask. A more appropriate question is "Are we, as a security team and organization, securing our share of our cloud consumption?"

The overwhelming majority of cloud data breaches and leaks are due to the customer, with Gartner, an IT research and consultancy company, predicting that through 2025, some 99 percent of cloud security failures will be the customer's fault (www.gartner.com/smarterwithgartner/is-the-cloud-secure). For this reason, it's imperative that all security practitioners understand their responsibilities.

Breakdown of the Shared Responsibility Model

The SRM delineates what you, the cloud customer, are responsible for, and what your cloud service provider (CSP) is responsible for. In the IaaS model, the CSP is responsible for security "of" the cloud—think physical facilities, utilities, cables, hardware, and so forth. The customer is responsible for security "in" the cloud—meaning network controls, identity and access management, application configurations, and data security.

Duties of the Shared Responsibility Model

That said, this division of responsibilities can change depending on what service model you use. At a basic level, the NIST definition of cloud computing explains three primary cloud service models:

- **Infrastructure-as-a-Service (IaaS):** Under the IaaS model, the CSP is responsible for the physical datacenter, physical networking, and physical servers/hosting.

- **Platform-as-a-Service (PaaS):** In a PaaS model, the CSP takes on more responsibility for things such as patching (which customers are historically terrible at and serves as a primary pathway to security incidents) and maintaining operating systems.

- **Software-as-a-Service (SaaS):** In SaaS, the customer can only make changes within an application's configuration settings, with the control of everything else left to the CSP. (Gmail is a basic example.) It is worth noting that even in the context of SaaS, there's much to be done when it comes to SaaS governance and security, which we discuss in depth later in this chapter.

Each comes with a trade-off, with the customer relinquishing control in exchange for more of a turnkey-managed experience with the CSP handling more of the operational activities and letting the customer focus on their core competencies. Many organizations find this paradigm compelling because managing compute and infrastructure generally isn't their core business and, instead, is typically an activity they have to perform to deliver their core services and products.

Each CSP has varying versions of the SRM. Figure 6.1 is an example from Microsoft's Azure SRM (`https://docs.microsoft.com/en-us/azure/security/fundamentals/shared-responsibility`).

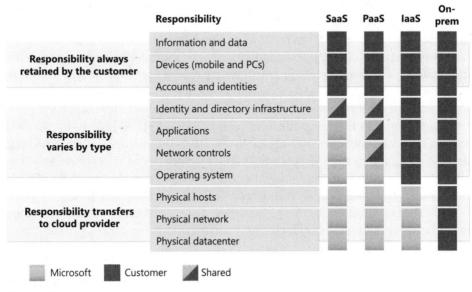

Figure 6.1

While the SRM involves nonsecurity issues such as contracts and financial implications, it also includes several security considerations. Security practitioners must understand what they are responsible for in the SRM based on the services they are consuming and their organization's implementations and architectures.

Remember how nearly all cloud data incidents occur on the customer side of the SRM? This is a major reason to understand the SRM and ensure you're doing your part of the model. Another thing we cannot emphasize enough is that while there may be a sharing of responsibilities, you cannot outsource accountability. As an organization, you're still ultimately the data owner and have accountability for that data and the stakeholders it belongs to, even if you decide to use a third party, such as a CSP, in your delivery of services and business to your customers or stakeholders. Although there may be contractual ramifications for CSPs involved in data breaches from their customers, the customers will suffer the consequences in terms of reputation, brand, and regulatory ramifications.

Your responsibilities depend on which of two primary security role perspectives you have: the technical security practitioner or the security executive. Technical security practitioners, such as cloud security engineers or cloud security architects, must understand what cloud services your organization uses; how to securely architect those solutions; and what configurations, settings, and controls are under your purview that you can influence and lead to a more robust security posture. In a glaring example of where firms are falling short, cloud-native vendor SysDig found in their 2023 "Cloud-Native Security and Usage Report" that 90 percent of granted permissions in cloud environments aren't used. This runs contradictory to the industry's push for zero trust and leaves a lot of opportunity for attackers to abuse compromised accounts (`https://sysdig.com/press-releases/sysdig-2023-usage-report`).

Technical security professionals should be intimately familiar with the platforms and services their organization uses and understand how to implement them securely. Cloud security engineers/architects often work with engineering and development teams. If you aren't able to guide them to a secure solution or spot risky configurations (remember how these account for most cloud data incidents), you could expose your organization to tremendous risk.

Look to your CSP for security resources. Amazon Web Services (AWS), for example, offers an incredible database of security documentation, broken down by categories (e.g., compute, storage, security, identity, and compliance), where you can find specifics associated with each of the services your organization uses. This includes a wide range of information, from how to securely configure the services, to what configurations you can manipulate, to troubleshooting guidance.

Key considerations for security executives include inventorying service usage (you must know what is being used within your organization or you cannot secure it), ensuring the services you use are compliant with your applicable regulatory frameworks, and understanding contractual/legal aspects such as CSP service-level agreements (SLAs), especially when it comes to things such as incident response planning. One such resource that one of the authors contributed to publishing is Cloud Security Alliance's Cloud Incident Response Framework (`https://cloudsecurityalliance.org/artifacts/cloud-incident-response-framework`).

Many organizations enter a partnership with the CSP and share responsibilities. This includes ensuring that the services you're using meet the regulatory frameworks to which you must adhere. The hyperscale CSPs make this information easy to find, with AWS and Microsoft Azure providing "services-in-scope" pages where you can determine what services comply with what frameworks and which are still in approval processes or yet to be assessed and evaluated. This helps ensure that your team not only builds robust and secure architectures and workloads in the cloud but also uses services that are compliant with your applicable frameworks to avoid compliance or regulatory issues and use services they have assurances around.

Security practitioners of all levels should strive to implement secure standards and best practices in their cloud environments. This could mean implementing security best practices from your respective CSPs or implementing something such as the Center for Internet Security (CIS) benchmark for your respective cloud environments (`www.cisecurity.org/blog/foundational-cloud-security-with-cis-benchmarks`).

A fundamental artifact when dealing with the SRM is the customer responsibility matrix (CRM), which lays out what controls are being provided by the CSP and what responsibilities are left to the cloud consumer. One place to find a CRM template and learn more about them is the Federal Risk and Authorization Management Program (FedRAMP). FedRAMP is a program that handles the authorization of cloud service offerings for consumption across the U.S. federal government (`www.fedramp.gov/updated-Control-implementation-summary-cis-and-customer-responsibility-matrix-crm-templates`).

A CRM is a critical tool for security practitioners to use. In the SRM, security controls are provided entirely by the CSP, a hybrid control (with responsibility falling on both the CSP and cloud customer), or entirely left to the customer. Security practitioners can leverage CRMs to gain a clear understanding of this security control delineation. These are often referred to security controls being fully, partially, or not inheritable, respectively.

Consuming cloud services can shift the responsibility of some security controls and activities to the CSP and let organizations focus on their core competencies. It creates a relationship of responsibilities that security professionals must understand and handle appropriately. Remember, most cloud data breaches will occur on the customer side of the SRM, and at the end of the day, you have the full accountability of your organization's reputation and the CSP represents another third-party provider that must be accounted for in the push for software transparency and software supply chain security.

The 4 Cs of Cloud Native Security

One helpful way to contextualize the cloud-native ecosystem is via the "4C's of Cloud Native Security" as described by the Kubernetes documentation, a container orchestrator illustrated in Figure 6.2 that is discussed here.

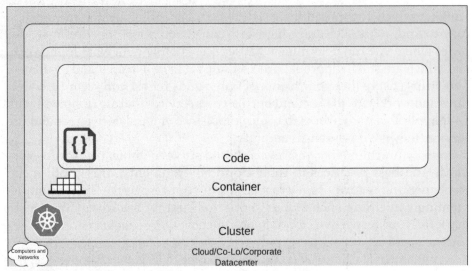

Figure 6.2

Source: https://kubernetes.io/docs/concepts/security/overview/#:~:text=The%20 4C's%20of%20Cloud%20Native%20security%20are,Clusters%2C%20Containers%2C%20 and%20Code. Kubernetes Documentation, The Kubernetes Authors, CC BY 4.0.

In this context, which is specific to containers and their orchestration, you have the cloud, clusters, containers, and code, with each layer inherently depending on the ones above (or preceding) it in terms of infrastructure in its various forms and the code that gets deployed onto it.

As discussed previously, the cloud paradigm has three agreed-upon service models as defined by NIST. One of the primary methods of cloud consumption is IaaS, where organizations utilize the CSP's physical facilities, utilities, personnel, and infrastructure to deploy operating systems and applications on. In this paradigm, the CSP is responsible for the underlying infrastructure, utilities, facilities, personnel, and general capital expenditure (CapEx) costs. The leading CSPs provide robust cloud services for consumption in key areas such as networking, compute, and storage. However, these services are still empowered by software, as is most of modern infrastructure. This means they are still vulnerable to software-related vulnerabilities and exploits. While cloud consumers are abstracted from the underlying infrastructure in the IaaS model, it doesn't mean they are fully insulated from the risks and threats that potentially impact it. That is exactly what happened in the case of the Log4j vulnerability. The major CSPs—AWS (`https://aws.amazon.com/security/security-bulletins/AWS-2021-006`), Azure (`https://msrc-blog.microsoft.com/2021/12/11/microsofts-response-to-cve-2021-44228-apache-log4j2`), and Google Cloud (`https://cloud.google.com/log4j2-security-advisory`)—all released advisories related to the impact of Log4j in their cloud service offerings.

These CSPs, much like the broader IT industry, use a myriad of open-source libraries and components to power their diverse portfolio of cloud services. Looking at the advisories from the CSPs mentioned, this single open-source software supply chain compromise had an impact across their portfolio of cloud-native services, and it does not stop there. These CSPs have revenue in the billions of dollars and support thousands of organizations and millions of individuals. As organizations build and deliver applications and services on top of these CSP offerings, a software supply chain compromise or vulnerability in the underlying service offerings can impact not just the consuming organizations but their business partners, customers, and stakeholders as well. For the hyperscale CSPs previously mentioned, those customers include even the most critical and sensitive workloads in the United States, as the CSPs are used by organizations such as the Department of Defense (DoD), the intelligence community, and Federal Civilian Executive Branch (FCEB) agencies.

This reality requires assurances for the services cloud customers are consuming and the associated software that powers them. While there are mature programs set in place, such as FedRAMP (`www.fedramp.gov`) or SOC2 (`https://us.aicpa.org/interestareas/frc/assuranceadvisoryservices/aicpasoc2report`), they traditionally have not looked at the software from the granular perspective of inventorying and understanding the underlying software supply chain that powers modern cloud-native service offerings and the associated risk with that software. These programs look at more traditional methods of assessing risk, such as CSP policies and processes, vulnerability scan results for underlying compute instances, and penetration tests. As the software supply chain increasingly becomes a point of concern for IT and cybersecurity leaders, we may see a shift where authorizing programs such as FedRAMP begin to ask for items such as SBOMs from CSPs for their software-oriented managed service offerings. The U.S. federal government has already signaled this intent with the release of Office of Management and Budget (OMB) Memorandum 22-18 (`www.whitehouse.gov/wp-content/uploads/2022/09/M-22-18.pdf`), which will have agencies potentially requesting artifacts, including SBOMs from third-party software producers selling software to the federal government, which of course includes cloud providers. It also requires third-party software vendors to provide self-attestations that they're following secure software development practices, such as NIST's Secure Software Development Framework (SSDF) and other NIST guidance on software supply chain security.

However, this is challenging, given the breadth and scale of the hyperscale CSPs such as AWS, Azure, and Google, who undoubtedly have massive software inventories powering their cloud service offerings. It also contrasts with the current approach that is largely based around third-party assessment organizations (3PAOs), where a third party evaluates the service provider and provides artifacts and attestations related to the provider's internal practices and security processes. Cloud and managed service offerings have typically strived to abstract some of the underlying complexity away from the consumer in exchange for the consumer experience and convenience. It is worth noting that, in the OMB 22-18 memo previously mentioned, it allows for software producers to self-attest to their use of secure development practices. However, it does allow for agencies to require a 3PAO if they believe it is warranted. Yet, how that would play out at scale for every cloud service is impractical, given the current landscape, tooling, and organizational capabilities.

While IaaS inevitably involves software, the conversation around software supply chain security is much more mature in other aspects of cloud-native architectures, such as containers, Kubernetes, code, and increasingly SaaS.

Containers

Continuing from traditional models of compute such as physical servers and virtual machines (VMs), the cloud-native ecosystem makes extensive use of containers. Therefore, it is important that we discuss containers and relevant software supply chain concerns when it comes to containers and their associated orchestration systems, such as Kubernetes.

As compute abstractions have matured, we have seen a shift from virtual machines (VMs) to containers. Containers, as defined by industry leader Docker, are "a standard unit of software that packages up code and all its dependencies, so the application runs quickly and reliably from one computing environment to another." Containers are far more lightweight, dynamic, and portable than their VM counterparts, which require a guest operating system for each VM (see Figure 6.3).

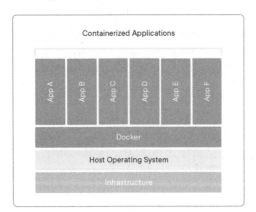
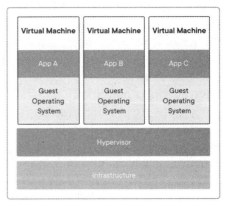

Figure 6.3

Source: www.docker.com/resources/what-container, last accessed March 27, 2023

One of the primary benefits of containers is that they allow developers to package their software code, relevant libraries, and dependencies into a lightweight artifact. This artifact is portable and able to be run across various hosting environments and infrastructures that support container-based deployments.

While this bundling is enormously beneficial to activities such as portability and efficiency, it also opens the door for insecure or vulnerable dependencies to be included in a container and then replicated at scale. This happens on a regular basis as well, with public container image repositories such as DockerHub, Google Container Registry, and others, where container images are available for anyone to consume and reuse.

In fact, a 2021 study by Palo Alto's Unit 42 Threat Research group found in a study of over 1,500 publicly available container images that known vulnerabilities existed in 96 percent of the images and 91 percent of the images had at least one critical or high vulnerability based on severity scores from sources such as CVSS (www.paloaltonetworks.com/content/dam/pan/en_US/assets/pdf/reports/Unit_42/unit-42-cloud-threat-report-2h-2021.pdf).

This study also points out that the more dependencies an image has, the more likely it is to have a higher vulnerability count on average. Therefore, efforts such as reducing the attack surface or minimizing the number of dependencies and code to only those required by the container and application to function is widely considered a security best practice.

Much like other forms of application and software delivery, deployment containers also warrant transparency. Using SBOMs for containers allows you to see every artifact in the container image, which aids in identifying vulnerabilities in your software supply chain and remediation throughout the software development life cycle. This includes from the source, build, staging, deploy, and runtime stages. Vulnerabilities can be introduced at any stage throughout the development cycle, so generating an SBOM throughout the process and stages can allow for visibility of the images throughout the life cycle and for any changes that introduce risk.

Despite the widespread prevalence of vulnerable images, innovative tooling is emerging to help provide transparency into a container and the software components and dependencies that it entails. Leading vendors such as Anchore have produced OSS tools that allow organizations to generate SBOMs. Anchore's SBOM tool is known as Syft and boasts a robust set of features and language support. Features include generating SBOMs for container images, filesystems, and more; support for Open Container Initiative (OCI) and Docker image formats; and the ability to support signed SBOM attestations using the in-toto framework. (Attestations are a concept we will discuss in other areas of the book such as Chapter 11, "Practical Guidance for Consumers.")

Syft supports the leading SBOM formats such as CycloneDX and SPDX as discussed in Chapter 4, "Rise of Software Bill of Materials." Another widely popular OSS scanner is Trivy, from the team at Aqua Security. It supports targeting container images, filesystems, Git repositories, and Kubernetes resources to identify CVEs, OS packages, and dependencies in support of SBOMs and misconfiguration in declarative infrastructure as code.

Container leader Docker has even added a native SBOM capability. In early 2022, Docker announced the ability to simply run `docker sbom` from the CLI of Docker Desktop and generate an SBOM for any Docker image (`www.docker .com/blog/announcing-docker-sbom-a-step-towards-more-visibility-into-docker-images`). This capability was developed with the collaboration of the open-source community and the Anchore team, using their Syft project that we previously discussed. The Docker team explained that this additional functionality is aimed at improving trust in the supply chain to see what is contained within images and making the process easy for developers in order to not impede productivity or velocity.

From a software supply chain perspective, containers and their associated ecosystem present a wide range of potential attack vectors and risks to consider. Although it would be difficult to enumerate every attack vector, we will certainly look at some of the primary ones here, including base images, operating systems, Git repositories, application code and dependencies, and OSS components. Container security is also further complicated due to the number of teams involved in development, security, and operations in cloud-native environments, coupled with the various security layers of securing containers. These involve the container image and software it contains, interactions between the container and host OS, as well as other containers running on the orchestration platforms. There are also attack vectors and risks associated with container networking and storage and the runtime environment the containers deploy to in production, which is often located on top of a Kubernetes cluster.

When discussing base images, much like any upstream component in a software supply chain, all downstream consumers and users can be impacted by risk introduced up the supply chain. Base images are a critical step in the container software supply chain because software applications running on containers inherit any security debt and vulnerabilities included in the base image on which the application is built. A key best practice recommended by several sources of container security guidance is to use a hardened base image. Typically, this means a base image has been hardened to reduce vulnerabilities and has also been stripped to only include the essentials required to be functional. This is often referred to as *attack surface reduction*, removing unnecessary components that can be taken advantage of to compromise the container and applications residing on them. Some of the most popular base images include Alpine, Ubuntu, and Debian.

Among the pushes to minimize the containers' attack surface is the emergence of what has become known as "distroless" container images. Distroless container images contain only the application and its runtime dependencies, thus removing components such as package managers, shells, or other programs that often accompany common Linux distributions. Minimizing the attack surface of containers is frequently cited as a best practice by sources such as NIST in their "Application Container Security Guide" (https://csrc.nist .gov/publications/detail/sp/800-190/final), as well as industry leaders such as Liz Rice in her book *Container Security* (O'Reilly Media, 2020), which discusses attack surface reduction among other container security recommendations. Distroless images have several benefits aside from reducing the attack surface, such as minimizing the noise of scanners due to false CVEs, reducing the burden of provenance, and being more efficient in terms of size, as cited in Google's Container Tools Distroless GitHub page (https://github.com/ GoogleContainerTools/distroless).

Software supply chain security startup Chainguard introduced Wolfi, a suite of distroless images with a far more secure footprint CVE-wise than most traditional container images (www.chainguard.dev/unchained/introducing- wolfi-the-first-linux-un-distro). Chainguard has also begun introducing the pursuit of memory-safe container images, which aligns with broader recommendations from sources such as the NSA on shifting the industry to more secure memory-safe languages and ecosystems.

Much like other OSS components, organizations often source container images from the open Internet, and when it comes to containers, one of the most popular sources is Docker Hub (https://hub.docker.com). As the name suggests, Docker Hub is run by Docker and is used to find and share container images with teams and organizations. To put the popularity of Docker Hub and the associated images it hosts in perspective, as of this writing there are 20 images on the site that have been downloaded *at least one billion times*. That said, much like any other software components, these container images often have several vulnerabilities in the image files, and organizations can inherit these vulnerabilities and technical debt by not doing due diligence before using them. As previously mentioned, studies have determined that over 90 percent of the images available publicly on Docker Hub contain known vulnerabilities, with an extremely high percentage of those including at least one critical or high vulnerability. Couple that with the billions of downloads, and you can imagine how many vulnerable containers are running in enterprise environments around the world.

Further studies by organizations such as software supply chain vendor Chainguard used container vulnerability scanning tools Trivy, Snyk, and Grype to evaluate some of the most popular base images by download count on Docker Hub (https://uploads-ssl.webflow.com/6228fdbc6c97145dad2a9c2b/624e233 7f70386ed568d7e7e_chainguard-all-about-that-base-image.pdf). Chainguard found that leading images such as Node, Debian, Ubuntu, and Red Hat UBI all have significant technical debt baked into the image. Vulnerability counts for these images ranged from 28 to as high as 800, depending on the image and the scanner used. The vulnerability severities ranged from low to critical, and only the Alpine: 3.15.0 image included no known vulnerabilities across the three vulnerability scanners used. As the study points out, the reason Alpine scored so well in comparison to the others is because it's a security-oriented base image that contains fewer than 10 packages. This is an example of attack surface reduction and base images created with security in mind in order to drive down organizational risk. Obviously, each layer of a containerized application potentially adds to the risk profile, but starting with a properly secure and minimal base image is recommended.

Not only is the base image a topic of concern, but organizations are increasingly adopting the practice of establishing internal repositories of hardened containers that have undergone attack surface reduction and hardening, and are signed by trusted entities. This mitigates the potential for teams to pull container images from public sources, so they might instead use internally approved and stored images that meet the organization's security and compliance requirements. One of the most visible and cited examples of this is the Department of Defense's (DoD's) Iron Bank (`https://p1.dso.mil/products/iron-bank`), which is a container repository of hardened, approved, and authorized container images for use within the U.S. Air Force (USAF) and more broadly the DoD. U.S. federal civilian agencies have leveraged these hardened images as well and followed suit, establishing their own internal repository of secure container images for use and deployment.

Public Git repositories represent another avenue where risk can be introduced in the container software supply chain. While CVEs associated with images is a great metric to gauge the security of containers, understanding the repositories they are sourced from is another measure that informs an organization's understanding of inherent or potential risk. A popular project that looks at the configuration and activities associated with public GitHub projects and their repositories is the OpenSSF Scorecard initiative, which we'll discuss in Chapter 7, titled "Existing and Emerging Commercial Guidance."

Application code, dependencies, and OSS components all present risks that can contribute to the vulnerability profile of a container image as well. Therefore, it is important to use application security best practices such as implementing static application security testing (SAST) and software composition analysis (SCA) scanning of containers going through continuous integration/continuous delivery (CI/CD) pipelines prior to introducing them to runtime environments. These tools can help identify vulnerabilities in the code within the container that can be remediated prior to being introduced to production, where a malicious actor may be able to exploit them.

That said, although shifting security left and identifying vulnerabilities in the pipeline or during the build prior to production are great practices, they do not alleviate the need for runtime container analysis and monitoring. Vulnerabilities may have been missed in the pipeline or new vulnerabilities may have emerged post-deployment, so organizations need container-runtime monitoring in place in addition to pipeline visibility. As mentioned by the Cloud Native Computing Foundation (CNCF) in their Cloud-Native Security Best Practices white paper (`https://cncf.io/blog/2022/05/18/announcing-the-refreshed-cloud-native-security-whitepaper`), cloud-native workloads require security controls throughout their entire life cycle, including at runtime. If the proper tools and visibility are in place, security teams can then be aware of vulnerabilities in the runtime environment, update the container image, and redeploy the no longer vulnerable image.

It is important to point out that modern applications are overwhelmingly composed of open-source code and components as well. Organizations such as security leader Snyk found that 80 percent of application code is composed of OSS (`https://snyk.io/wp-content/uploads/Snyk-Docker-Container-Security.pdf`). This open-source code, of course, contains both direct and transitive dependencies, each of which includes its own respective vulnerabilities. In addition to OSS code and components, container images are created in layers, and each layer in terms of tools, libraries, and additional components represents the potential for the introduction of risk. By governing and controlling the additional code and layers that are added to container files, organizations can control the risk that gets introduced.

Another key concern when working with containers is the host infrastructure itself. As previously mentioned, this means Kubernetes clusters are operating as an orchestrator, but there are also concerns such as the underlying VMs. These concerns include the hardening of the VM, its operating system of choice, and control of the networking associated with the host instance(s). We explore this more in the next section.

Kubernetes

Container orchestration is often defined as automating the operational effort to run containerized workloads and services. While there are several potential container orchestration tools of choice, Kubernetes is inarguably the industry leader in terms of adoption and use (`https://kubernetes.io`).

Kubernetes originated as a container orchestration project at Google and has rapidly grown in adoption and use. A 2021 survey by the CNCF found that 96 percent of respondents report using Kubernetes, with 70 percent of them saying they use Kubernetes in production (`www.cncf.io/wp-content/uploads/2022/02/CNCF-AR_FINAL-edits-15.2.21.pdf`). There are an estimated 3.9 million Kubernetes developers worldwide with dramatic year-over-year (YoY) increases. In a similar Red Hat survey (`www.redhat.com/en/enterprise-open-source-report/2022?intcmp=701f2000000tjyaAAA`), 85 percent of IT leaders agreed that Kubernetes is either extremely or very important to their cloud-native application strategies.

As previously mentioned, the origins of Kubernetes date to early internal projects at Google, most notably the Borg system around 2003. This project grew into a project called Omega, which was another cluster management system Google introduced in 2013. Finally, in 2014, Google open sourced Borg and introduced it as Kubernetes. Kubernetes's adoption and growth has only accelerated from that point, with additional versions and capabilities and a robust ecosystem of enthusiasts. Related industry events such as KubeCon, a conference oriented around Kubernetes and the cloud-native ecosystems, boasts participants from industry leaders as well as highlighting some of the emerging capabilities and innovations in the space.

Despite the rapid growth of Kubernetes, several software supply chain organizations are still associated with the use and implementation of Kubernetes and its associated technologies. Kubernetes architecturally consists of several components within the Kubernetes cluster. Among those components is the Kubernetes API server. The Kubernetes API server validates and configures data for Kubernetes objects, including pods, services, replication controllers, and other Kubernetes entities.

In 2022, the organization Shadow Server, which actively scans the entire IPv4 space of the Internet daily, was able to find 380,000 publicly exposed Kubernetes API servers (`www.shadowserver.org/news/over-380-000-open-kubernetes-api-servers`). Their research points out that 84 percent of the known Kubernetes instances they can find were publicly exposed and returning HTTP 200 OK responses. Many security and Kubernetes experts have pointed out that this doesn't mean these clusters are insecure or vulnerable, often owing their presence to default configurations from managed Kubernetes services from CSPs. However, it does show how minor misconfigurations could expose the clusters, containers, and code running on them. Genuine misconfigurations could allow malicious actors to compromise the clusters and their workloads, and potentially pivot laterally to other organizational assets.

Another contributing factor associated with supply chain threats for Kubernetes is the fact that Kubernetes is implemented via manifest files. These are declarative YAML or JavaScript Object Notation (JSON) configuration files that describe how Kubernetes clusters should be run, defining the desired state of various Kubernetes API objects. This means they are written in code and able to be saved, stored, and shared like other forms of traditional code and configuration files.

Managing complex Kubernetes deployments with a variety of resources can be a complex undertaking. Typically, organizations will use Helm charts, a packaging format for a collection of files describing a related set of Kubernetes resources. Helm charts, much like Kubernetes resources, are often described in YAML format. They are stored, shared, and available in places such as Artifact Hub, a web-based application that enables finding, installing, and publishing packages and configurations for various CNCF projects, including Kubernetes.

While using preexisting Helm charts and configuration files can expedite time to implementation and deployment, doing so also comes with risks that traditional software code has, such as malicious or vulnerable code or configurations. For example, Palo Alto's research group Unit 42 looked at Kubernetes and Helm in their "2H 2021" white paper (`https://paloaltonetworks.com/prisma/unit42-cloud-threat-research-2h21.html`). The researchers utilized a tool called "helm-scanner" to evaluate Helm charts and YAML files on Artifact Hub and found that over 99 percent of the chart's containers had insecure configurations and almost 10 percent had at least one critical or highly insecure configuration.

The researchers also pointed out that, much like code, Helm charts often have dependencies on other charts and that 62 percent of the misconfigurations they identified in the charts were due to dependent charts. They also pointed out that the higher the dependency count, the higher the average misconfiguration count was. These misconfigurations included items such as over-privileged containers and insecure network configurations. So, although modern applications and workloads are often being deployed on containers orchestrated by Kubernetes, the configuration files and charts for Kubernetes are often replicated and shared with inherent vulnerabilities and misconfigurations themselves, potentially threatening all the workloads residing on these clusters.

In the context of Kubernetes, configurations and declarative manifests pose their own risk, but malicious actors are often after the workloads Kubernetes orchestrates and use the life cycle of container images to infiltrate the Kubernetes supply chain. These attack vectors may include things such as base images, application code and dependencies, repositories, OSS components, and other associated resources. If nefarious actors can get malicious code to run on containerized workloads, particularly without proper Kubernetes security configurations in place, they can impact not just the single workload but also other potential workloads in the clusters or, more broadly, an organization's enterprise systems, depending on the architecture and configurations in place. Ensuring proper supply chain security in the context of Kubernetes will mean ensuring that you have a secure Kubernetes architecture and configuration in place.

Some recommendations for organizations to start on this front are, of course, Kubernetes documentation and best practices, but also utilizing industry guidance in the form of sources such as the Kubernetes CIS Benchmark (`www.cisecurity.org/benchmark/kubernetes`) or Kubernetes Defense Information Systems Agency (DISA) Security Technical Implementation Guide (STIG). These guidance sources focus on core activities such as securing the control plane components of the Kubernetes architecture, including the master node, controller manager, scheduler, and so on. They also include controls and configurations related to properly implementing secure policies and role-based access control (RBAC), network policies, and secrets management. Failing to implement these security practices and configurations can compromise workloads within the nodes and clusters and potentially allow lateral movement to other systems in the enterprise environments they are connected to.

Organizations often also make use of managed Kubernetes service offerings from CSPs, such as Google's Kubernetes Engine (GKE) or Amazon's Elastic Kubernetes Service (EKS). Using these managed Kubernetes offerings alleviates some of the administrative overhead with "rolling your own" Kubernetes (e.g., owning the entire control plane activities and configurations). However, using managed Kubernetes offerings doesn't come without its own issues. There are still secure configurations within the CSP environment that are required in areas such as identity and access management (IAM), encryption and key management, networking, and the metadata service for the nodes running the workloads, coupled with the inherent nature of trusting and being reliant on the cloud provider.

One of the best resources for learning about securing Kubernetes clusters is the Kubernetes documentation page (`https://kubernetes.io/docs/tasks/administer-cluster/securing-a-cluster`). Sources such as the CIS Kubernetes Benchmark, DISA Kubernetes STIG, and NSA Kubernetes Security Guide are also reputable resources, but users should also ensure more broadly that cloud-native security best practices specific to the cloud platform they're using are also addressed if they're running in the cloud.

Organizations can use tooling to ensure Kubernetes clusters and deployments are hardened according to the guidance previously mentioned, as well as Kubernetes security best practices. Some examples include kube-bench from Aqua Security (`https://github.com/aquasecurity/kube-bench`), an OSS tool that checks whether deployed Kubernetes configurations align with the CIS Kubernetes Benchmark. Much like Kubernetes itself, kube-bench uses tests written in YAML, which can be modified as the benchmark evolves. Another notable tool also from Aqua is kube-hunter, which looks for security weaknesses in Kubernetes clusters. kube-hunter can be run on a machine or endpoint and uses an IP to conduct remote scanning. In addition, it can be run on a machine in the cluster or even as a pod within a cluster. One unique aspect of kube-hunter is that it supports not only an audit/assessment mode but also an active-hunting mode, which can change the state of a cluster to exploit vulnerabilities that are discovered. For this latter reason in particular, the kube-hunter documentation specifically states that this tool should *not* be used on clusters that you do not own, which includes consuming managed Kubernetes offerings.

Organizations looking to understand the various attack tactics and techniques associated with Kubernetes can also take advantage of resources such as the Threat Matrix for Kubernetes by Microsoft (`www.microsoft.com/en-us/security/blog/2020/04/02/attack-matrix-kubernetes`), shown in Figure 6.4.

Initial Access	Execution	Persistence	Privilege Escalation	Defense Evasion	Credential Access	Discovery	Lateral Movement	Impact
Using Cloud credentials	Exec into container	Backdoor container	Privileged container	Clear container logs	List K8S secrets	Access the K8S API server	Access cloud resources	Data destruction
Compromised images in registry	bash/cmd inside container	Writable hostPath mount	Cluster-admin binding	Delete K8S events	Mount service principal	Access Kubelet API	Container service account	Resource hijacking
Kubeconfig file	New container	Kubernetes CronJob	hostPath mount	Pod / container name similarity	Access container service account	Network mapping	Cluster internal networking	Denial of service
Application vulnerability	Application exploit (RCE)		Access cloud resources	Connect from proxy server	Applications credentials in configuration files	Access Kubernetes dashboard	Applications credentials in configuration files	
Exposed dashboard	SSH server running inside container					Instance Metadata API	Writable volume mounts on the host	
							Access Kubernetes dashboard	
							Access tiller endpoint	

Figure 6.4

Much like MITRE ATT&CK, this resource helps organizations understand the attack surface of their environments, as well as the various tactics used by malicious actors. Microsoft took a similar approach with their Threat Matrix but tailored it to be Kubernetes specific, including activities such as exposing Kubernetes secrets and exploiting cluster internal networking, among many others, as demonstrated in Figure 6.4. These tactics range from the stages of Initial Access all the way through Impact, much like MITRE ATT&CK.

Another similar resource is the MITRE ATT&CK Matrix for Kubernetes (www .weave.works/blog/mitre-attack-matrix-for-kubernetes), which has been evangelized by Weaveworks. It uses phases similar to those in the Microsoft Threat Matrix and also includes a collection phase, which focuses on techniques that adversaries use for gathering information, specifically for gathering images from a private registry. Although there are differences and similarities between the Weaveworks and Microsoft matrices, both resources help organizations understand the various phases of Kubernetes-focused attacks and the associated tactics malicious actors can potentially use to exploit Kubernetes environments and orchestrated workloads. In addition to implementing resources discussed previously, such as CIS Benchmarks, DoD STIGs, and Kubernetes Threat Matrices, organizations should also be looking to adopt emerging frameworks such as Supply Chain Levels for Software Artifacts (SLSA), discussed in our next chapter.

Kubernetes also supports various multitenancy models that use its construct of clusters and namespaces to facilitate efficiency, cost savings, and scalability of cloud-native workloads (www.weave.works/blog/mitre-attack-matrix-for-kubernetes). It is important for organizations deploying workloads to Kubernetes to understand the tenancy model(s) they are using and the potential security and

compliance concerns, particularly if a security incident or data breach was to occur that could have a cascading impact across tenants if poor security hygiene and blast radius controls exist. For a detailed look at the risks of multitenancy in cloud-native environments, cloud security leader Wiz published what they have called the "PEACH Framework," which is a mnemonic including factors such as privilege, encryption, authentication, and connectivity hardening as well as hygiene. This framework can be applied to Kubernetes deployments as well as broader multitenant cloud environments (`www.datocms-assets`
`.com/75231/1671033753-peach_whitepaper_ver1-1.pdf`).

There is also support for SBOM within the Kubernetes ecosystem. Most notably, this includes the OSS Kubernetes bom utility, which leverages code written for Kubernetes to generate SBOMs for their projects (`https://github`
`.com/kubernetes-sigs/bom`). The Kubernetes bom tool supports creating SBOMs from files, images, and Docker images in tarballs, sets of files packaged together into a single file. You can also pull images from registries and analyze them with the bom tool. It produces these artifacts in Software Package Data Exchange (SPDX) SBOM format and can be exported to an in-toto provenance attestation. In-toto is a framework that goes beyond the last mile or final artifact focus and is designed to ensure integrity of a software product all the way from initiation to end-user installation, making it transparent what steps were performed, by whom, and in what order (`https://in-toto.io/in-toto`). These provenance attestations from in-toto allow for generating verifiable claims about any aspect of how a piece of software was produced. SPDX manifests can be created with a simple `bom generate` command using the Kubernetes bom tool.

Serverless Model

Building on the compute abstraction and evolution of VMs and containers, some organizations have taken their adoption journey further, depending on their use case, and have begun using what is known as the *serverless model*. At a high level, the serverless model allows development teams to build and run cloud-native applications without the need to manage the underlying servers. In the cloud paradigm of IaaS, PaaS, and SaaS, there are some similarities to PaaS and SaaS in the context of not needing to manage infrastructure and servers, but the primary difference is that with the serverless model, rather than consuming an application from an SaaS provider, the developer is deploying their code onto the cloud platform and having it hosted and executed by the cloud provider. The cloud provider handles the underlying infrastructure, including administrative overhead such as scaling and patching of the servers and instances to host the code running.

One of the most popular examples is AWS's Lambda service, which lets you run code without the need to provision or manage servers. The code is run in a highly available compute infrastructure model and handles underlying logging of the instances as well. Other cloud providers such as Google and Microsoft Azure offer similar serverless capabilities.

In software supply chain security, concerns still exist, even in the serverless model. The code that is run in the serverless model functions still may contain OSS components or vulnerable code, which can present risks to organizations running in a serverless architecture. Additionally, the underlying functions-as-a-service (FaaS) and infrastructure in the cloud, as previously discussed, is also powered by software, each of which contains various software components, potentially including OSS.

SaaSBOM and the Complexity of APIs

Creating an SBOM for contained entities such as software delivered on premises or a container image can be complex. Creating an SBOM for dynamic and rapidly changing environments with a myriad of interrelationships such as cloud and SaaS can be another level of difficulty.

Discussions have emerged around the concept of an SBOM for SaaS, which has been dubbed an *SaaSBOM*. Cloud and SaaS introduce vendor-managed deployment models where the consumer doesn't own or control the underlying physical infrastructure, hosting environment, operating system, or even the application. The application is merely consumed as-a-Service, with the consumer having limited control over the configurations and modifications that can be made to the application.

A more formal definition is NIST's 800-145 Definition of Cloud Computing:

> **The capability provided to the consumer is to use the provider's applications running on a cloud infrastructure. The applications are accessible from various client devices through either a thin client interface, such as a web browser (e.g., web-based email), or a program interface. The consumer does not manage or control the underlying cloud infrastructure including network, servers, operating systems, storage, or even individual application capabilities, with the possible exception of limited user-specific application configuration settings.**

The proliferation and popularity of SBOMs grew in early 2021, and many practitioners in the industry began asking how this push for SBOMs would work in highly dynamic and complex environments such as SaaS (another method for application use, unlike traditional software delivery and consumption). One of the authors of this book co-published an article in September 2021 titled "The Case for a SaaS Bill of Materials" (`www.csoonline.com/article/3632149/the-case-for-a-saas-bill-of-material.html`). As the article points out, defining what exactly is software in the context of SaaS is challenging. Modern SaaS is often built on existing IaaS and PaaS environments, often owned by other CSPs. That underlying IaaS and PaaS is often defined "as-code" and includes physical and virtual components, all of which include their own software. This creates a situation of complexity when defining software in the context of SaaS, due to the myriad of code and software components involved as well as the various relationships and entities of ownership included. That said, many in the industry are rallying around SaaSBOMs in the context of services and data flows as the focal point. CISA's SBOM Working Group includes a Cloud Working Group, and many professionals in the audience there have advocated for this position. The use of SBOMs for SaaS is also cited in the Cloud Security Alliance (CSA) publication "SaaS Governance Best Practices for Cloud Customers," of which one of this book's authors led the publication (`https://cloudsecurityalliance.org/artifacts/saas-governance-best-practices-for-cloud-customers`).

To further add to the challenge, the vendors often use tools to maintain and operate the underlying cloud environments as well as the SaaS residing on top of them. Some of the most notable are Ansible, Chef, and Terraform, all of which help configure, deploy, and govern cloud infrastructure on which SaaS relies. Of course, there are other systems and software involved in facilitating the delivery of SaaS, such as CI/CD pipelines and IAM software.

All these entities are composed of software and are often changing dynamically and rapidly, making defining their exact software component composition challenging. Proposed approaches include having the SaaS vendor determine the entirety of technological components, potentially just within their control, on which the SaaS application relies to be able to provide an SaaSBOM to the application consumers. Though challenging, this approach could be possible, because the SaaS provider should at least have access and an understanding of the components used in the application delivery under their direct control.

As we've alluded to, this does not solve the challenge of providing SaaS application consumers with a detailed SBOM of the underlying IaaS and PaaS providers' software and systems, all of which are critical dependencies to the SaaS application.

CycloneDX SaaSBOM

We are not the only ones to recognize this challenging aspect of SBOM adoption and maturity for the industry. One of the industry-leading SBOM formats, CycloneDX, a project managed by Open Worldwide Application Security Project (OWASP), has put forth an SaaSBOM model of their own, as shown in Figure 6.5.

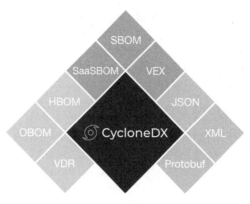

Figure 6.5

Source: OWASP Foundation, Inc. `https://cyclonedx.org/capabilities/saasbom`, last accessed March 27, 2023

The CycloneDX SaaSBOM information recognizes that modern software relies on a number of external services and can even consist entirely of services. For this reason, they have worked toward making CycloneDX capable of representing various service types, including microservices, FaaS, systems of systems (SoS), and of course, SaaS. CycloneDX points out that SaaSBOMs can be complementary to infrastructure-as-code (IaC), which also provides a logical representation of complex systems. In the case of IaC, this includes cloud architecture components such as networking, computing, and access control, all defined in an as-code model.

CycloneDX states that SaaSBOMs can provide a similar logical representation, including all services, service dependencies, relevant URLs, and even the directional flow of data between services and systems.

As previously mentioned, SaaS consists of a collection of independent applications and services in each architecture to deliver applications to consumers. CycloneDX's SaaSBOM capability allows for the inventory of services and software components into a single BOM or independent BOMs. CycloneDX recommends decoupling SaaSBOMs from an SBOM for large systems due to the reality that the Cloud and SaaS involves dynamic services and deployment scenarios. The SaaSBOM can be represented as a single entity with many SBOMs associated with it, with the SBOMs representing the associated services that work in unison to deliver the SaaS application.

Because each independent service can obviously have its own unique vulnerabilities, CycloneDX also supports the ability reference components, services, and vulnerabilities within a BOM from other systems and BOMs as well. This is referred to as a BOM-Link (`https://cyclonedx.org/capabilities/bomlink`) and supports two general scenarios that are referencing one BOM from another BOM and referencing a specific component or service from one BOM to another.

CycloneDX also recommends decoupling Vulnerability Exploitability eXchange (VEX) and BOMs because whereas a BOM may not change until the system inventory does, a VEX can change more frequently, as new vulnerabilities may emerge that are associated with already existing and in-use software components.

Tooling and Emerging Discussions

As is evident from our discussion, implementing an SaaSBOM, or an SBOM in general as it relates to the complex and dynamic world of the cloud, is no easy feat. It will inevitably require new processes and tooling to facilitate its widespread adoption, given that it is unrealistic for humans to keep up with this rapid pace of change in software component inventory and associated vulnerabilities.

Therefore, there are increasing calls for further discussion on the topic of tooling and capabilities to help address these gaps in the context of cloud and SaaS for SBOMs. In July 2022, CISA held a series of listening sessions on several topics, among them "Cloud & Online Applications" (`www.federalregister`
`.gov/documents/2022/06/01/2022-11733/public-listening-sessions-on-`
`advancing-sbom-technology-processes-and-practices`). These events weren't intended to seek consensus, but the conversations were used to foster open dialogue on the topic of SBOMs for SaaS and cloud applications.

Furthermore, the Department of Homeland Security (DHS) Science & Technology (S&T) Directorate is encouraging technology companies to help develop automated SBOM tooling. This is due to DHS S&T realizing the complexity of managing SBOMs at scale, including for SaaS. In their announcement, S&T acknowledged that attacks looking to exploit vulnerabilities in software can lead to outages and damage to safety and critical systems on which society depends. For more information, see "DHS S&T Seeks Solutions to Software Vulnerabilities" at

```
https://dhs.gov/science-and-technology/news/2022/07/11/
st-seeks-solutions-software-vulnerabilities
```

Usage in DevOps and DevSecOps

As the adoption of cloud and cloud-native architectures has emerged and continues to become prevalent, another trend has occurred: the shift from traditional waterfall software development to an era of DevOps, or more recently, DevSecOps. Without getting into a philosophical debate, DevOps can be summarized as a set of practices that bridge the divide between software development and operations, or in the case of DevSecOps, software development, security, and IT operations. The movement has origins dating back to the early 2000s with individuals such as Patrick Debois, Andrew Shafer, Gene Kim, and Jez Humble, who have contributed to the ecosystem. This has coincided with the evolution of cloud computing, and organizations have increasingly used cloud-native technologies to facilitate business outcomes with agile and DevOps methodologies. For a better understanding of DevOps, we recommend books such as *The DevOps Handbook* (2nd edition, IT Revolution Press, 2021) or *The Phoenix Project* (5th Anniversary edition, IT Revolution Press, 2018).

Many of the technologies touched on in other sections of this chapter, such as cloud, SaaS, CI/CD, Kubernetes, containers, and infrastructure as code, have all played a part in successful DevSecOps journeys and implementations. In the context of software supply chain security and DevSecOps, a robust ecosystem of tooling has emerged. A quick look at the CNCF landscape (`https://landscape.cncf.io`) shows a thriving variety of tools in areas such as CI/CD, automation and configuration, and scheduling and orchestration, all of which play a heavy role in modern DevSecOps environments. It is worth emphasizing that although tools and technologies have facilitated successful DevOps transformations, DevOps is not tooling or technology; it is a methodology and a set of practices. Many tools have been adopted to support DevOps, and some of the common approaches, such as CI/CD, have allowed for the integration of tools to tackle software supply chain challenges.

Tools such as Syft and Grype are commonly being used in toolchains to enable the creation of SBOMs as well as scanning of those SBOMs for vulnerabilities associated with software components going through the toolchain prior to their deployment to production environments. DevOps uses source code management (SCM) and Git repositories, CI/CD pipelines, GitOps styles of declarative deployment, and more. All these tools and methodologies have converged to enable iterative software delivery from source code to runtime. They also enable teams and organizations to leverage tooling to gain better visibility of the components involved in source code, container images, insecure IaC, or Kubernetes configurations, which have culminated in cloud-native deployment architectures, each with its own software supply chain concerns.

Organizations like NIST have started to plead the case that DevSecOps practices can help identify, assess, and mitigate risk for the software supply chain (`www.nccoe.nist.gov/sites/default/files/2022-07/dev-sec-ops-project-description-draft.pdf`). The perspective, as laid out in the white paper "Software Supply Chain and DevOps Security Practices," aims to provide risk-based recommendations for secure DevOps environments. It also seeks to align with other NIST guidance such as SSDF and 800-161/C-SCRM. This guidance takes a very CI/CD pipeline-centric approach to integrating software supply chain security into DevSecOps environments.

One fundamental aspect of agile and DevOps is a shift away from traditional waterfall software development and a focus on more iterative and incremental software delivery. Some may argue that the incremental nature of agile and

DevOps could potentially facilitate managing software supply chain security concerns. As organizations are incrementally producing and releasing software, toolchains can be used to identify software components, correlate vulnerabilities, aggregate those metrics, and empower organizations to make risk-informed decisions related to software supply chain concerns. Using DevSecOps tooling and an emphasis on shifting security left, or earlier in the SDLC, vulnerable software components can be identified before being introduced into runtime environments. Many claim that this approach is more efficient from a cost perspective but that it also reduces the likelihood of exploitation, given that the vulnerability isn't able to be exploited in production by malicious actors if it is caught and remediated earlier.

Not only does DevSecOps provide an opportunity to catch vulnerable software components earlier in the SDLC and offer improved transparency, but highly capable DevSecOps teams are able to respond better to software supply chain concerns and incidents. Research supports these claims, most notably the DevOps Research and Assessment (DORA) team, which is run by Google. In the "2022 Accelerate State of DevOps Report," the DORA team found that practices such as pre-deployment security scanning were effective at finding vulnerable dependencies, which led to fewer vulnerabilities in production applications (`https://services.google.com/fh/files/misc/2022_state_of_devops_report.pdf`).

As the DORA team has conducted their research over the years, they have created specific metrics, which are now recognized as the DORA metrics. The four key metrics that they use to gauge the performance of software development teams are as follows:

Deployment Frequency   How often an organization successfully releases to production.

Lead Time for Changes   The amount of time it takes a commit to get into production.

Change Failure Rate   The percentage of deployments causing a failure in production.

Time to Restore Service   How long it takes an organization to recover from a failure in production. This is also often referred to as mean time to recovery (MTTR).

These four metrics support two key themes: velocity for deployment frequency and lead time for changes and stability for failure rate and time to restore service. These metrics help gauge a team's ability to release software at the pace of business/mission demands, while also ensuring those releases do not compromise the resiliency of the system. It may seem counterintuitive initially to think of fast-moving teams as stable, but as industry experts point out, it is the practice of software development and delivery without compromising stability that helps these teams excel at doing just that. Teams that do not frequently release software to production and take exponentially longer to do so often struggle with changes that fail as well as an inability to restore systems from failures. In this context, high-performing DevOps teams can be thought of as building muscle memory or, more appropriately, competency.

Summary

In summary, the 2022 State of DevOps Report, the DORA team's Supply Chain Levels for Software Artifacts (SLSA), and NIST's SSDF identify processes and practices related to securing the software supply chain. We explored how DevOps and DevSecOps are much more than tooling—they are a collection of cultural practices and methodologies. DevSecOps methodologies place teams in a position to mitigate software supply chain concerns, and recent studies have now begun to support that perspective.

In this chapter, we discussed some of the complexity and nuance associated with software transparency in the cloud-native paradigm. This included the fundamental service models associated with the cloud, the 4 C's of cloud-native, and also SBOMs in the context of SaaS. We also discussed how high-performing teams using mature DevSecOps practices can achieve more secure software supply chain outcomes.

Existing and Emerging Commercial Guidance

As the conversation around software supply chain security has matured, many organizations have begun providing robust guidance, frameworks, and resources for the industry to bolster their security posture against this style of attacks. In the coming chapters, we discuss some of these resources and the organizations that provide them, which include the Cloud Native Computing Foundation (CNCF), National Security Agency (NSA), and the National Institute of Standards and Technology (NIST), among several others.

Supply Chain Levels for Software Artifacts

With the increase of software supply chain attacks, it became clear that there was a need for a comprehensive end-to-end framework for defining both software supply chain attacks and methods for mitigation. In June 2021, the Google Open Source Security Team launched the Supply Chain Levels for Software Artifacts (SLSA) effort (`https://security.googleblog.com/2021/06/introducing-slsa-end-to-end-framework.html`). The effort's goal is to ensure that the integrity of software artifacts is maintained throughout the software supply chain life cycle.

SLSA includes four levels, and each provides higher levels of integrity assurances but with coinciding levels of maturity and rigor from those implementing it. Organizations have various needs that guide the SLSA levels they pursue, driven by their specific industry and regulatory or security requirements. Much like other security endeavors, SLSA is a process that will take time and effort to achieve. Figure 7.1 shows the four levels and describes each.

Level	Description	Example
1	Documentation of the build process	Unsigned provenance
2	Tamper resistance of the build service	Hosted source/build, signed provenance
3	Extra resistance to specific threats	Security controls on host, non-falsifiable provenance
4	Highest levels of confidence and trust	Two-party review + hermetic builds

Figure 7.1

Source: The Linux Foundation, `https://slsa.dev/spec/v0.1/levels`, last accessed March 27, 2023

SLSA provides a framework that covers the software path all the way from the originating developer to the downstream consumer and user, including the software's interaction with source code repositories, build systems, package repositories, and all the steps in between. Figure 7.2 indicates each point in the software supply chain where a malicious actor can compromise the integrity of the software artifacts downstream that consumers are using in production environments.

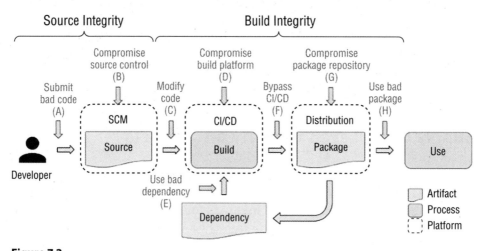

Figure 7.2

Source: `https://security.googleblog.com/2021/06/introducing-slsa-end-to-end-framework.html`, Google

If the malicious actor can submit bad code at the source code repository, it could introduce vulnerabilities into downstream activities that are carried out throughout the build process. The introduction of bad code is not the only concern associated with source code management, as the source code management (SCM) system itself could be attacked and compromised, impacting both the code stored in it and the downstream build and distribution activities that it facilitates.

This threat applies to both self-hosted and cloud-offered SCMs. In the self-hosted scenario, the organization self-hosting the SCM is responsible for its security from an infrastructure and hosting perspective, whereas in the cloud-based scenario, the cloud service provider (CSP) owns the responsibility for the underlying infrastructure and the platform and, to an extent, the application itself, if it is delivered as a Software-as-a-Service (SaaS).

The attack tree associated with the compromise of an SCM is depicted by researcher François Proulx in his article "SLSA Dip—At the Source of the Problem!" (`https://medium.com/boostsecurity/slsa-dip-source-of-the-problem-a1dac46a976`). Figure 7.3 shows example attack vectors that a malicious actor can use to compromise SCM repositories, such as GitHub.

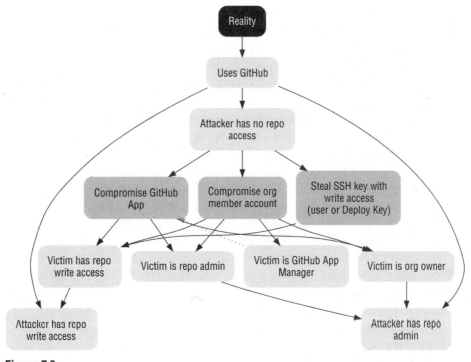

Figure 7.3

Continuing with the potential software supply chain threat model, a malicious actor could use approved build processes and infrastructure but introduce code not matching what should have been used from the SCM. This is an example where code provenance information is critical to ensure that the code being used is from the intended source and hasn't undergone tampering or integrity attacks. SLSA defines provenance as "verifiable information about software artifacts describing where, when, and how something was produced." The higher you move up the SLSA levels, the more rigorous the requirements for provenance become.

The build platform is another critical part of the software supply chain and makes an enticing target for attackers. This attack vector was used in the Solar-Winds incident, which led to a compromise of the build system and malware being inserted into the software build of the SolarWinds Orion IT management product. It was then downloaded and installed by downstream SolarWinds customers, which included over 18,000 organizations, many of which were government entities, and this fact inarguably contributed to the subsequent Cybersecurity Executive Order (EO) we have previously mentioned. This attack was discussed in our landmark cases section in Chapter 1, "Background on Software Supply Chain Threats."

Another potential avenue of attack is that the malicious actor can inject a benign dependency, which subsequently can be modified to produce malicious behavior. A real-life example is the `event-stream` npm package, where someone volunteered to take over maintenance duties for the project but ended up adding a malicious dependency named `flatmap-stream`. This was particularly impactful because the `event-stream` package was downloaded over 1.9 million times weekly!

Malicious actors have also taken advantage of opportunities to upload malicious packages that downstream consumers download and are impacted by. The most notable example is the Codecov incident, which involved malicious actors using compromised credentials to upload malicious packages into Codecov's cloud storage. From there, the Codecov breach impacted hundreds of customer networks as well, because the malicious actors used Codecov to attack downstream customer networks. If consumers had been using provenance verification methods, they could have identified that the downloaded artifact was not as expected from the source code repository.

SLSA also emphasizes *software attestations*, which they define as "authenticated statements (metadata) about a software artifact or collection of software artifacts" (`https://slsa.dev/attestation-model`).

SLSA lays out a general model for representing software attestations, as shown in Figure 7.4.

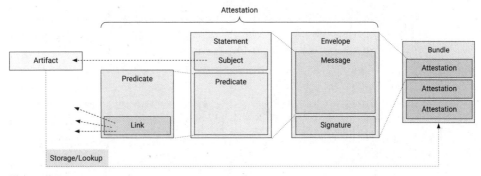

Figure 7.4

In early 2023, SLSA introduced their release candidate (RC) specification, which was the first major update since SLSA's original release in June 2021. Significant changes include the division of SLSA into multiple SLSA tracks to measure particular aspects of the software supply chain. The RC specification also simplified and clarified aspects of the original specification and provided new guidance on provenance verification. That said, as of this writing, the specifics of each proposed track haven't been fully defined and will be addressed in future versions of SLSA. If you're interested in learning more about the 1.0 release candidate, visit `https://slsa.dev/blog/2023/02/slsa-v1-rc`.

Google Graph for Understanding Artifact Composition

In a slyly named follow-up to the SLSA framework, Google, along with partners such as Citi and Purdue University, also announced an open source software (OSS) effort named the Graph for Understanding Artifact Composition (GUAC), shown in Figure 7.5. Per their announcement, "GUAC addresses a need created by the burgeoning efforts across the ecosystem to generate software build, security and dependency metadata" (`https://security.googleblog.com/2022/10/announcing-guac-great-pairing-with-slsa.html`).

The announcement acknowledges the numerous OSS efforts being led by groups such as OpenSSF, along with software supply chain efforts for software bill of materials (SBOM) formats, as contributing to the conversation of securing the digital supply chain. That said, a lot of information needs to be collated and made sense of. From SBOM formats such as Software Package Data Exchange (SPDX) and CycloneDX, to attestations for frameworks like SLSA and the various vulnerability databases we have discussed, such as National Vulnerability Database (NVD), Global Security Database (GSD), and Open Source Vulnerabilities (OSV), organizations find themselves trying to make sense of all the data.

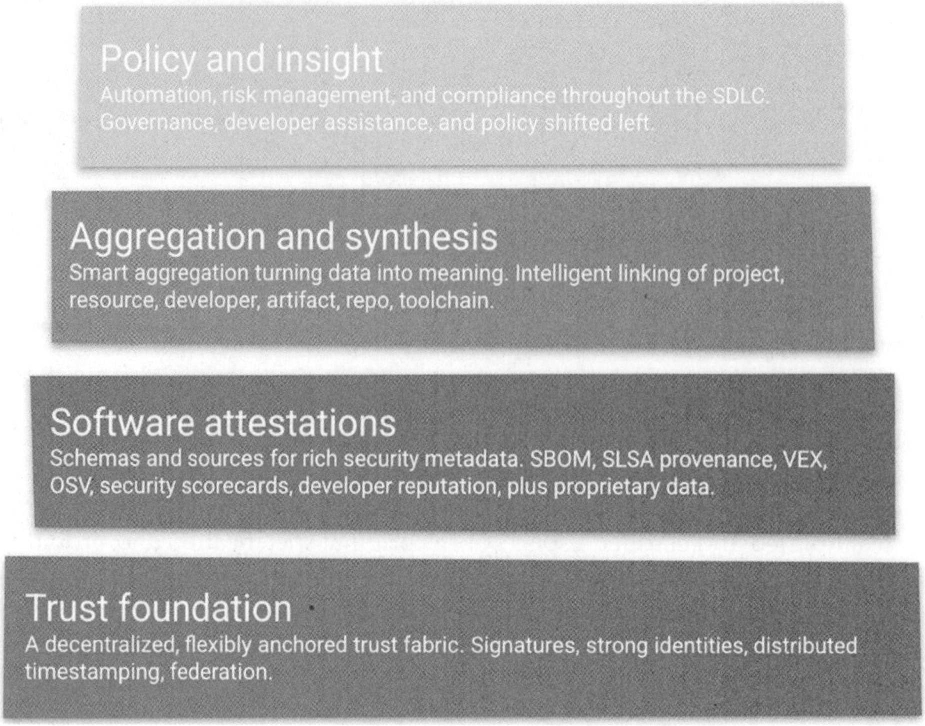

Policy and insight
Automation, risk management, and compliance throughout the SDLC. Governance, developer assistance, and policy shifted left.

Aggregation and synthesis
Smart aggregation turning data into meaning. Intelligent linking of project, resource, developer, artifact, repo, toolchain.

Software attestations
Schemas and sources for rich security metadata. SBOM, SLSA provenance, VEX, OSV, security scorecards, developer reputation, plus proprietary data.

Trust foundation ·
A decentralized, flexibly anchored trust fabric. Signatures, strong identities, distributed timestamping, federation.

Figure 7.5

While all the information is useful, the GUAC effort points out the need to combine and synthesize all the information for a comprehensive picture of software supply chain risks. GUAC consolidates the various metadata sources into graph databases and relationships, which benefit in-use cases such as auditing and risk management as well as developer empowerment.

Per the announcement from Google, GUAC focuses on four key areas:

- Collection
- Ingestion
- Collation
- Query

Collection includes sources such as OSV and GSD or even internal repositories. Ingestion allows for taking in upstream data sources such as artifacts, projects, and resources. Collation takes the raw metadata from the various sources and assembles it into a normalized graph to show relationships between entities such as projects/developer, vulnerabilities, and software versions. Lastly, the ability to query enables searches against the assembled graphs and associated metadata, querying for artifacts such as SBOMs, project scorecards, vulnerabilities, and others. See Figure 7.6.

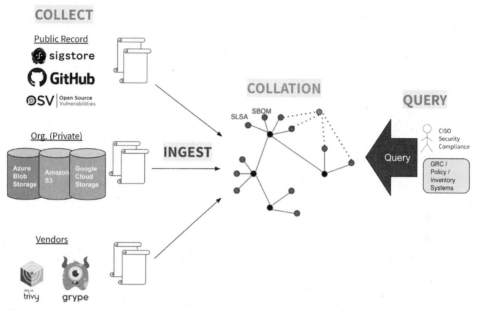

Figure 7.6

As pointed out in Figure 7.6, Collection, Ingestion, Collation, and Querying enable various personas and use cases such as governance, risk, and compliance (GRC) and policy professionals, chief information security officers (CISOs), and even developers. As the announcement mentions, understanding the impact of a specific OSS vulnerability requires aggregating and analyzing tremendous amounts of data across the enterprise and broader ecosystem. GUAC aims to make all this information actionable, focusing on empowering users to answer these three fundamental questions:

1. How can we prevent supply chain compromises?
2. Are the right safeguards in place?
3. If an event occurs, has our organization been impacted?

These three questions have three topic areas, as illustrated in Figure 7.7:

■ Proactive

■ Preventive

■ Reactive

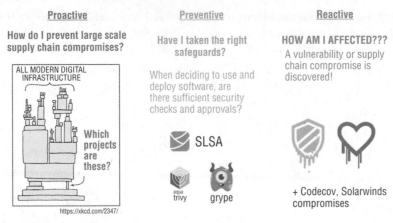

Figure 7.7

Proactive aims to understand the most critical components in your software supply chain and your primary weak points and exposures. Preventive focuses on ensuring that applications being deployed align with your organization's policies and requirements. Reactive enables your organization to understand where it has been impacted as vulnerabilities emerge.

CIS Software Supply Chain Security Guide

As the industry continues to mature software supply chain practices, we have seen guidance from groups such as NIST, the Open Source Security Foundation (OpenSSF), and the Center for Internet Security (CIS). In this section, we discuss the recently published CIS Software Supply Chain Security Guide (`https://github.com/aquasecurity/chain-bench/blob/main/docs/CIS-Software-Supply-Chain-Security-Guide-v1.0.pdf`). This guide was created in collaboration with Aqua Security, who created an open source tool named `chain-bench` to help you audit your software supply chain stack for compliance with the CIS guide (`https://github.com/aquasecurity/chain-bench`).

The intent of the CIS benchmark for the Software Supply Chain Security Guide is to provide a platform-agnostic high-level set of best practices that subsequently can be used to build platform-specific guidance for platforms like GitHub, GitLab, and others.

The guide consists of five core areas:

- Source Code
- Build Pipelines
- Dependencies
- Artifacts
- Deployment

It also follows the phases of the software supply chain, from source to deployment, and touches on the various potential threat vectors present throughout that process. As you can see in Figure 7.8, it is reminiscent of another emerging framework, SLSA, as well as the existing Open Worldwide Application Security Project (OWASP) Software Component Verification Standard (SCVS) framework.

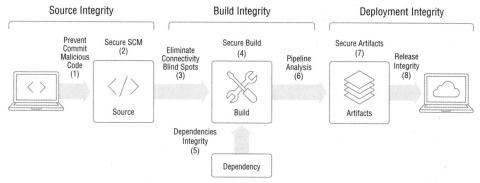

Figure 7.8

Collectively the guide covers more than 100 recommendations across the five categories discussed. Let's step through each of the five categories, highlighting why the area is relevant as well as some of the notable recommendations included in it.

Source Code

As mentioned, the guide follows the software supply chain life cycle, so inevitably source code is right at the top of the list, given that it is the first phase of that life cycle. As the guide states, source code serves as the source of truth for the remainder of the processes/phases.

When dealing with securing source code, you will be looking to secure the code as well as the source code management system, which can be exploited by malicious actors to compromise the source code itself. The guide points out that securing source code involves everything from the developers, sensitive data in the code, and the source code management platform itself.

The Source Code category itself is broken down into subsections:

- Code Changes
- Repository Management
- Contribution Access
- Third Party
- Code Risks

These subsections include critical recommendations, all of which relate to source code security. In the Code Changes subsection, some notable examples include ensuring that the code changes are tracked in version control, scanning code merges for risks, and ensuring that the code changes require the approval of two strongly authenticated users. Controls such as these attempt to ensure that changes are tracked, risks are mitigated prior to allowing code changes, and peer/two-person code reviews from users with appropriate authentication measures occur.

In the Repository Management subsection, security controls are recommended, such as ensuring SECURITY.md files are posted in public repositories and cleaning up inactive repositories. These measures help protect the integrity of repositories, guide security and/or vulnerability feedback, and prevent repository sprawl and lack of governance.

Controlling contribution access is another fundamental measure used to validate that the integrity of code is addressed. In the Contribution Access subsection, recommended controls include requiring multifactor authentication (MFA) for code contributions, implementing least-permissive access control to repositories, and limiting Git access to specific allow-list IP addresses. Taking these steps improves the security of the code contribution process and source code, granting access to only those who are authorized, who have authenticated appropriately, and who are coming from approved IP addresses.

Third-party applications in code repositories pose a risk to organizations. These include integrations with third-party tools to enable enhanced functionality or capabilities as well as developer productivity. Taking steps such as ensuring that an administrator approves installed applications, removing stale applications, and implementing least-permissive control can go a long way. These fundamental controls in the Third Party subsection minimize the organization's attack surface and limit the blast radius should a third-party application be compromised.

Mitigating code risks is a key activity that an organization must perform when dealing with their source code security. In the Code Risks subsection, risk controls such as scanning code for sensitive data, like secrets and secret sprawl, particularly in cloud-native DevOps environments, are recommended. Also included is the need to scan for vulnerabilities in code via static application security testing (SAST) and practices such as using software composition analysis (SCA) and emerging SBOM tooling and practices to look for vulnerabilities in OSS components.

Build Pipelines

As defined by the CIS Guide, build pipelines are used to take raw files of source code and run a series of tasks to achieve a final artifact as an output. This equates to the latest version of a software/application that is stored and eventually deployed. The Build Pipeline sections include the build environments, build workers, pipeline instructions, and pipeline integrity. The guide stresses that many of the recommendations are related to self-hosted build platforms versus as-a-service SaaS offerings. That said, as-a-service offerings such as SaaS-based offerings have their own unique risks, which we have touched on in Chapter 6, "Cloud and Containerization."

For the build environment, the guide recommends controls such as dedicating pipelines to single repositories, using pipeline infrastructure and configurations that are immutable, and ensuring that the activities of the build environment are logged. These controls ensure that organizations avoid issues like drift and configuration deviations, lack of visibility/logging when things go awry, and facilitating automation during the creation of the build environments, which minimizes the risk of manual activities. These controls aid in avoiding issues such as human error that can lead to data exposure and misconfigurations that malicious actors can take advantage of.

Build workers, called *runners*, present a core component of the infrastructure for pipeline operations and a target for those seeking to wreak havoc. Workers can check out code, perform testing, and even push code to the registry, all of which can be used for nefarious purposes. Security controls here include single-use build workers, segregation of duties among the build workers, and implementation of runtime security. These activities attempt to ensure that runtime events are monitored for malicious behavior patterns, limit the potential attack of a build worker to its assigned duty rather than the broader environment, and minimize the risk of data theft.

Pipeline instructions are used to convert source code into final artifacts. When tampered with, the instructions can be used to perform malicious activities. Security controls include defining build steps as code, clearly defining inputs and outputs, and scanning pipelines automatically for misconfigurations. These controls ensure that the build steps are immutable and repeatable and have anticipated inputs/outputs, and that scans can identify misconfigurations to avoid backdoors or compromises.

Maintaining pipeline integrity is a critical control and includes verifying that the pipeline, necessary dependencies, and the artifacts it produces are all as they should be and unaltered. Key controls in this area include attempting to ensure that artifacts are signed upon release, that dependencies are validated prior to use, and that the pipeline is producing reproducible artifacts. These controls validate that artifacts are signed by a trusted entity, dependencies are vetted prior to consumption, and the pipeline is producing artifacts consistently to ensure tampering hasn't occurred. The guide also recommends not only producing an SBOM for each component of the software or build process, but also ensuring that the SBOM is signed to further attest to its validity. These recommendations align with guidance from NIST and OpenSSF and leverage technologies such as

Sigstore, which we covered in our discussions of SBOMs and software signing in Chapter 4, "Rise of Software Bill of Materials."

Dependencies

The CIS guide recognizes the fundamental role dependencies play in the software supply chain. There is an emphasis on the reality that dependencies generally come from third-party sources such as Log4j and can cause massive damage when exploited. In fact, studies such as those from Sonatype and EndorLabs show that six out of seven vulnerabilities come from transitive dependencies.

Third-party packages require proper governance and use, including efforts to establish trust and manage their use appropriately. Third-party packages impact not just your software but downstream consumers of your software as well, as was evident with Log4j and its associated flurry of notifications from vendors whose software was impacted. Security controls here include verifying third-party artifacts and open source libraries, requiring SBOMs from third-party suppliers, and requiring/verifying signed metadata of the build process. These steps help mitigate the risk of using malicious or high-risk third-party components, leading to an understanding of what is inside the software of a supplier/vendor and ensuring that artifacts haven't been compromised during the build process.

The guide calls for validating packages to understand how and if to use them at all, and it includes a combination of policy and technical controls such as establishing organization-wide guidance for dependency use, scanning packages for known vulnerabilities, and maintaining awareness of ownership changes. These controls help govern the use of packages while also ensuring that existing packages aren't vulnerable and keeping track of ownership implications that can lead to malicious activity by new owners.

Artifacts

Artifacts, as defined by the CIS guide, are packaged versions of software that are stored in package registries. The guide stresses the need to secure artifacts throughout the life cycle, from creation all the way to deployment into an environment.

Verification controls are required, such as ensuring artifacts are signed by the pipeline and then encrypted before distribution as well as controlling who can perform decryption. Such controls ensure that the artifacts have integrity and confidentiality, limited to those authorized to view decrypted copies of the artifacts.

Fundamental access controls for artifacts must be put in place. This area often deals with registries that store artifacts, ensuring that prior to delivery to a customer they haven't been tampered with through a myriad of attack vectors. Controls include governing the number of permitted users who can upload new artifacts and implementing MFA for user access. This pursues the goal of separating user management from the package registry to an external authentication mechanism/server.

Package registries represent another component of the attack surface and are where organizational artifacts are stored. While the goal is to protect the artifacts, you can't do that without also protecting the registries that store them. Controls include auditing configuration changes to the package registry and cryptographically verifying artifacts in the package registry.

Origin traceability, or code provenance, is another best practice that's getting increased attention. It's the process of ensuring that both the organization and its customers understand where an artifact originates and that it's coming from a trusted source. It is imperative to ensure that artifacts contain information about their origin through methods such as SBOMs and metadata. Organizations should also use proxy registries to proxy requests of internal packages from public registries. This recommendation aligns with Appendix F of NIST's 800-161r1 (`https://nvlpubs.nist.gov/nistpubs/SpecialPublications/NIST .SP.800-161r1.pdf`), which calls for establishing internal registries of known validated components. NIST 800-161 Appendix F has its own web page (`www .nist.gov/itl/executive-order-14028-improving-nations-cybersecurity/ software-security-supply-chains`).

Deployment

Finally, we have the development phase—the last phase of the software supply chain, where artifacts are deployed to runtime environments. Controls in this phase include both the deployment configuration and the deployment environment.

For the deployment configuration, it's recommended that you separate deployment configuration files from source code, track deployment configuration changes, and use scanners to secure Infrastructure-as-Code (IaC) manifests. Misconfigurations or vulnerabilities in deployment configurations can make the deployment environment vulnerable.

The deployment environment recommendations include making deployments automated and reproducible and limiting access to those who need it. These recommendations ensure that deployments are immutable, avoid configuration deviations, and limit access to minimize threats.

While software supply chain security is still an evolving field, the CIS Guide, coupled with guidance from other organizations mentioned throughout this book, serves as a beacon of light in a historically shadowy area of cybersecurity. The software supply chain is an incredibly complex and fragile ecosystem that presents systemic risk due to the countless organizations, consumers, suppliers, and industries it impacts. Be sure to keep an eye out for subsequent platform-specific CIS benchmarks that build on the controls and recommendations cited in the CIS Software Supply Chain Guide.

CNCF's Software Supply Chain Best Practices

Another source of industry guidance that's regularly cited in the conversation about software supply chain security is the CNCF's Software Supply Chain Best Practices white paper (`https://github.com/cncf/tag-security/blob/main/supply-chain-security/supply-chain-security-paper/CNCF_SSCP_v1.pdf`). Released in 2021, this white paper covers securing source code, materials, pipelines, artifacts, and deployments. It cites the SolarWinds incident as a key issue driving attention to the software supply chain and is built around four fundamental principles:

- Each step in the supply chain must be trustworthy.
- Each step in the supply chain must use automation.
- Build environments must be properly defined and secured.
- Mutual authentication must be present for all entities in the supply chain environment.

The white paper also recognizes that various assurance personas and risk appetites exist across organizations and industries. Not all organizations have the same assurance requirements; a weapons system operating in the Department of Defense (DoD) will have much more rigorous security requirements than a simple web application that isn't processing sensitive data. Organizations can use the recommendations in the white paper based on their specific risk tolerance and assurance requirements to mitigate software supply chain risks.

The white paper uses the three assurance levels of Low, Moderate, and High. Low-assurance environments are those where little development time is dedicated to safeguarding the integrity (or security) of the product. Moderate includes reasonable assurance requirements that align with most deployments and serves as the baseline in the paper. Lastly, high-assurance environments require that products be untampered with, resist unauthorized changes, and employ high-fidelity attestations and verification processes.

As Figure 7.9 shows, the white paper draws parallels to traditional supply chains that would be associated with raw materials, products, and manufacturing. It points out that, much like how technology adopted Agile and DevOps practices from lean manufacturing, the software supply chain can leverage insights from manufacturing.

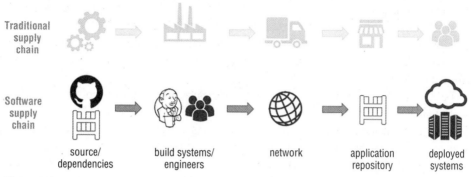

Figure 7.9

Source: CNCF Supply Chain Best Practices Whitepaper (`https://github.com/cncf/tag-security/blob/main/supply-chain-security/supply-chain-security-paper/CNCF_SSCP_v1.pdf`). GitHub

That said, despite the similarities with a manufacturing supply chain, the white paper also emphasizes some key differences. Primarily, the reality is that software supply chains are intangible and include virtual and digital components that aren't as visible as those in the physical realm. Other key differences include the fact that software supply chains do and will continue to evolve more rapidly, due to their technology-centric nature. Last is the presence of reuse and the complexity of the digital supply chain. Many often use the phrase "turtles all the way down," meaning it is an infinite regression in most cases, with several levels of direct and transitive dependencies. Many products and supply chains are pieces or components of other products or supply chains. This reality can produce some challenges, especially as data shows that most vulnerabilities are prevalent among transitive rather than direct dependencies, but most organizations don't understand the full extent of their transitive dependencies.

Much like in a physical supply chain, each step in the digital and software-driven supply chain presents the potential for the introduction of risk—hence, the emergence of frameworks such as SLSA, along with the associated best practices to mitigate risks at each step of the software supply chain life cycle. Much like broader cybersecurity and technology, software supply chains are only as strong as their weakest link, so vulnerabilities in one aspect of the supply chain can have a cascading impact on the remainder of the supply chain and all downstream consumers and stakeholders, as we've seen several times with both vendors and OSS components.

The CNCF's guidance emphasizes some key themes, such as Verification, Automation, Authorization in Controlled Environments, and Secure Authentication. These themes are critical to ensuring robust assurance throughout the entire software supply chain life cycle and occur throughout the document in their various recommendations and recommended controls.

Verification is key to ensuring integrity from one stage to the next, and automation helps facilitate repeatable and immutable processes. The rightsizing of permissions for both machines and human entities ensures that each entity and stage can only conduct the activities explicitly defined and required for it. While it is a long-standing security best practice, this least-permissive approach is also being emphasized in the industry's push for zero trust, so there are parallels in this regard.

Lastly, secure authentication ensures mutual authentication between entities in the supply chain, using authentication methods aligned with the assurance level of the environment and the organizations involved. The guidance covers five stages of the supply chain—securing the source code, securing materials, securing build pipelines, securing artifacts, and securing deployments—and we discuss each of them in the following sections.

Securing the Source Code

Software supply chains originate from source code. Creating and securing this source code is a foundational activity that has the potential to impact the integrity of the entire downstream supply chain. The CNCF's guidance points out that identity access management (IAM) serves as the most critical attack vector in this regard across any platform or vendor, and it applies to both humans and machine entities with access to source code repositories. This claim is substantiated by reports such as Verizon's 2022 Data Breach Investigations Report (DBIR; www.verizon.com/business/resources/reports/dbir), which shows that compromised credentials are involved in upward of 60 percent of data breaches.

Source code security recommendations cover the five themes previously mentioned. These include verification activities, such as implementing signed commits to ensure both the integrity and nonrepudiation of source submissions or modifications. There are more traditional methods such as GNI Privacy Guard (GPG) keys or Secure/Multipurpose Internet Mail Extensions (S/MIME) certificates, but there are also innovative emerging solutions such as GitSign (https://github.com/sigstore/gitsign), which uses Sigstore to facilitate "keyless" signing. This is an increasingly appealing method of signing artifacts and metadata due to the reduced overhead associated with traditional signing and key management activities.

Automation can also be used to secure source code and associated repositories. One such area is the issue of exposed secrets. In this context, secrets are items such as credential files, Secure Shell (SSH) keys, access tokens, and application programming interface (API) keys. Secret sprawl, which is the spread and distribution of sensitive credentials, is a significant problem, especially in cloud-native DevSecOps environments that include a declarative approach and the opportunity to commit secrets in various manifests and configuration files.

GitGuardian, a company that focuses on secrets management, has produced highly informative reports, such as the State of Secrets Sprawl 2022 report (`www.gitguardian.com/state-of-secrets-sprawl-report-2022`), which dives deep into the issue. Some alarming metrics include over 3,000 occurrences of secrets detected per application security engineer in 2021 and over 6 million publicly exposed secrets in 2021, which was twice as high as 2020. One of this book's authors has written an article covering the state of secrets management and the impact that poor practices can have (`www.csoonline.com/article/3655688/keeping-secrets-in-a-devsecops-cloud-native-world.html`). These exposed secrets have the potential to grant access to malicious actors and cause havoc across environments. The problem doesn't seem to be improving either, with the release of the State of Secrets Sprawl 2023 report from GitGuardian finding over 10 million new secrets exposed in public GitHub repositories. 2022 also saw secrets involved in some shape or fashion in security incidents that impacted some of the industry's most notable organizations, such as Uber, NVIDIA, Microsoft, and Slack (`www.gitguardian.com/state-of-secrets-sprawl-report-2023`).

Implementing controlled environments for source code repositories offers an opportunity to mitigate several risks through corresponding controls, including establishing and adhering to contribution policies that govern code contributions. In line with the earlier recommendation to rightsize permissions, there are opportunities to align roles and associate permissions with functional responsibilities within the organization as well. Organizations can take this further by using context-based access control mechanisms that examine factors such as time of day and device posture to provide dynamic, time-based access, as is common in zero-trust environments. Another fundamental recommendation that is often made in many areas of cybersecurity is to enforce a separation of duties so that the author of a request cannot also be its approver.

Authentication is an activity that helps grant initial access to a source code repository by an entity, either human or machine. Some of the recommendations here include activities such as enforcing MFA for accessing the repositories and using SSH keys to facilitate developer access. These keys should have an associated rotation policy to ensure that if the keys are compromised, they are limited in their ability to have a negative impact in terms of malicious access and activities. For machine or service entities, organizations should adopt short-lived and ephemeral credentials. These credentials can allow access for machines and services, such as pipeline agents, but also mitigate the impact of credential compromise as the keys are constantly being generated, utilized, and discarded. As mentioned previously, compromised credentials are one of the most common attack vectors for malicious actors, so using short-lived credentials can mitigate that impact.

Securing Materials

In the context of software supply chains, the CNCF's guidance discusses materials as dependencies and libraries whether they are direct or transitive. This section most closely relates to the overarching concept of the book, which focuses on software supply chain transparency and security. The guidance mentions that some high-assurance environments may have the need to use only trusted repositories while blocking access to others. It is also worth mentioning that NIST 800-161r1's guidance recommends establishing internal repositories of known trusted components for development use, which we will discuss in Chapter 8, "Existing and Emerging Government Guidance," which covers NIST's 800-161r1 guidance.

The CNCF guidance emphasizes that organizations should be using risk management methodologies when it comes to the second- and third-party software they are consuming. While it's customary practice for both organizational and open source projects to publish Common Vulnerabilities and Exposures (CVEs) for vulnerable code, the guidance points out that CVEs are also a trailing metric, meaning they're informing the consumer once a vulnerability has been discovered and published; the code they're consuming is already vulnerable. It's important for organizations to make use of other metrics as well, which can inform consumers of the risk associated with projects and code that tie to metrics such as operational health. One such project is the OpenSSF's Scorecard project, which we will discuss in the upcoming section "OpenSSF Scorecard."

Organizations consume software components from external entities, so verifying those third-party libraries and components is critical and includes methods such as using checksums and verifying signatures. Organizations can (and should) also be using methods such as SCA and SBOM generation to determine whether any vulnerable open source components exist in the software they are consuming. Once organizations have used SCA and SBOMs, they can begin to track dependencies between their consumed OSS components and the systems they belong to as part of their broader software asset inventory efforts. An organization can start to produce a supply chain inventory that encompasses not just OSS components but also software vendors, suppliers, and sources used across the organization.

Another risk the guidance warns against is the possibility for malicious code to be included in compiled software such as binaries or tarballs, which are compiled rather than in source code or text format. For this reason, the guidance recommends that organizations build their libraries from source code, as opposed to using already compiled software, which may have been compromised by malicious actors. Much like the recommendation to create a software supply chain inventory, the guidance advises that organizations have an inventory of trusted package managers and repositories and control their access to limit the introduction of code from unapproved sources.

Organizations should also take advantage of automation to secure materials they're consuming from external parties. This area includes scanning software for vulnerabilities, licensing implications, and identifying both direct and transitive dependencies associated with ingested software.

Securing Build Pipelines

The CNCF SSCP guidance draws parallels between an assembly line in a manufacturing context and the build pipelines in the context of the software supply chain ecosystem, going so far as to call build pipelines the "heart of a software factory." The pipeline assembles many of the materials discussed earlier and from sources such as source control repositories and third-party providers. These build pipelines consist of various components such as build steps, workers, tools, and a pipeline orchestrator, each of which we also discuss in the later section "The Secure Software Factory Reference Architecture."

Securing the build pipelines requires hardened build steps and associated outputs to ensure that neither the build pipeline nor its processes are compromised. Malicious actors know that, if they can compromise the build pipeline, they can distribute malicious software to downstream consumers, who will be unaware that the upstream build process was compromised.

CNCF recommends some key steps to secure the build pipeline:

- Using a single repository for all the build components
- Documenting the steps and associated inputs/outputs
- Using methods such as the signing of artifacts and metadata to ensure the integrity of the build process

Organizations should also subject their build pipeline and infrastructure to threat modeling and automated security testing, much as they would other production systems and environments. To put it bluntly, your build systems should be treated like production systems from a security perspective because their outputs are ultimately what make it into runtime environments. If those outputs are compromised, production runtime environments are also compromised.

While not specifically cited by CNCF's publication, one excellent source of guidance on this topic is the newly formed OWASP Top 10 CI/CD Security Risks project. As the project says, CI/CD environments, processes, and systems are at the core of modern software delivery. The project points out that abusing CI/CD environments has led to several notable security incidents such as SolarWinds, Codecov, and others, impacting thousands of downstream consumers and organizations (`https://owasp.org/www-project-top-10-ci-cd-security-risks`).

The guidance points out core components of the modern build environments such as the pipeline orchestrator, build worker, and sourcing from secured artifact repositories (see Figure 7.10). The entities collaborate to perform steps such as building and linking dependencies, building the application, testing it and publishing it to a secure storage repository, and ultimately deploying it. Compromising these processes and entities has downstream ramifications for deployment environments.

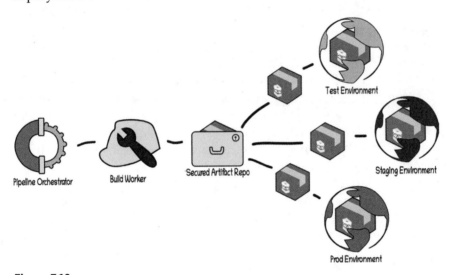

Figure 7.10

Source: `https://project.linuxfoundation.org/hubfs/CNCF_ SSCP_v1.pdf`. The Linux Foundation

Verification is another critical activity that the guidance emphasizes. This area includes activities such as using cryptography to validate policy adherence, validating environments and dependencies before usage, and validating the runtime security of the build workers, as depicted in Figure 7.10. The guidance cites producing end-to-end cryptographic guarantees as one option.

Another emphasis is the use of reproducible builds for high-assurance and high-risk environments. To summarize, reproducible builds enable taking given inputs and creating output that can be cryptographically attested. This means malicious or unintentional modifications can be identified and acted upon. This practice shows up in other sources of guidance such as SLSA, and as many point out, it isn't a trivial endeavor and can be costly in terms of time and resources. This is why it's a practice reserved for high-assurance environments.

Other notable practices and capabilities include:

- Automating creation of the build environment
- Distributing builds across different infrastructure environments
- Using automation to standardize pipelines across teams and projects
- Provisioning the secured orchestration environment to host the software factory (see the upcoming section "CNCF's Secure Software Factory Reference Architecture")

Securing Artifacts

After the build phase has been completed, artifacts and software are produced along with the metadata that is associated with them. Various methods can be used to secure these artifacts and ensure their integrity, such as signing, which CNCF recommends and which should be done at each stage of the artifact's life cycle.

CNCF's guidance recommends that organizations perform verification by signing every step in the build process and validating those signatures that are generated. They cite The Update Framework (TUF) and SPIFFE and SPIRE as examples of projects that can be used to support the attestations required throughout the process. SPIFFE and SPIRE aim to provide a uniform identity control plane across modern and heterogeneous infrastructure. SPIFFE and SPIRE support includes securing microservices communication, enabling secure authentication, and cross-service authentication for zero-trust security models (`https://spiffe.io`). Organizations can embrace automation by using TUF and Notary to manage the signing of artifacts and storing of the associated metadata and outputs.

Organizations should also take steps to limit the artifacts a given party is able to sign, and time-bind those abilities and associate them with periodic reviews. Time-binding involves setting time constraints on the validity of credentials and access. Once the artifacts are produced, prior to distribution organizations should encrypt them and do so in a format that only authorized platforms and consumers have the ability to decrypt. Following these steps ensures that the artifacts are provided with integrity throughout their various life cycle stages and that the end consumers or recipients, whether individuals or non-person entities, have properly scoped permissions and access control in place.

Securing Deployments

The concluding section of the CNCF SSCP white paper is the Securing Deployments section. Once again, CNCF emphasizes the importance of TUF in this activity and the need to be able to both detect and prevent malicious activity.

Verification is presented as a key activity that must occur once software artifacts are deployed, meaning that the client receiving the software artifact can verify its integrity and can also verify the associated metadata. This means that they could verify the signature of an SBOM if one was created and verify that it was signed by an authorized party.

CNCF's Secure Software Factory Reference Architecture

To many the term *factory* related to software production may seem bizarre. Most still associate *factory* with the collection, manipulation, and manufacturing of physical materials such as steel, automobiles, or consumer electronics. However, software, which, ironically, powers most modern factory environments, is increasingly produced in a manner that has some parallels to a factory. The term *software factory* generally refers to the collection of tools, assets, and processes required to produce software in an efficient, repeatable, and secure manner.

This term has taken hold in both the public and private sectors and is recognized by organizations such as MITRE and VMware, among others. The Department of Defense (DoD) has a robust ecosystem of some 29 software factories, most notably Kessel Run, Platform One, and the Army Software Factory. The software factory construct is also spreading to U.S. federal civilian agencies with programs such as the Centers for Medicare and Medicaid (CMS) program, batCAVE. The term is also being acknowledged by industry-leading organizations such as CNCF, who have released their Secure Software Factory Reference Architecture. Let's take a closer look.

The Secure Software Factory Reference Architecture

CNCF defines a software supply chain as "a series of steps performed when writing, testing, packaging and distributing application software to end consumers." The software factory is the logical construct in aggregate that facilitates the delivery of software and, when done correctly, ensures that security is a key component of that application delivery process.

The CNCF Secure Software Factory (SSF) Reference Architecture (`https://github.com/cncf/tag-security/blob/main/supply-chain-security/secure-software-factory/Secure_Software_Factory_Whitepaper.pdf`) guidance builds on previous CNCF publications such as the Cloud Native Security Best Practices (`https://github.com/cncf/tag-security/tree/main/security-whitepaper`) and Software Supply Chain Best Practices (`https://github.com/cncf/tag-security/blob/main/supply-chain-security/supply-chain-security-paper/CNCF_SSCP_v1.pdf`). The reference architecture emphasizes existing open source tooling with a focus on security. It also rallies around four overarching principles from the Software Supply Chain whitepaper:

- Defense in Depth
- Signing and Verification
- Artifact Metadata Analytics
- Automation

Each principle is required to ensure secure software delivery from inception and code to production.

The reference architecture also makes it clear that it isn't focused on areas of concern such as code scanning and signing, but instead has a deeper focus on code provenance and build activities. The rationale for this focus is that downstream activities such as static application security testing/dynamic application security testing (SAST/DAST) are reliant on validating the provenance and that the identity of the party you are receiving something from is a trusted entity. These may be identities tied to a human user or a machine identity. The combination of a signature and validating that it is coming from a trusted source is key to the assurance of provenance.

Each entity in a secure software factory (SSF) has dependencies, whether those are related to broader organizational IAM systems, source code management, or downstream consumers' dependence on the SSF itself for attestations and signatures of artifacts they are using.

The SSF has several components, some of which are considered core components, management components, and distribution components. The core components are responsible for taking inputs and using them to create output artifacts. The management components focus on ensuring the SSF runs in alignment with your policies. Lastly, the distribution components move the products of the factory for downstream consumption safely.

Core Components

These core components include your scheduling and orchestration platform, pipeline framework and tooling, and build environments. All SSF components use the platform and associated orchestration to conduct their activities. The pipeline and associated tooling allow the facilitation of the workflow to build software artifacts. The guidance emphasizes that the pipeline should be subject to the same requirements as your workloads. This is intended to point out that the pipeline is part of your attack surface and can be exploited to impact downstream consumers, much as it did in SolarWinds. This emphasis is echoed by emerging frameworks like SLSA.

Lastly, you have your build environment, which is where your source code is converted into machine-readable software products referred to as *artifacts*. Mature build environments are working to provide automated attestations regarding the inputs, actions, and tools used during the build to validate the integrity of the build process and associated outputs/artifacts.

Organizations such as TestifySec (`www.testifysec.com`) are innovating to ensure that organizations can detect process tampering or build compromises. A notable example is the project Witness, which aims to prevent tampering of build materials and verify the integrity of the build process from source to target (`https://github.com/testifysec/witness`).

Management Components

The management components include the Policy Management Framework and attestors and observers. In the SSF context, your Policy Management Framework is what helps codify organizational and security requirements such as IAM, assigned worker nodes, and authorized container images. These policies will look different for each organization due to differing risk tolerances and a myriad of applicable regulatory frameworks. The Policy Management Framework is particularly crucial as we watch the push for zero-trust unfold.

Determining who is allowed to do what and in what context is key to enforcing tenets of zero trust such as least-permissive access control. You don't want to deploy containers that were pushed by unauthorized individuals or even containers from sources you don't trust or aren't signed by a source you trust, and so on. Given that the cloud-native context often infers that you're using containers and an orchestrator such as Kubernetes, you have entities such as node attestors, workload attestors, and pipeline observers. These verify the identity and authenticity of your nodes and workloads as well as the verifiable metadata associated with pipeline processes.

Distribution Components

Rounding out the key components identified in the SSF are your distribution components, including an artifact repository and admission controller. The outputs of your pipeline process produce artifacts, which are stored in your artifact repository. These can include items such as container images, Kubernetes manifests, SBOMs, and associated signatures. Increasingly, we see a push to use solutions such as Sigstore to sign not just code but SBOMs and attestations. This is emphasized in the previously discussed Linux Foundation/OpenSSF OSS Security Mobilization Plan (`www.csoonline.com/article/3661631/the-open-source-software-security-mobilization-plan-takeaways-for-security-leaders.html`). Following your artifact repository, you have admission controllers, which are responsible for ensuring that only authorized workloads can be run by your scheduling and orchestration components. These controllers can enforce policies such as what sources are allowed into a build and what components are allowed onto a node host, and that the components used are trusted and verifiable.

Variables and Functionality

The SSF guidance understands that SSF inputs and outputs will vary. Inputs include items such as source code, software dependencies, user credentials, cryptographic material, and pipeline definitions. Outputs include items such as software artifacts, public signing keys, and metadata documents. The white paper also discusses the SSF functionality such as a project moving through the

SSF, and ultimately, providing secure outputs and artifacts that are attested to and have a level of assurance to establish trust with downstream consumers.

Wrapping It Up

At first glance, the SSF reference architecture will seem complex, and that's because it is. Delivering software in modern cloud-native environments involves many moving parts and accompanying processes to ensure that what is being both consumed and produced can be done with a level of assurance that aligns with an organization's risk tolerance.

The complexity also emphasizes both how challenging it is to tie it all together and how fraught with opportunity for missteps and misconfigurations the system can be, leading to a cascading downstream impact on consumers across the ecosystem, all of which are powered by software in the modern economy. It's often said that defenders must be right all the time and that malicious actors must be right just once. In complex cloud-native environments fraught with staffing challenges and cognitive overload, it could be akin to looking for a particular needle in a pile of needles, rather than a haystack.

Microsoft's Secure Supply Chain Consumption Framework

As one of the largest contributors and consumers of OSS, it should come as no surprise that Microsoft has also created a software supply chain security framework called the Secure Supply Chain Consumption Framework (S2C2F). Microsoft first officially announced the S2C2F in August 2022 but stated they have been using it internally to secure their own development practices as early as 2019. Taking it a step further, Microsoft contributed the S2C2F to the OSS community in November 2022 by having it formally adopted by industry OSS leader OpenSSF (www.microsoft.com/en-us/security/blog/2022/11/16/microsoft-contributes-s2c2f-to-openssf-to-improve-supply-chain-security).

Let's dive into the framework a bit to see what it covers and aims to achieve. Microsoft states the framework's goal is to lay out the core concepts of securely consuming OSS dependencies and to implement core practices of secure OSS consumption. Much like similar frameworks, the framework emphasizes the critical role OSS plays across the software ecosystem and broader industries as well when it comes to driving both productivity and innovation. Microsoft states the guidance is broken into two sections:

- The solution-agnostic and maturity-oriented section aimed at individuals such as security executives

- The implementation section, which is focused on actual software developers and their security peers, which makes it informative at the organizational level while still being actionable at the tactical level

S2C2F has three high-level goals:

- To provide a strong OSS governance program
- To improve the mean time to remediate (MTTR) for resolving known vulnerabilities in OSS
- To prevent the consumption of compromised and malicious OSS packages

The three framework goals work in tandem with these three core concepts:

- Scale
- Continuous process improvement
- Control of all artifact inputs

Figure 7.11 illustrates these goals and core concepts.

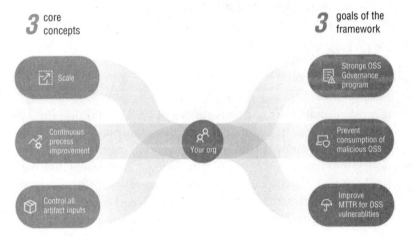

Figure 7.11

Source: https://github.com/ossf/s2c2f/blob/main/specification/Secure_Supply_Chain_Consumption_Framework_(S2C2F).pdf. GitHub

While the core concepts may sound simple on the surface, they can be incredibly complex and daunting in large enterprise environments that are developing software. As the S2C2F points out, the modern software developer consumes OSS in a myriad of ways. Developing standardized ways to consume OSS and having developers stick to them makes it possible to secure OSS.

Bringing a governed and structured approach to OSS consumption across *all* the organization's development teams is critical. Like most security frameworks, S2C2F is a journey that organizations embark on, and for this reason it is framed as a maturity model that focuses on continuous process improvement. Organizations can prioritize specific requirements for earlier implementation and make changes as new threats and risks emerge.

Lastly, practices and maturity implemented in isolation aren't efficient and don't address the broad attack and risk surface of the modern enterprise. For that reason, S2C2F is oriented around scale as a core concept as well. One specific example the guidance points out is the advocacy for a centralized internal registry that developers use, which was also a recommendation in sources such as NIST's Software Supply Chain guidance, 800-161 r1.

As the framework points out, this model falls apart as soon as a single developer decides to pull OSS components from anything outside of the internal registry and the internal registry itself requires overhead and management, which has an associated burden and cost. S2C2F was designed, as they state, to secure OSS consumption at scale without the centralization approach advocated for in other guidance we have covered. This thought process should resonate for organizations advocating for or taking a more decentralized approach.

S2C2F is a combination of tools and requirements across a capability maturity road map focused on secure OSS ingestion through governance. The S2C2F guidance discusses common OSS supply chain threats, covering not just the threats but also real-world examples of the attacks occurring, and then maps them to specific S2C2F requirements. Examples S2C2F provides range from accident vulnerabilities in OSS code or containers to intentional backdoors and malicious activity in repositories and packages. The guidance draws from sources such as Google's Software Supply Chain Threats, which addresses threats from source, build, deployment/runtime, and dependencies (`https://cloud.google.com/ software-supply-chain-security/docs/attack-vectors`). The threats listed also include more benign sources, such as OSS components that have reached end of life and are no longer addressing vulnerabilities, and maintainers simply failing to address vulnerabilities in a timeframe desired by consumers.

S2C2F Practices

As mentioned, S2C2F includes a set of solution and vendor-agnostic practices that can help organizations secure their OSS supply chain usage. Leaders such as compliance, security, and engineering managers as well as CISOs can reference these practices to identify gaps in their organizations' secure OSS usage and governance. Let's now step through these practices to understand what they entail.

The first practice cited is Ingestion. As S2C2F points out, the first step of securing a software supply chain is controlling artifact inputs, which includes packaged and source code artifacts. The practice here is aimed at enabling organizations to ship assets despite external OSS sources being either compromised or unavailable. Packaged artifacts include items such as Linux package repositories or Open Container Initiative (OCI) registries. Organizations need to proxy those external sources and save copies of what is required. On the source code artifact front, the practice advocates mirroring external source code repositories internally and caching packages locally to enable organizations to continue operating in adverse situations, thus demonstrating business continuity. It also allows organizations to conduct security scans and even contribute fixes upstream, or to fix the code locally in situations where this is desired rather than contributing upstream.

After Ingestion, the next practice is Scanning, with the goal of ensuring that the consuming organization and individuals have visibility of vulnerabilities associated with the OSS component. As S2C2F states, trust is built by getting visibility into the security posture of the component being consumed. By scanning the ingested OSS component, the organization can identify misconfigurations, vulnerable code, known vulnerabilities, or extraneous code that can increase the potential attack surface. There are plenty of OSS and proprietary scanning tools organizations can use to fulfill this practice.

Once an organization has ingested and scanned an OSS component, they need to inventory it so that they understand where their OSS components exist in production environments. A perfect example S2C2F uses is the Log4J incident. Organizations that had accurate OSS component inventories were far better equipped to respond to the incident than organizations that lacked this inventory. As other critical vulnerabilities emerge in OSS components, organizations with inventories can quickly respond by remediating or triaging the vulnerable or compromised components and systems.

Having scanned and inventoried ingested components is a great start, but as we all know, software ages like milk—meaning there will inevitably be a need to update and patch components that are in the production environments. Therefore, the next practice is having the capability to update components as needed. It is well known that when a vulnerability gets publicly disclosed, it is often a race between an organization's ability to patch or remediate the vulnerability and a malicious actor's ability to exploit it.

For this reason, the practice of updating and patching vulnerable components at scale across the enterprise's OSS footprint is critical. Another consideration here is that the OSS components are generally maintained by volunteers with no associated service level agreements (SLAs) for vulnerability remediation. So, consumers must be prepared to implement virtual patching and other mitigating controls if the OSS maintainer hasn't provided remediations directly.

Having a standardized process around OSS ingestion and use is one thing, but you must inevitably be able to audit your environments to identify components that deviated from the process or that pose a risk to your organization.

Therefore, the next practice in the guidance is auditing. This means organizations can audit their OSS components and validate that they have gone through their standardized process of ingestion, scanning, and inventory; otherwise, governance starts to fall apart.

While auditing is great, organizations must be able to do something about ungoverned OSS components that are discovered. Therefore, enforcement is the next practice in the guidance. If a developer were to bypass established processes and introduce ungoverned OSS components from untrusted sources, then organizations must be able to remediate this deviation. The example the guidance provides is the enforcement of rerouting DNS traffic or establishing gates in the build process to break builds if unverified OSS components are introduced. Increasingly, malicious actors make attempts to compromise the build process or infrastructure to lead to compromised binaries and artifacts.

Next up in the guidance is the practice of being able to rebuild every OSS artifact being deployed from source code. This can become key if malicious actors have been able to insert a malicious OSS package with a backdoor or make unauthorized changes to generated binaries during the build.

The S2C2F emphasizes that for key artifacts or business-critical high-value assets, it may be necessary to create a chain of custody from the original source code for every single artifact used to create a production service or version of an application. This practice is focused on enabling developers who have that dependency on key OSS components to ingest the source code, rebuild it, modify it if needed such as by signing, and then cache the rebuilt artifact for internal use.

This practice points directly to *reproducible builds*, which are practices in software development for creating an independently verifiable path from source to binary code (`https://reproducible-builds.org/docs/definition`). This leads to bit-by-bit identical copies of all relevant artifacts. You'll notice this practice is prevalent in other emerging guidance, such as SLSA, particularly for higher levels of maturity.

The final practice in S2C2F is being able to fix issues and contribute back upstream. S2C2F states that "I can privately patch, build and deploy any external artifact within 3 days of harm notification and confidentially contribute the fix to the upstream maintainer." This is a very mature practice because it switches the onus from strict dependence on the maintainer to the software consumer being an active contributor to an OSS project or component. This is exactly the type of behavior being advocated for by researchers who we've touched on in other parts of the text, such as the research by Chinmayi Sharma titled "A Tragedy of the Digital Commons."

That said, the guidance states this is only for extreme scenarios and temporary risk mitigation when an upstream maintainer isn't able to provide the public fix within the acceptable window of risk for your organization. It comes across as a recognition of allowing the maintainer to take the appropriate action but also being willing to help when appropriate, which is the ethos of the OSS community. S2C2F also advocates several ways organizations can contribute to the OSS community such as financial support directly or through foundations, participating in bounty programs, advocating best practices, and being an active participant in key OSS projects.

S2C2F Implementation Guide

Like other frameworks such as SLSA, S2C2F is oriented around four levels of maturity, ranging from minimum OSS governance all the way to advanced threat defense, each with their own associated activities, as illustrated in Figure 7.12.

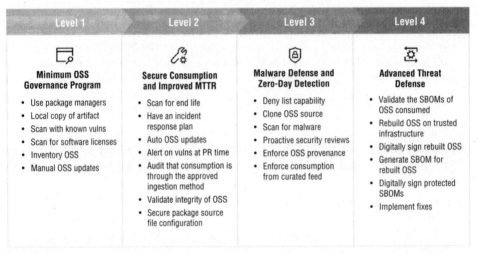

Level 1	Level 2	Level 3	Level 4
Minimum OSS Governance Program	**Secure Consumption and Improved MTTR**	**Malware Defense and Zero-Day Detection**	**Advanced Threat Defense**
• Use package managers • Local copy of artifact • Scan with known vulns • Scan for software licenses • Inventory OSS • Manual OSS updates	• Scan for end life • Have an incident response plan • Auto OSS updates • Alert on vulns at PR time • Audit that consumption is through the approved ingestion method • Validate integrity of OSS • Secure package source file configuration	• Deny list capability • Clone OSS source • Scan for malware • Proactive security reviews • Enforce OSS provenance • Enforce consumption from curated feed	• Validate the SBOMs of OSS consumed • Rebuild OSS on trusted infrastructure • Digitally sign rebuilt OSS • Generate SBOM for rebuilt OSS • Digitally sign protected SBOMs • Implement fixes

Figure 7.12

Source: `https://github.com/ossf/s2c2f/blob/main/specification/Secure_Supply_Chain_Consumption_Framework_(S2C2F).pdf`. GitHub

Level 1 includes basic activities such as caching packages internally, doing basic inventory and fundamental scanning, and updating OSS in your environment. Level 2 builds on that by driving down mean time to recovery (MTTR) for patching vulnerable components and performing incident response. Level 3 involves creating a deny list of known malicious or untrusted components and sources, scanning for malware present in the OSS components, and enforcing provenance. Lastly, Level 4 is considered aspirational, meaning it is a level of maturity that most organizations won't meet, with the exceptions of the most resourced and sensitive organizations in the industry. Activities at this level include rebuilding OSS on trusted build infrastructure and creating and digitally signing SBOMs for the rebuilt OSS components.

While these four levels of maturity and associated capabilities or requirements are helpful, organizations need to understand how to approach assessing themselves or others against the levels. S2C2F provides two high-level steps: preparing for the assessment and then actually performing it. Preparing involves ensuring the organization is comfortable engaging with the development and engineering teams to inquire about the tooling, capabilities, and workflows the guidance discusses. The guidance goes on to provide a series of example questions that can be used as part of an assessment. These questions involve understanding how OSS is consumed currently in projects, where it comes from, as well as existing governance and security practices as discussed in the preceding core concepts, goals, and levels of maturity of the framework.

After an assessment has occurred, organizations should have a better understanding of their current maturity levels across the capabilities and practices the framework recommends. This understanding empowers organizations to plan for improvements to address deficiencies or areas of weakness that were discovered during the assessment process. Organizations can then make targeted investments and initiatives to improve capabilities and practices that they deem the most critical, based on their respective goals and risk tolerance.

S2C2F lays out the framework's requirements across a matrixed table that includes the practice, requirement ID, maturity level, requirement title, and associated benefit to the organization for implementing the practice. Knowing that tooling is a core component and meets the various requirements and maturity levels, the guidance also provides tooling availability and recommendations, which include existing free tools, tools from Microsoft, and proposed tools that Microsoft is also working on.

The S2C2F guide is a welcome addition to the dialogue on supply chain security, and the contribution of the framework by Microsoft to OpenSSF shows Microsoft's commitment to the OSS community and to helping the industry tackle this problem.

OWASP Software Component Verification Standard

Unlike frameworks such as NIST's Secure Software Development Framework (SSDF), which is created by government organizations, OWASP's Software Component Verification Standard (SCVS) is a community-driven effort focused on the software supply chain. It mainly focuses on reducing risk in the software supply chain by identifying relevant activities, controls, and best practices that can be implemented throughout the software supply chain life cycle. OWASP's SCVS is also referenced throughout the NIST SSDF guidance, which will be discussed in Chapter 8. Released in 2020, Version 1.0 of SCVS is led by Steve Springett, along with several other contributors and reviewers.

SCVS is broken out into six control families, each of which contains multiple controls for various aspects of software component verification and processes:

- Inventory
- SBOM
- Build Environment
- Package Management
- Component Analysis
- Pedigree and Provenance

SCVS Levels

Much like SLSA, SCVS uses levels—the higher the level, the more controls associated with it. SCVS has three levels. Level 1 is for low-assurance requirements and basic controls. Level 2 is for moderately sensitive software and situations where additional rigor is warranted. Level 3 is for the most high-assurance environments due to data sensitivity or mission criticality. Let's take a deeper look at each of these levels to understand some of the fundamental controls associated with them.

Level 1

As the SCVS guide states, Level 1 lays the groundwork for all subsequent levels and higher levels of assurance. Much like other frameworks, Level 1 includes some fundamental activities, most notably having an accurate inventory. In the world of software, this increasingly involves creating an SBOM to understand the software components involved in your applications. Level 1 also involves using continuous integration (CI) in pursuit of producing repeatable builds. Popular CI platforms include CircleCI, Jenkins, GitLab, and GitHub, among others. Continuous integration involves developers merging all their working copies of code to the shared main repository. CI involves both technology and practices, such as the CI or build service as well as the cultural aspect of developers learning to frequently integrate their code changes. Lastly, Level 1 calls for performing analysis of third-party components with publicly available tools and intelligence. Various tools can help with analyzing and identifying relevant publicly disclosed vulnerabilities associated with the third-party software components, which we will dive into more deeply in the following sections. SCVS also includes Levels 2 and 3, each of which adds additional rigor or requirements to the baseline Level 1.

Level 2

Level 2 of SCVS, as stated by OWASP, focuses on software-intensive organizations that have some level of maturity around risk management in place within their environments. Level 2 builds on the controls identified in Level 1 by bringing in additional stakeholders and parties to the mix, such as nontechnical professionals who may be involved in areas such as contracts and procurement.

Level 3

Level 3 is the most rigorous of the SCVS levels and focuses on both auditability and end-to-end transparency throughout the software supply chain. This level is often reserved for the most highly regulated and sensitive industries as well as the most mature organizations.

OWASP recommends that organizations use SCVS in pursuit of incremental improvement of software supply chain security. They also recommend organizations tailor SCVS to fit the security and compliance requirements most relevant to the organizations using the standard. This is a unique perspective that advocates for flexibility over uniform baselining as is often done by other security standards and frameworks.

With that said, let's dig into the control families and associated controls as defined by SCVS.

Inventory

Having an accurate inventory has long been a critical security control, as cited in sources such as the SANS and subsequent CIS Critical Security Control frameworks. Despite being cited, it has also long been a challenge that organizations struggle with, so it is no surprise to see Inventory as the initial control family listed in the SCVS standard. In the SCVS context, the focus is on having an inventory of all the components used in the creation of software and the controls advocated for reaching across single applications, organization-wide inventories, and bolstering software transparency related to software acquisition. SCVS, much like the broader push for software transparency, advocates for having organization-wide software inventories, which includes both first-party and third-party software components, including OSS code.

Level 1 in the Inventory family focuses on key activities such as knowing direct and transitive components at build time, as well as using package managers to manage third-party binary components. Level 1 also includes having a comprehensive inventory of third-party components in a machine-readable format and generating SBOMs for publicly and commercially available applications. Level 2 builds on these controls by also requiring SBOMs for new software procurements. This is an example of a control that extends beyond the cyber practitioner and begins to involve other nontechnical stakeholders, such as acquisition professionals who can begin to ask for these artifacts as part of procurement.

Level 3 within the Inventory family begins to add more rigorous controls such as continuously maintaining SBOMs for all systems and knowing the component types throughout the inventory. Not only does Level 3 require knowing the component type, but it also requires knowing the component's function and, more importantly, the point of origin for all components. This is often referred to as *provenance* as it relates to the software supply chain.

Software Bill of Materials

The software bill of materials (SBOM) is a key component and security control family within the SCVS framework. SCVS states that organizations with mature development practices are creating SBOMs as part of their build pipeline activities and doing so in a machine-readable format. SCVS recognizes that there are multiple SBOM formats, such as CycloneDX and SPDX, and organizations need to align with the format(s) that best fit their use cases, as well as potentially more than one format, to meet things such as functional and contractual requirements and to be able to work with the diverse vendor ecosystem.

Level 1 of the SBOM family lays out some fundamental controls such as having a structured and machine-readable SBOM present, assigning unique identifiers to SBOMs, and using metadata such as timestamps. Building on these controls, SCVS calls for having SBOMs with complete accurate inventories for all the components the SBOM describes and analyzing the SBOMs for any relevant vulnerabilities associated with the components. Lastly, there are requirements to ensure component identifiers are derived from native ecosystems where possible and to have accurate licensing information for the components contained in the SBOMs.

Building on the Level 1 requirements, Level 2 in the SBOM family adds controls such as not only having the SBOMs signed by the publisher, supplier, or certifying authority, but also performing signature verification activities. Level 2 also calls for SBOMs having accurate inventory of all test components for an application and metadata about the asset or software the SBOM is describing. Lastly, there is a requirement to have components defined in the SBOM to have valid SPDX license IDs or expressions if applicable.

Level 3 adds even more controls to the SBOM family of activities. These include identifying the component point of origin in a machine-readable format, such as PURL, as well as having valid copyright statements for the software components defined in the SBOM. Additionally, Level 3 calls for having detailed provenance and pedigree information for components defined in the SBOM and using file hashes such as SHA-256 for components defined in the SBOM.

Build Environment

SCVS acknowledges the complexity of modern build environments, including source code and package repositories, CI/CD processes, testing activities, and the supporting network infrastructure and services that make software builds and delivery possible. As SCVS mentions, each of these entities and activities in the build environment and pipeline presents possible attack vectors for malicious actors, as well as opportunity for traditional failures and misconfigurations to occur. This is perhaps best articulated by other frameworks such as SLSA and their illustration of the various attack vectors and potential points of compromise in the modern pipeline and build process.

The Build Environment control family is the largest of the SCVS standard, with over 20 controls associated with it. Level 1 involves fundamental controls such as having repeatable build processes and documentation associated with build instructions and using CI pipelines. It also involves controls such as ensuring that the application build pipeline can only perform builds from source code in the version control systems and ensuring build time changes to source and binaries that are well known and defined. Lastly, Level 1 calls for having checksums of all first- and third-party software components that are documented for every build.

Level 2 of the Build Environment controls begins to add activities such as build pipelines not allowing for the modification of builds outside of the job performing the build or the alteration of package management settings or executing code outside of the context of a job's build script. Level 2 also calls for enforcing authentication and authorization and default deny settings on the build pipeline. Given the build pipeline itself can be compromised due to outdated systems and software, Level 2 calls for having an established maintenance cadence for the build pipeline tech stack. Lastly, Level 2 requires having checksums of all components accessible and delivered out-of-band when components are packaged or distributed.

The final requirements in Level 3 include items such as requiring separation of concerns/duties for modifying system settings in the build pipeline and retaining a verifiable audit log of all system changes and build job changes. There are also requirements for monitoring compilers, version control systems (VCSs), development utilities, and software development kits (SDKs) for tampering and malicious code. The controls call for ensuring that unused direct and transitive components have been both identified and removed from the application, which contributes to attack surface reduction and minimizing the potential attack vectors for malicious actors.

Package Management

SCVS points out that modern-day OSS components are often published to ecosystem-specific package repositories such as Maven, .NET, and

NPM. Organizations are increasingly being directed toward establishing internal repositories of not only first-party components but also trusted third-party components, with guidance such as NIST 800-161r1 and the NSA Secure Guidance for Developers both recommending this approach. SCVS notes that package managers are often invoked during the build process, and there are several business and technical benefits for their use but security considerations as well.

Level 1 controls for the Package Management family include ensuring binary components are retrieved from a package repository and that their contents align with an authoritative point of origin for OSS components. The repository must also support auditing/logging when these components are updated and verifying the integrity of the packages when they're retrieved from a remote repository or filesystem. Package managers should also enforce encryption such as Transport Layer Security (TLS) for data exchanges and ensure that the TLS certificate chains are validated or fail securely when they cannot be. Failing securely means when the TLS certificate chains cannot be validated, the system defaults to a secure state rather than allowing ongoing functionality and activities to occur. The package manager must also not execute component code, and package installation data should be available in machine-readable formats.

Advancing the controls from Level 1, Level 2 in the Package Management family calls for strong authentication for the package repository, including using MFA. Organizations may want to specifically focus on phishing-resistant MFA (www.yubico.com/resources/glossary/phishing-resistant-mfa/?gclid=CjOK CQjwj7CZBhDHARIsAPPWv3fXCG329UPlV7Oz3WZvIvcdHfJeDqo60tPOHaa9KsNcX Z2BZK5N_voaAvhqEALw_wcB), given recent incidents involving compromised or abused MFA (www.malwarebytes.com/blog/news/2022/08/twilio-data-breach-turns-out-to-be-more-elaborate-than-suspected#:~:text=Earlier%20 this%20month%2C%20messaging%20service,more%20elaborate%20than%20 originally%20assumed). In addition to strong authentication, Level 2 calls for ensuring that the package repositories support the ability to conduct security incident reporting and notify the publishers of security issues. There are controls to require that the package repositories are able to verifiably correlate component versions to source code in VCS as well as requiring code signing for publishing packages to the production repository.

Finally, Level 3 in the Package Management family adds a handful of additional controls to the mix. These include ensuring package repository components have been published with MFA and automated security incident reporting, including the notification of users for security issues. There is also the requirement that the package repository perform SCA prior to publishing components and then make those results available to software component consumers and analysis and assurance.

Component Analysis

The fifth control family in SCVS is Component Analysis, which is the process of identifying potential areas of risk from using OSS and third-party components, which includes not only direct but also transitive components. Organizations need to understand any inherent risk associated with OSS and the third-party components they use in their applications and systems. OSS and third-party software use is pervasive, with a large majority of modern applications composed of OSS and third-party software components. Organizations must understand both the components they are using and any vulnerabilities and risks associated with those components.

In pursuit of understanding vulnerabilities, organizations most commonly refer to sources such as the NIST National Vulnerability Database (NVD) to look for known vulnerabilities. In addition to known vulnerabilities, organizations should also be familiar with other data, including terms such as component version currency, component type, function, and quantity. It means understanding whether the component is out of date or end of life and likely to be vulnerable, as well as understanding the component type and any associated implications for its upgrades and risk. Organizations should understand the component's function to identify duplicative components and only use higher-quality components to minimize risk. Organizations should also understand the component quantities in their inventories, as it becomes increasingly difficult to manage component sprawl. Lastly, organizations must understand license types associated with the components they are using, as there may be distribution requirements, limitations, and conflicts that pose business risk.

Level 1 of the Component Analysis family involves activities such as being able to analyze components with linters and static analysis. An emphasis is placed on automation for activities such as identifying publicly disclosed vulnerabilities associated with components and identifying non-specified component versions in use or outdated components. Organizations must also have automated processes for identifying component quantities in use and licensing associated with the components.

Level 2 takes these steps further by ensuring components are analyzed via linting and static analysis, including on every upgrade of a component, as well as automating the process of identifying component types in use.

Key distinctions for Level 3 involve automating the process of identifying confirmed exploitability, end of life/support for components, and component functions.

Pedigree and Provenance

The last of the control families is Pedigree and Provenance, which is critical because it's difficult to trust or understand the risk associated with software consumption without understanding both the quality of what you are consuming and where it originated, and the chain of custody involved in its delivery.

Level 1 in the Pedigree and Provenance family involves having provenance of modified components documented as well as analyzing modified components with the same level of rigor as unmodified components. Control is also included to ensure that the organization understands the risks unique to the modified components and their associated variants.

Building on Level 1, Level 2 adds controls to ensure that organizations have documented verifiable pedigree of component modifications and are uniquely identifying modified components.

The lone control for Level 3 involves having a chain of custody that's auditable for source code and binary components.

Open Source Policy

While not a formal control family within the SCVS, the guidance lays out recommendations for organizations more broadly around their use of OSS. Although the use of OSS is rampant and involved in many modern applications that organizations produce and consume, many organizations have poor security maturity when it comes to governing its consumption and use.

SCVS recommends that organizations establish an OSS policy that is supported and enforced by cross-functional stakeholders. These policies should cover critical considerations related to OSS, such as understanding the age of components in use, setting requirements for using old major or minor revisions, and keeping components continuously updated with automation capabilities. Organizations should also establish guidance for excluding components with known vulnerabilities, or at least a stance on the level of acceptable risk. At-risk components should have defined MTTR criteria as well as restrictions on using end-of-life components due to their inherent risks. Some organizations may even have a prohibited components list due to vulnerabilities, national security concerns, or other factors.

As previously mentioned, while the use of OSS is overwhelmingly common, many organizations have not taken the time to codify their stance on OSS in formal policy and guidance. We have begun to see some organizations leading the way, going beyond policies and establishing open source program offices (OSPOs) (`www.linuxfoundation.org/resources/open-source-guides/creating-an-open-source-program`) to help govern and drive organizations' use of OSS within the software they produce as well as OSS consumers.

OpenSSF Scorecard

Everyone knows the phrase "software is eating the world" (`https://a16z` `.com/2011/08/20/why-software-is-eating-the-world`) by Marc Andreessen, dating back to well over a decade now. Software powers nearly every aspect of modern society, both personally and professionally, and it is critical to the modern economy and even national security—this is not debatable. Given that reality, it can also be said that OSS has eaten the software industry. It is estimated by groups such as the Linux Foundation and others that free and open source software (FOSS) constitutes 70 to 90 percent of any modern software solution or product (`www.linuxfoundation.org/blog/blog/a-summary-of-census-ii-open-` `source-software-application-libraries-the-world-depends-on`). Not only is modern software largely composed of OSS components, but IT leaders are also more likely to work with vendors who also contribute to the OSS community (`www.redhat.com/en/enterprise-open-source-report/2022`).

Many reasons exist for the rampant use of OSS such as flexibility, cost savings, innovation through community-enabled projects, and even better security through the ability to review code and have more "eyeballs" on the code, especially for large OSS projects. That said, OSS is not without its own concerns, including vulnerabilities and CVEs for affected code. CVE is a project by MITRE that strives to "identify, define and catalog publicly disclosed cybersecurity vulnerabilities" (`cve.mitre.org`). However, as noted by the CNCF Software Supply Chain Best Practices white paper, CVEs are a "trailing metric," meaning that CVEs are the enumerations of vulnerabilities that have been *publicly* disclosed. They are also but one of the potential risks and vulnerabilities associated with software.

For this reason, it's recommended that organizations make use of other methods to evaluate the state of security for a specific OSS project they are consuming, with one of the most notable being OpenSSF's Scorecard project (`http://openssf` `.org`), which we will discuss next.

Security Scorecards for Open Source Projects

In late 2020, the OpenSSF announced their project dubbed "Scorecard," which aims to autogenerate a security score for OSS projects to help consumers and organizations make risk-informed decisions about their OSS consumption. Organizations are making overwhelming use of OSS dependencies, but determining the risk of consuming those dependencies remains a largely manual activity, particularly at scale across the software ecosystem. The Scorecard project seeks to alleviate some of that burden using their automated heuristics and security checks, on a scoring scale of 0–10 (see Figure 7.13).

Name	Description	Risk Level
Binary-Artifacts	Is the project free of checked-in binaries?	High
Branch-Protection	Does the project use Branch Protection?	High
CI-Tests	Does the project run tests in CI, e.g. GitHub Actions, Prow?	Low
CII-Best-Practices	Does the project have a CII Best Practices Badge?	Low
Code-Review	Does the project require code review before code is merged?	High
Contributors	Does the project have contributors from at least two different organizations?	Low
Dangerous-Workflow	Does the project avoid dangerous coding patterns in GitHub Action workflows?	Critical
Dependency-Update-Tool	Does the project use tools to help update its dependencies?	High
Fuzzing	Does the project use fuzzing tools, e.g. OSS-Fuzz?	Medium
License	Does the project declare a license?	Low
Maintained	Is the project maintained?	High
Pinned-Dependencies	Does the project declare and pin dependencies?	Medium
Packaging	Does the project build and publish official packages from CI/CD, e.g. GitHub Publishing?	Medium
SAST	Does the project use static code analysis tools, e.g. CodeQL, LGTM, SonarCloud?	Medium
Security-Policy	Does the project contain a security policy?	Medium
Signed-Releases	Does the project cryptographically sign releases?	High
Token-Permissions	Does the project declare GitHub workflow tokens as read only?	High
Vulnerabilities	Does the project have unfixed vulnerabilities? Uses the OSV service.	High

Figure 7.13

The Scorecard project is not aiming low either; they scan the one million most critical OSS projects based on direct dependencies and publish the results to a public dataset on a weekly basis. In addition to leveraging this publicly available dataset, organizations can run Scorecard against their own GitHub projects by using GitHub Actions. Then when there is a change in the repository, GitHub Actions runs and provides alerts to the maintainers of those projects.

The Scorecard project uses a scoring scale of Critical, High, Medium, and Low, which are severity levels that many security practitioners are familiar with. The Scorecard project runs a standard list of checks against all the projects that it is targeted for, whether for public projects or if you are using it natively in your own GitHub repositories. For those interested, you can dive into what some of those checks are. They include fundamental security practices such as using branch protection and cryptographically signing releases. To detect the presence of unfixed vulnerabilities, the Scorecard project uses the OSV Vulnerability Database (`http://osv.dev`), a distributed vulnerability database for OSS that uses OpenSSF OSV format. OSV, at its core, is an aggregation of other vulnerability databases using the OSV schema, such as GitHub Security Advisories and the Global Security Database, among others. OSC also supports both APIs and command-line interface (CLI) tools for scanning SBOMs in either CycloneDX or SPDX formats, which we discussed in Chapter 3, "Vulnerability Databases and Scoring Methodologies."

How Can Organizations Make Use of the Scorecards Project?

As mentioned previously, organizations are making widespread use of OSS. However, the practice of conducting due diligence, governance, and risk management of OSS consumption is still in its infancy. We are seeing a big push to bolster the software supply chain's resiliency and mature organizations' software supply chain security practices, NIST's Cybersecurity Supply Chain Risk Management Practices for Systems and Organizations, NIST's SSDF, the OpenSSF OSS Security Mobilization Plan, SLSA, and many other best practices and sources of guidance have emerged. All touch on the need to govern an organization's consumption of OSS and to ensure that this consumption aligns with the organization's risk tolerance.

While that may sound straightforward on the surface, the idea of doing that across the entire robust ecosystem of OSS projects and components that organizations are consuming is not so trivial. OpenSSF's Scorecard project provides an automated way to get security and risk insights into over one million leading OSS projects, and allows organizations to use the project natively for their own software and projects.

Organizations can use Scorecard via the CLI for projects they do not own, as well as use a package manager for projects such as npm, PyPi, or RubyGems. Scorecard is also available as a Docker container and can be deployed via this route as well.

The Scorecard project meets biweekly and has an active Slack channel. It is led by facilitators from companies such as Google, Datto, and Cisco, among others. Since its inception, Scorecard has grown in popularity and is listed as having over 3,000 Stargazers, or users, who have bookmarked the project. As organizations continue their push to mature their OSS consumption governance practices, the project will inevitably grow in popularity. There is also the opportunity for organizations and individual contributors to participate in the project, including submitting checks to be considered for the scoring assessment. Organizations can also customize their use of Scorecard and run only specific checks potentially aligned with their organizational or industry-specific security requirements.

Scorecard provides a critical capability that automates a robust set of assessment criteria that would be impractical for organizations to do manually, either on public projects they are consuming or internal projects they want to assess. It is well known that despite the value and innovation that OSS brings, most FOSS projects are understaffed and led by uncompensated volunteer contributors.

This is not to say organizations should not make use of OSS projects, but rather that they should have some rigor around the projects they consume and the risk those projects present. The Scorecard project exactly fits that need in an easy-to-use capacity. It does all of this while assessing OSS projects for security concerns that align with best practices such as signing, SAST, and more, already advocated for by both public and private security leaders.

The Path Ahead

While OSS offers tremendous benefits, many concerns and studies find that FOSS developers largely don't prioritize security. A study by the Linux Foundation's OpenSSF and Harvard University's Laboratory for Innovation Science found that the average FOSS developer spends only about 2.3 percent of their time on improving the security of their code (www.darkreading.com/application-security/open-source-developers-still-not-interested-in-secure-coding). This warrants organizations consuming OSS components taking various measures, such as vetting OSS components prior to consumption and using SBOMs to understand the vulnerabilities associated with their OSS consumption and where those components reside within the enterprise, so they are better positioned to respond to the next Log4j type situation.

To obtain more specific guidance, organizations can reference NIST's recommended practices for Open Source Software Controls, which were published in response to the Cybersecurity Executive Order (EO) 14028, Improving the Nation's Cybersecurity (www.nist.gov/itl/executive-order-14028-improving-nations-cybersecurity/software-security-supply-chains-open). These include tiered capabilities based on the maturity of the organization: Foundational, Sustaining, and Enhancing. Within those tiers are capabilities such as using SCA source code reviews to identify vulnerable components, prioritizing the use of programming languages with built-in guardrails, and automating the process of collecting, storing, and scanning OSS components into hardened internal repositories prior to introducing them to production environments.

It should be evident by now that there's no panacea or silver bullet to securely using OSS, or any software for that matter. That said, with the right combination of people, processes, and technology, in that order, organizations can reap the benefits of OSS while driving down the risk of its use as well.

Summary

In this chapter we discussed existing and emerging guidance for software supply chain security. This included efforts such as SLSA as well as resources from Microsoft, CNCF and others. In the following chapter we will discuss existing and emerging guidance from Government entities.

Existing and Emerging Government Guidance

In this chapter, we will discuss existing and emerging publications addressing software supply chain security from governmental and public sector organizations. These publications build on existing commercial guidance that we discussed in the previous chapter and account for some of the unique requirements of the Department of Defense (DoD), U.S. Federal Civilian Executive Branch (FCEB) agencies, and the National Security Agency (NSA), among others.

Cybersecurity Supply Chain Risk Management Practices for Systems and Organizations

In early 2020, the National Institute of Standards and Technology (NIST) first released special publication (SP) 800-161, "Cybersecurity Supply Chain Risk Management (C-SCRM) Practices for Systems and Organizations." However, as with many other resources discussed throughout this book, the Cybersecurity Executive Order (EO) 14028 warranted an update to the original NIST C-SCRM publication. The Cybersecurity EO's Sections 4(b), 4(c), and 4(d) specifically focused on software supply chain concerns, and because of that, NIST published their response and guidance in 800-161 Revision 1 Appendix F, the "Response to Executive Order 14028's Call to Publish Guidelines for Enhancing Software Supply Chain Security." Rather than embed the guidance within the broader

800-161 document, NIST published it online as a stand-alone resource (`www`
`.nist.gov/itl/executive-order-14028-improving-nations-cybersecurity/`
`software-security-supply-chains`).

Before diving into the specific guidance provided by NIST, we should revisit
what the EO's Section 4 details. Section 4 calls for the Secretary of Commerce,
acting through NIST, to work with the government, industry, and academia
to identify existing—or to develop new—standards, tools, and best practices
to align with Section 4 of the EO. This section included criteria for evaluating
software and security practices of developers and suppliers. In addition, this
evaluation was tasked to occur within 30 days of the EO's publication. Moving
beyond that, within 180 days of the publication, the director of NIST was required
to publish primary guidelines to enhance software supply chain security that
aligned with the requirements from Section 4.

Within one year after the EO's publication, the director of NIST was tasked
with publishing additional guidelines and procedures for periodic review and
maintenance of the guidelines that NIST had published on the topic. To produce
their initial guidance published online, NIST pulled insights from SP 800-161r1,
along with various position papers submitted to NIST prior to their June 2021
"Enhancing Software Supply Chain Security Workshop" (`https://csrc.nist`
`.gov/Events/2021/enhancing-software-supply-chain-security-workshop`),
working groups, and of course, the NIST EO page itself.

NIST's 800-161r1 guidance strives to inform the acquisition, use, and maintenance of third-party software and services that agencies are using as part of
their IT programs. This guidance can be integrated into their C-SCRM programs
as well as used to help inform acquisition and procurement activities. It can be
implemented and used by not only federal agencies but also relevant suppliers
looking to bolster their software supply chain practices and processes. This
guidance will become pertinent as these best practices and requirements work
their way into federal contracting language and become required of software
suppliers looking to sell to the U.S. federal government.

NIST also provided a relationship map to illustrate the relationship between
their various publications such as 800-37r2, 800-53r5, and the Secure Software
Development Framework (SSDF), which is discussed later in the section "NIST's
Secure Software Development Framework." These documents can be used for
both the purchase of secure software by the government and the attestation by
industry to these best practices and requirements. Figure 8.1 demonstrates the
relationship between the various publications.

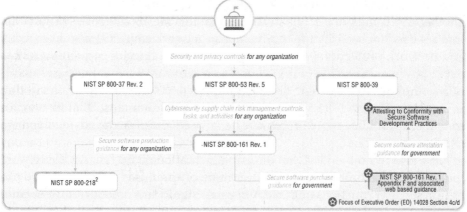

1. Secure Software Development Framework (SSDF) Version 1.1: Recommendations for Mitigating the Risk of Software Vulnerabilities

Figure 8.1

Source: www.nist.gov/itl/executive-order-14028-improving-nations-cybersecurity/software-security-supply-chains-guidance, Unites States Department of Commerce, Public domain

Critical Software

One of NIST's key requirements from the EO was to define *critical software*. NIST's definition of critical software is "any software that has or has direct software dependencies upon one or more components with these attributes." Critical software

- Is designed to run with elevated privileges or managed privileges
- Has direct or privileged access to networking or computing resources
- Is designed to control access to data or operational technology
- Performs a function critical to trust
- Operates outside of normal trust boundaries with privileged access

Anyone reading this list can quickly agree that this is a complicated set of criteria that would make most software potentially critical. For that reason, let's unpack some of the previously listed criteria. First, *direct software dependency* must be defined. NIST defined direct software dependency as other software components such as libraries and packages that are directly integrated into or necessary for the operation of the specific software being discussed (www.nist.gov/itl/executive-order-improving nations cybersecurity/critical-software-definition-faqs#Ref_FAQ2). They also specify that this doesn't include interfaces or services of otherwise independent products. *Critical to trust* can be another confusing phrase. NIST clarifies that this means categories of software that are used for security functions such as network control endpoint security and network protection (`www.nist.gov/itl/executive-order-improving-nations-cybersecurity/critical-software-definition-faqs#Ref_FAQ3`). NIST emphasizes that their definition applies to software in any form that is purchased for and deployed in production environments. That means, for example, it wouldn't apply to software being used for research and development (R&D) use cases.

NIST also recommended that the implementation phase for critical software requirements initially focus on stand-alone on-premises software serving in critical security functions or that could cause significant potential harm if compromised, with following phases focusing on other software such as cloud, hybrid, and source code management, among others.

NIST goes on to provide a preliminary list of software categories they deem critical along with rationale for their inclusion. The list includes categories such as Identity, Credential and Access Management (ICAM), Operating Systems, Web Browsers, Endpoint Security, Network Control, and several others. The rationale is their critical access and functions could potentially compromise the security and integrity of a system if vulnerable and exploited.

For those looking to dive deeper into the conversation around critical software as defined by NIST, check out the Critical Software Definition FAQ page that answers some frequent questions and concerns at `www.nist.gov/itl/executive-order-improving-nations-cybersecurity/critical-software-definition-faqs`.

Security Measures for Critical Software

Beyond just defining critical software, NIST also provided guidance on security measures for what they dub *EO-Critical Software*. NIST used position papers from the community, virtual workshops, and inputs from the Cybersecurity and Infrastructure Security Agency (CISA) and the Office of Management and Budget (OMB), among other sources, to determine what security measures may be appropriate for critical software.

The primary scope NIST defined for the security measures was the *use* of critical software, not the development and acquisition of it. That said, there are other sources of guidance, such as SSDF, that deal with software development, and 800-161r1 itself, which more broadly covers C-SCRM and acquisition of software. NIST's objectives for critical software security measures involve protecting the software and associated platforms from unauthorized access and usage. It also strives to prevent exploitation and to protect the confidentiality, integrity, and availability of the data being used by the software and platforms.

NIST acknowledges that incidents will occur, so organizations must be able to quickly detect, respond to, and recover from incidents. In addition, organizations must work to improve human actions and behaviors that could impact and influence critical software and platforms. This acknowledgment is critical, given sources such as Verizon's 2022 Data Breach Investigation Report (DBIR), which stated that upward of 60 percent of data breaches involve a human element but that organizations spend only 3 percent of their security budgets on the human aspect.

NIST's guidance goes on further to define a set of robust security practices and processes that can be used to protect critical software. It also acknowledges that the list isn't exhaustive or all-encompassing and will grow and evolve over time as the risk landscape changes.

Now, let's dive into some of NIST's security measures to see what NIST has defined as fundamental security measures for critical software. It is worth noting that NIST's discussion of security measures for critical software pulls from many sources such as other NIST publications, along with resources from CISA, OMB, NSA, and more.

Multifactor authentication (MFA) is one of the first listed recommendations. Authentication factors typically include the following:

- Something you know
- Something you have
- Something you are, such as usernames and passwords
- Physical tokens
- Biometric sources

MFA is a frequently cited security best practice by public and private sector organizations alike. This authentication type moves beyond basic authentication measures such as usernames and passwords by adding authentication factors, including SMS text codes, phone calls, approval via authentication applications on mobile devices, and even form factors like the personal identity verification (PIV) or common access cards (CACs), along with popular examples such as YubiKeys. (For more on YubiKeys, check out www.yubico.com.) Adding these factors can make it significantly more difficult for a malicious actor to compromise credentials, depending on the secondary authentication source.

It is worth noting, however, that even MFA is not infallible and can be compromised by methods such as SMS phishing (https://thehackernews.com/2022/08/twilio-suffers-data-breach-after.html). Therefore, NIST's guidance calls for MFA use that is impersonation-resistant for not just all administrators, but for all users as well. This is also sometimes referred to as *phishing-resistant* MFA, and typically authentication methods such as passwords, SMS, and security questions are not considered phishing resistant. Some core tenets of phishing-resistant

MFA include a strong binding between the authenticator and user identity, eliminating shared secrets, and ensuring responses only go to trusted parties. Examples of phishing-resistant MFA include FIDO2 and PIV smart options (`www.yubico.com/resources/glossary/phishing-resistant-mfa`).

Building on the recommendation of MFA for all users, NIST also recommends uniquely identifying and authenticating each service and following least-privileged access management principles. These controls ensure proper access control and can limit the blast radius of malicious cyber activities. Least-privileged access control is also a fundamental tenet of the broader push for zero trust, as defined by NIST in their 800-207 publication, Zero Trust Architecture (`https://nvlpubs.nist.gov/nistpubs/SpecialPublications/NIST.SP.800-207.pdf`).

While least-privileged access control can limit the impact of malicious activities, so can NIST's next recommendation, which is to employ boundary protection, such as network segmentation, and use software-defined perimeters. Perimeter delineation works by ensuring that an incident in one area of a system and environment doesn't have a cascading impact across the entire system or even on external systems to which it connects.

To meet the second objective of protecting the confidentiality, integrity, and availability of data used by critical software and software platforms, NIST provides a series of key controls and practices organizations can adhere to, including establishing and maintaining a data inventory. It's impossible for an organization to protect its data without having a proper inventory of what it has. A popular saying in cybersecurity says that "you can't defend what you don't know exists."

Much like the network-level access controls previously discussed, an organization's data and resources should also be secured by using fine-grained access control. NIST recommends protecting data at rest by using encryption that aligns with NIST's cryptographic standards (`https://nvlpubs.nist.gov/nistpubs/SpecialPublications/NIST.SP.800-175Br1.pdf`). The same goes for data in transit; the NIST recommendation is to use not only encryption but also mutual authentication when possible.

Mutual authentication is when two parties authenticate each other at the same time, using supportive authentication protocols such as Internet Key Exchange (IKE), Secure Shell (SSH), and Transport Layer Security (TLS). Doing so ensures that the data is encrypted in transit so that (1) the data isn't exposed to unauthorized parties who may gain access to it, and (2) they can mitigate some types of attacks such as on-path attacks, replays, and spoofing. These types of attacks include trying to capture data in transit, replicate it, or mimic a valid entity in an exchange by a malicious actor. The last NIST recommendation for this objective is not just backing up data but also exercising backup restoration and being prepared to recover data. It acknowledges that despite the presence of controls such as encryption and mutual authentication, incidents can and do happen that compromise organizational data—and that when they do, organizations must be capable of restoring their data from valid backups.

The third objective for securing critical software as defined by NIST is the need to identify and maintain critical software platforms and software residing on those platforms to protect it from exploitation. Controls in this area include establishing and maintaining software asset inventory. Software asset inventory is also recommended by groups such as the Center for Internet Security (CIS) in their CIS Critical Security Controls guidance (`www.cisecurity.org/controls`).

Inventorying and managing software allows better software governance and control to ensure that only authorized software is installed and executed on systems. Software inventory, of course, goes beyond the broad-level inventory of software products and down to component-level inventory with the software bills of materials (SBOMs) discussed extensively throughout this book. In addition to having a software inventory, organizations should ensure that they are using patch management best practices, that they are identifying, documenting, and mitigating known vulnerabilities and doing so in a documented change control process. Software platforms, and more broadly software in general, also requires configuration management best practices. These best practices include activities such as implementing hardened security configurations and monitoring platforms and software for unauthorized changes.

As previously discussed, NIST recognizes that despite implementing these best practices and security controls, incidents can and will happen. Therefore, the fourth objective includes being able to quickly detect, respond to, and recover from threats and incidents that impact critical software and platforms.

To achieve the response and recovery capabilities desired, organizations must properly log all necessary information about any security events. To implement logging best practices, organizations should make use of guidance such as NIST's Guide to Computer Security Log Management and vendor-specific guidance for their products and platforms (`https://nvlpubs.nist.gov/nistpubs/Legacy/SP/nistspecialpublication800-92.pdf`). Critical software must be continuously monitored, and this can be done in conjunction with the use of endpoint security protection products or services, often referred to as endpoint detection and response (EDR) tooling. EDR tooling helps identify, review, and minimize the attack surface and exposure to known threats, control what software executes, and assist with recovering from incidents when they do occur. Organizations must implement network security protection for critical software and platforms to detect threats at all layers of the stack and help prevent them, as well as provide any necessary telemetry to security operation and other staff responding to the incidents. To be effective at incident response, NIST recommends training all security operations and incident response team members based on their specific roles and responsibilities.

The last objective, which focuses on strengthening the understanding and performance of human actions that contribute to the security of critical software and platforms, is a people-centric objective. This objective includes activities such as training the users of critical software and platforms based according to their roles and responsibilities, including those administrators who often have elevated permissions. Lastly, it recommends broad security awareness training for all users and administrators of critical software and platforms and measuring the effectiveness of the training to drive improvement and better outcomes.

Software Verification

Another key component of NIST's Cyber EO Section 4 guidance involves publishing guidelines for recommending the minimum standard for vendors' testing of their source code. It includes both manual and automation testing, such as code review tools, static application security testing (SAST), dynamic application security testing (DAST), and penetration testing. Much like the other sections of its guidance from Section 4 of the EO, NIST took the approach of gathering position papers (`www.nist.gov/itl/executive-order-improving-nations-cybersecurity/enhancing-software-supply-chain-security`) from the community and hosting workshops (`www.nist.gov/itl/executive-order-improving-nations-cybersecurity/enhancing-software-supply-chain-security`).

NIST emphasizes that a key aspect of ensuring that software is securely built is frequent and thorough testing early in the software development life cycle (SDLC) by developers. Verification is defined by NIST as

> **a discipline employed to increase software security, encompassing many static and active assurance techniques, tools and related processes to identify and remediate security defects while continuously improving the methodology and supporting processes**
>
> *Source:* `www.nist.gov/itl/executive-order-improving-nations-cybersecurity/recommended-minimum-standards-vendor-or-0`

Citing SSDF, NIST states that verification is necessary to identify vulnerabilities and verify compliance with security requirements. NIST stresses that no single type of testing or standard is all-encompassing and instead clarifies its guidance as high-level guidelines.

Before diving into the specifics of the verification testing methods proposed, it is worth noting that NIST states that while the Cyber EO uses the term *vendors* for testing, developers often ingest software from outside sources and, therefore, will do their own verification as well if using software from another source.

In the published guidance, NIST recommends 11 types of testing and methodologies as well as supplemental techniques that we will discuss soon (`https://nvlpubs.nist.gov/nistpubs/ir/2021/NIST.IR.8397.pdf`). At a high level, NIST's guidance discusses the need to gain assurance that developed software does what the developers intended it to do, while also being sufficiently free of vulnerabilities throughout its life cycle. Gaining this assurance involves various activities such as threat modeling, automated testing (SAST/DAST), dynamic analysis, correction of unacceptable bugs or findings, and use of similar techniques for any associated libraries, packages, and services. While many of these activities are touched on in the previous chapter covering commercial guidance, we'll briefly cover them here from the perspective as defined by NIST, relevant to their Cybersecurity EO guidance.

Threat Modeling

NIST recommends using threat modeling early in the SDLC to identify design-level security issues. You will gain a conceptual understanding and visualization of a system and begin to profile potential attacks, along with their relevant goals and methods of exploitation that materialize in potential threats. Through threat modeling, organizations are attempting to identify potential threats, weaknesses, and vulnerabilities, and then define mitigation plans aligned with those threats. NIST points to the Department of Defense (DoD) DevSecOps Reference Architecture diagram, shown in Figure 8.2, as an example of how threat modeling fits into the methodology of DevSecOps as part of system development and planning activities.

DevSecOps is not a linear activity (e.g., waterfall), and threat modeling shouldn't be either. It should be done as part of frequent and iterative system and software delivery.

Automated Testing

In its guidance, NIST makes it clear that automated testing can be as simple as a script to automate static analysis or as complicated and automated as the creation of entire environments, including running testing and verifying testing success. Organizations may make use of simple tools for testing web-enabled applications and fields or more complex tooling that involves modules and subsystems. The recommendations include automated verification to ensure that new weaknesses aren't reported by static analysis, the tests run iteratively, the results are accurate, and the use of automation reduces the need for human analysis and effort, which can be both resource intensive and faulty. Organizations using modern development systems such as Git and CI/CD pipelines can make the verification processes automated and repeatable upon commits and pull requests.

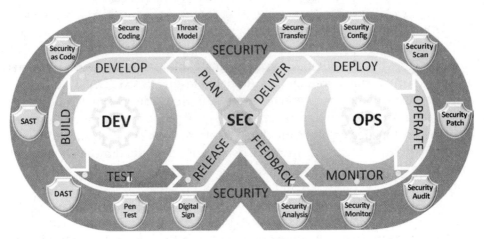

Figure 8.2

Source: DoD Enterprise DevSecOps Reference Design v1.0 (`https://dodcio.`
`defense.gov/Portals/0/Documents/DoD%20Enterprise%20DevSecOps%20`
`Reference%20Design%20v1.0_Public%20Release.pdf?ver=2019-09-26`
`-115824-583`, Unites States Department of Defence, Public domain)

Code-Based or Static Analysis and Dynamic Testing

NIST distinguishes between two approaches of code-based or static analysis and execution-based testing, which they provide examples of, such as SAST and DAST, respectively. Code-based static analysis reasons about the code as it is written in its native format, whereas dynamic analysis involves execution-based dynamic testing and analysis that entails program execution. Like the DevSecOps methodology mentioned earlier for automated testing, NIST recommends conducting static code analysis as soon as code is written, in iterative small chunks. This approach is more efficient and effective than waiting to perform SAST on a final product, since flaws and vulnerabilities can be addressed earlier in the SDLC.

Review for Hard-Coded Secrets

NIST recommends using heuristic tools to look for hard-coded secrets in application code. These secrets might involve things such as credentials, encryption keys, API keys, and access tokens. This is particularly challenging in cloud-native environments due to the expansive use of APIs, tokens, and credentials, and one of this book's authors touched on that topic in an article titled "Keeping Secrets in a DevSecOps Cloud-Native World" (`www.csoonline.com/article/3655688/keeping-secrets-in-a-devsecops-cloud-native-world.html`). Studies show that compromised credentials are involved in a substantial portion of data breaches, so organizations should bolster their secrets management capabilities to negate these risks.

Run with Language-Provided Checks and Protection

In the guidance, NIST also recommends using prebuild checks that various programming languages, both compiled and interpreted, offer. NIST also emphasizes that some languages are not *memory-safe*, which is where programmers are prevented from introducing specific types of bugs related to how memory is used in an application and recommend enforcing memory safety. In addition to using built-in enforcement capabilities, organizations can use measures such as static analyzers or "linters" to look for dangerous functions and parameters. It is worth noting that other guidance, such as the OpenSSF Open Source Security Mobilization Plan, discussed in the previous chapter, recommends moving the industry toward memory-safe languages and away from legacy languages that have some increased inherent risk related to memory safety.

Black-Box Test Cases

Unlike previously discussed test types, black-box tests aren't tied to specific pieces of code but instead focus on functional requirements and validating what software should not do. These tests include things like denial of service and input boundaries and are conducted without the internal knowledge and assumptions that come with source code analysis and threat modeling.

Code-Based Test Cases

Code-based test cases involve the specifics of the code itself. This may involve activities such as testing the number of items and interactions software can handle and validating it through test cases. NIST recommends executive test suites with a minimum of 80 percent statement coverage.

Historical Test Cases

When the NIST guidance uses the phrase *historical test cases*, it is referring to what is commonly called *regression testing*. Regression testing is prevalent among mature security teams who implement tests to validate the *absence* of a previously discovered and remediated vulnerability. This type of testing is important due to situations such as configuration and hygiene drift, where insecure configurations and system states can reoccur. Regression tests help validate that is not the case.

Fuzzing

Another software verification method NIST recommends is *fuzzing* or *fuzz testing*, which is an automated testing method that operates by injecting invalid, malformed, or unexpected inputs into software to identify defects and vulnerabilities. Once these are injected into the system, the fuzzing tool watches for how the system responds, such as crashing or leaking information that shouldn't have been exposed. The Open Worldwide Application Security Project (OWASP) has a comprehensive fuzzing page for those looking to learn more at `https://owasp.org/www-community/Fuzzing`.

Web Application Scanning

Often referred to as dynamic application security testing (DAST) or interactive application security testing (IAST), web application scanning is applicable when software provides a web service. Both tools perform similar activities as fuzzing, but they both perform them for a web application as they look for anomalies or failures. The world's most popular web application scanner is the OWASP Zed Attack Proxy (ZAP; `www.zaproxy.org`).

Check Included Software Components

NIST's final recommended minimum standard for developer-testing listing is to check included software components. NIST states the goal of this activity is to gain assurance that the included code is *at least* as secure as code developed locally. As we have discussed throughout this book, tools such as software composition analysis (SCA) can help identify OSS libraries, packages, and dependencies your software is using. These tools query against vulnerability databases such as NIST's National Vulnerability Database (NVD) to look for *known* vulnerabilities in these components. Given that most modern software is overwhelmingly composed of OSS components, this activity is particularly important.

NIST also provides additional background and supplemental information about all the techniques we've discussed, which are worth diving into if you're looking for even further details about such testing techniques and how to implement them successfully.

NIST's Secure Software Development Framework

As discussed in several sections of this book, the Cybersecurity Executive Order (EO) 14028 has wide-reaching impacts across areas such as zero trust, cloud computing, and of course, software supply chain security. As part of the Cybersecurity EO, the government is required to "only purchase software that is developed securely." The EO directed NIST to issue guidance that identifies practices that enhance the security of the software supply chain. NIST did exactly that. In collaboration with the industry, NIST published the Secure Software Development Framework (SSDF) Version 1.1, along with other software supply chain security guidance. This section discusses SSDF in depth, what it is, and why it matters.

The SSDF points out that few SDLC models explicitly address software security. A common phrase many in the industry are familiar with is "bolted on, not baked in" when it comes to cybersecurity. Cybersecurity is often an afterthought in developing digital systems and is often addressed later in the SDLC, rather than earlier, when security best practices and requirements can be integrated into software and systems from the outset. It is worth noting that the SSDF Version 1.1 released in 2022 builds upon an original SSDF version from April 2020. To facilitate the SSDF's update, NIST held a workshop with participants from the public and private sectors and received over 150 position papers to be considered for the SSDF update.

The intended audience for the SSDF includes both software producers such as product vendors, government software developers, and internal development teams and software acquirers or consumers. While the SSDF was specifically created for use by federal agencies, the best practices and tasks it contains apply to software development teams across all industries and can be used by many diverse organizations. It is also worth noting that the SSDF is not prescriptive but descriptive; it does not specifically say how to implement each practice and instead focuses on secure software outcomes and allows the organization to implement practices to facilitate those outcomes. This is logical, given the infinite ways to secure software and the unique people, processes, and technologies that make up every organization producing and consuming software. The guidance also clarifies that factors such as an organization's risk tolerance should be considered when determining which practices to use and the resources to invest in achieving said practices.

NIST has defined minimum recommendations for federal agencies that are acquiring software or products containing software from producers and vendors. These recommendations include several key provisions to help ensure that the government is not acquiring insecure software and products. As agencies procure software, NIST recommends that they use SSDF terminology to organize their communications around secure software development requirements. NIST also recommends that vendors attest to SSDF development practices throughout their SDLC. An often-contentious topic is that of attestation, which is evidence or proof of something. Typically, attestation from a process perspective can be done firsthand, also known as *self-attesting*, or by an independent third party, such as a third-party assessment organization (3PAO).

The use of a 3PAO adds to the assurance of the attestation because it is made by a theoretical third party rather than the party who is being assessed. That said, 3PAO compliance regimes also come with additional overhead in terms of time and cost to accompany their potential increased rigor. For example, FedRAMP, which is the authorization process for cloud service providers (CSPs) looking to offer their services in the federal market, requires that CSPs undergo a third-party assessment.

However, as of this writing, despite the program being in existence for 10 years, there are only roughly 250 FedRAMP-authorized cloud service offerings. If a 3PAO approach was taken for software producers under SSDF, it would undoubtedly have a similar impact in terms of limiting the pool of qualified vendors authorized to sell software to the government. However, NIST has stated in its guidance that depending on the risk tolerance of the agency and software consumers, a third-party attestation could be warranted in some situations. Critics have urged government agencies not to take this approach because of the impact it would have on SSDF adoption, and pointed to examples of delays in other similar programs, such as the DoD's Cybersecurity Maturity Model Certification (CMMC), which has experienced several setbacks (`https://insidedefense.com/daily-news/delay-publicly-releasing-cmmc-process-guide-attributed-potential-national-security`), some of which are related to the complexity of implementing a 3PAO process for a new compliance certification.

SSDF Details

The NIST SSDF, as mentioned, is aimed at advocating for the use of fundamental and recognized secure software development best practices. One way that makes SSDF unique is that rather than creating guidance from scratch entirely, it uses many known and implemented established sources of guidance such as the Building Security in Maturity Model (BSIMM) by Synopsys and the Software Assurance Maturity Model (SAMM) from OWASP, among several others.

SSDF's robust set of secure software development practices are broken into four distinct groups:

- Prepare the Organization (PO)
- Protect the Software (PS)
- Produce Well-Secured Software (PW)
- Respond to Vulnerabilities (RV)

Within those practices, you have elements that define the practice, such as Practice, Task, Notional Implementation Example, and Reference, which maps the practice to tasks. As previously mentioned, the latest version of SSDF addresses requirements from the Cybersecurity EO, so it also includes mapping to specific EO Section 4e requirements. The desired goal of using the SSDF practices is to reduce the number of vulnerabilities included in the release of software and the impact of those vulnerabilities being exploited if they are undetected or unmitigated.

Prepare the Organization (PO)

Preparing the organization for secure software development is a logical first step for any organization looking to develop secure software. Practices in this group encompass defining security requirements for software development, which includes requirements for the organization's software development infrastructure and security requirements that organization-developed software must meet. Of course, these requirements must be communicated to all third parties who provide commercial software components to the organization for reuse as well.

Defining Roles and Responsibilities is another fundamental step that organizations must take. It includes roles for all parts of the SDLC and provides appropriate training for the individuals in those roles. The guidance emphasizes the need to get upper management or the authorizing officials' commitment to secure development and ensure that individuals involved in the process are aware of that commitment. This is often referred to as getting *executive buy-in*.

Modern software delivery involves supporting toolchains that use automation to minimize the human effort associated with software development and to lead to more consistent, accurate, and reproducible outcomes. Tasks in this area involve specifying the tools and tool types that must be used to mitigate risks and how they integrate with one another. Organizations should also define recommended security practices for using the toolchains and ensure the tools are configured correctly to support secure software development practices.

Organizations should also define and use criteria for software security checks. This includes implementing processes and tooling to safeguard information throughout the SDLC. Toolchains can be used to automatically inform security decision-making and produce metrics around vulnerability management.

Lastly, organizations should implement secure environments for software development. This typically manifests as creating different environments such as Development, Testing, Staging, and Production. These environments are segmented to limit the blast radius of a compromise impacting other environments and allow for differing security requirements, depending on the environment, as well as provide improved configuration management and the control of configuration drift, which is where actual configurations don't align with desired configurations.

These environments can be secured through methods such as MFA, conditional access control, or least-permissive access control, and by ensuring that all activities are logged and monitored across the various development environments to enable better detection, response, and recovery. Securing the environment also means that the endpoints developers and others interacting with the environments use are hardened to ensure they do not introduce risk. You will notice there are several parallels to these recommendations with the current guidance and best practices for zero trust.

Protect the Software (PS)

Moving on from protecting the organization is protecting the software (PS) itself. Practices in this group involve protecting the code from unauthorized changes, verifying code integrity, and protecting each software release.

Protecting all forms of code from unauthorized changes and tampering is critical to ensure the code is not modified either intentionally or unintentionally in a form that compromises its integrity. Code should be stored in methods that align with least-permissive access control based on its security requirements, which looks different from OSS code or proprietary code. Organizations can take measures such as using code repositories that support version control and commit signing and review by code owners and maintainers to prevent unauthorized changes and tampering. Code can also be signed to ensure its integrity with methods such as cryptographic hashes.

Not only does the code's integrity need to be maintained, but there must be methods for software consumers to validate this integrity. This is where practices such as posting hashes on well-secured websites come into play. Code signing should be supported by trusted certificate authorities that software consumers can use as a measure of assurance or trust in the signature.

Finally, each software release should be protected and preserved. It can be used to identify, analyze, and eliminate vulnerabilities tied to specific releases. It also facilitates the ability to roll back (in the case of compromised releases) and restore to "known good" states of software and applications. Protecting and preserving software releases allows consumers to understand the provenance of code and the associated integrity of the code provenance.

Produce Well-Secured Software (PW)

Now that requirements have been codified and development environments and the endpoints that access them have been addressed, the organization can focus on producing well-secured software. This is not to say that these practices do not occur concurrently throughout the life of an organization or program, but they do build upon one another while also warranting revisiting and revising, as necessary.

You will note that, in the PO section of the SSDF, security requirements were defined and documented. Now, software must be designed to meet those security requirements. This is where organizations can use methods of risk modeling such as threat modeling and attack surface mapping to assess the security risk of the software being developed. Organizations can train development teams in methods such as threat modeling to facilitate empowered development teams capable of understanding the threats to the systems and software they develop and measures to reduce those risks. By using data classification methods, organizations can prioritize more rigorous assessments of high sensitivity and elevated risk areas for risk mitigation and remediation. Organizations should also review software design regularly to ensure that it meets security and compliance requirements that the organization has defined. This includes not only internally developed software but also software that is being procured or consumed from third parties. Depending on the nature of the software being consumed, organizations may be able to work with software designers to correct failures to meet security requirements, but this does not apply in situations such as OSS, where there are no contracts or associated agreements such as SLAs.

Organizations are encouraged to reuse existing, well-secured software rather than duplicating functionality. This reuse has a myriad of benefits such as lowering the cost of development, speeding up capability delivery, and reducing the potential of introducing new vulnerabilities into environments. It is common for large enterprise organizations to experience *code sprawl*, which is the uncontrolled growth of code, particularly in the era of "as-code" where infrastructure and even security in cloud-native environments can be defined as code. This as-code approach supports concepts such as modularity, reuse, configuration-as-code, and hardened code templates and manifests, which can be safely used elsewhere in organizations or even beyond. That said, as mentioned by the Palo Alto Unit 42 study discussed in Chapter 6, "Cloud and Containerization," if these manifests and code templates include vulnerabilities, they now become replicated at scale as well, so proper governance and security rigor is required.

Organizations or even teams within organizations that reuse existing software and code should ensure that they review and evaluate code for security and misconfiguration concerns as well as understand the provenance information associated with the code they are reusing. A similar recommendation that the SSDF makes is to create and maintain well-secured software components and repositories in house for development reuse, which is like the recommendations made in NIST 800-161r1.

Source code created by the organization should align with the secure coding practices adopted by the organization and advocated by industry guidance.

These practices include steps such as validating all inputs, avoiding unsafe functions and calls, and using tools to identify vulnerabilities in the code.

Respond to Vulnerabilities (RV)

While organizations may have defined security requirements, prepared their environments, and even strived to produce secure software, vulnerabilities will inevitably arise. The reality is that identifying all vulnerabilities during development is simply impossible, and as time goes on, vulnerabilities will be discovered. As we have discussed, the longer software has been around, the more likely it is that vulnerabilities will be discovered by researchers, malicious actors, and/or others.

Organizations should be working to both identify and confirm vulnerabilities on an ongoing basis. This includes monitoring vulnerability databases, using threat intelligence feeds, and automating the review of all software components to identify any new vulnerabilities. These practices are key, since new vulnerabilities will inevitably emerge from the initial time the code may have been scanned and examined. Organizations should also have policies centering around vulnerability disclosure and remediation, and as previously mentioned, define the necessary roles and responsibilities to address vulnerabilities as they emerge. With regard to vulnerability disclosure, teams often will strive to have product security incident response teams (PSIRTs), which we discuss in depth in Chapter 10, "Practical Guidance for Suppliers."

Not only will organizations need methods to identify and confirm vulnerabilities, but they will also need to remediate vulnerabilities in a method that aligns with the risk that vulnerabilities pose. It means having a process in place to assess, prioritize, and remediate software vulnerabilities. Using tools and governance, organizations can then make risk-informed decisions such as remediating, accepting, and in some cases, transferring the risk if possible. Organizations that are producing software also need established methods in place to develop and release security advisories to software consumers that help them understand the software's vulnerabilities and the potential impact to them as consumers, and the steps necessary to resolve the vulnerability, if possible.

Lastly, organizations should take steps to identify the root causes of vulnerabilities through analysis, which helps reduce their frequency in the future by addressing the root cause, rather than just an individual vulnerability.

As evident from the vast array of secure software development tasks and practices discussed, no organization of significant size or scale will always have the ability to do all these practices correctly. That said, organizations can take steps to codify their secure software development practices by using the SSDF as a guide and helping to ensure that proper steps are taken to secure software throughout the SDLC.

NSAs: Securing the Software Supply Chain Guidance Series

In 2022, the NSA, along with CISA and the Office of the Director of National Intelligence (ODNI), set out to release guidance on software supply chain security. It is a three-part series focused on the perspective of developers, suppliers, and customers, each with its own specific guidance based on their roles and activities in the software supply chain.

This series was provided through what the NSA calls the *Enduring Security Framework (ESF)*, which is a public–private cross-sector working group led by the NSA and CISA, aimed at providing guidance addressing high-priority threats to the nation's critical infrastructure.

We discuss each of the publications in the following sections and their specific recommendations. This guidance was released in the same manner as the software life cycle, which flows from developers, suppliers, and customers; therefore, it will be covered in the same order in which it was released.

In the following section, we will look at the NSA's software supply chain security guidance, its various parts, and its overarching takeaways. The announcement for the publication (www.nsa.gov/Press-Room/News-Highlights/Article/Article/3146465/nsa-cisa-odni-release-software-supply-chain-guidance-for-developers) emphasizes the role the developer plays in creating secure software and states that the publication strives to help developers adopt government and industry recommendations for doing so. The second and third releases focus on the supplier and the software consumer, given the unique role each plays in the broader software supply chain and its resilience.

At a high level, the documents are organized into three parts:

- Security Guidance for Software Developers
- Recommended Practices Guide for Suppliers
- Recommended Practices Guide for Consumers

The guidance notes the unique roles developers, suppliers, and customers play in the broader software supply chain ecosystem (see Figure 8.3).

Security Guidance for Software Developers

First up in the NSA series of guidance is the "Recommended Practices Guide for Developers." Software supply chain attacks are far from a new phenomenon, with sources such as the Cloud Native Computing Foundation (CNCF) offering a catalog of supply chain compromises referring back to 2003. There is also the IQT Labs Software Supply Chain Compromises—A Living Dataset, which also dates to 2003 (https://github.com/IQTLabs/software-supply-chain-compromises).

The latter represents IQT Labs' attempt to produce a living dataset of publicly reported software supply chain compromises. But while the software supply chain attacks may have a 20-year track record, the pace at which they have been occurring is accelerating based on published research, such as this USENIX article from Dan Geer, Bentz Tozer, and John Speed Meyers, titled "For Good Measure—Counting Broken Links: A Quant's View of Software Supply Chain Security," shown in Figure 8.4 (www.usenix.org/system/files/login/articles/login_winter20_17_geer.pdf).

Developer Security Activities	Supplier Security Activities	Customer Security Activities
• Architecture & Design Review • SW Threat Modeling • Attack Surface Analysis • Coding Standards • Secure Software Development • Secure Library Checks (Composition Analysis) • Code & Executable Testing • Secure Build & Delivery	• Security Deliver Software • Protect Code Pipeline • Ensure Security Requirements are Met • Verify 3rd Party Software • Test Executable Code • Configure Secure Defaults • Notify Customers of Vulnerabilities • Respond to Vulnerabilities	• Security Requirements Definition • SCRM Requirements Definition • Security Acceptance Testing • SCRM & Product Integrity Validation • Implement Risk & Security Controls for Product Deployment • Product Lifecycle Management Security & SCRM Controls & Processes

Figure 8.3

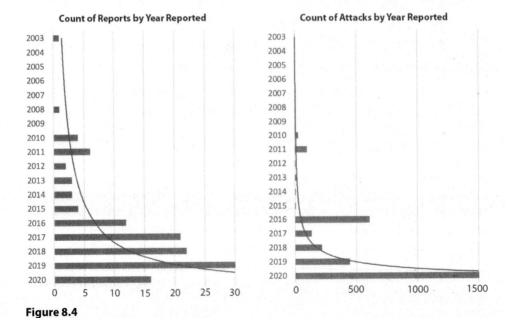

Figure 8.4

Within the context of the software producers' perspective, they are the supplier, providing features and capabilities to customers, with those features and capabilities being driven and created by developers. This inevitably places the suppliers and their development teams in the dichotomy of speed to market (or mission in the public sector) contrasted with the rigors of secure and resilient software or software-enabled products.

Secure software begins with an SDLC, and the NSA's guidance cites many options teams can use, such as NIST's SSDF (`https://csrc.nist.gov/Projects/ssdf`), Carnegie Mellon University's (CMU)'s Secure Software Development Life Cycle Processes (`https://resources.sei.cmu.edu/asset_files/whitepaper/2013_019_001_297287.pdf`), and others such as the OpenSSF Secure Software Development Fundamentals courses announced in 2022 (`https://openssf.org/training/courses`).

The guidance stresses not just using secure software development processes but also producing tangible artifacts and attestations that are used for validation by both the software producer and consumer, to have assurances related to the security and resiliency of the software.

These processes and activities include best practices such as threat modeling, SAST, DAST, and pen testing, and use secure release activities such as digital signing. A notable example is the increased adoption of Sigstore, a standard for signing, verifying, and protecting software. The adoption and use of Sigstore is also cited in the OpenSSF's Open Source Security Mobilization Plan as a method to deliver enhanced trust in the software supply chain.

So, let's now take a look at the various sections of the NSA's Developer Guidance.

Secure Product Criteria and Management

A core part of producing secure products is having organizational secure development policies and procedures in place along with the accompanying budget and schedule to facilitate secure product development. This, of course, presents potential friction, where there is a myopic focus on speed to market or resource constraints, because the time, expertise, and effort to implement some security best practices will inevitably have a cost associated with them.

In a nod to some of the great DevSecOps work underway within the Department of Defense (DoD), the NSA's guidance uses a Secure Software Development process diagram from the DoD's DevSecOps Fundamentals Playbook (`https://dodcio.defense.gov/Portals/0/Documents/Library/DoDEnterpriseDevSecOpsFundamentals.pdf`). However, unlike the DoD's example, which cited Dev,

Sec, and Ops as the three entities within the infinity loop, the NSA example overlays the three entities it discussed in the introduction of the guidance:

- Developers
- Suppliers
- Customers

Rather than organizational teams that contribute to the software development process (as in the DoD example), these are the entities involved in producing and consuming secure and resilient software products and extend beyond a single organizational boundary, implying the software supply chain context intended.

The NSA's guidance provides several examples of threats that may occur when developing and delivering software products: malicious adversaries, the introduction of vulnerable third-party components, exploitation of the build process, and compromise of the delivery mechanism facilitating the transportation of the product to the customer. Software producers should have security-focused processes in place to mitigate these risks, such as creating threat models, defining release criteria, and documenting and publishing their security procedures and processes for releasing software. Many other examples are also provided in the guidance that are worth reviewing.

While far from new, some of the practices recommended are increasingly gaining in popularity. For example, threat modeling has been advocated by industry leaders like Adam Shostack, Robert Hurlbut, and many others for several years. (*Threat modeling* is thinking of what could go wrong and how to prevent it.) There are great sources of guidance on threat modeling like the Threat Modeling Manifesto and OWASP Threat Modeling projects.

Threat modeling can be done across the software development life cycle and is recommended by NIST for critical software that the federal government uses. Defining critical software was required by NIST for the Cybersecurity EO, and more guidance can be found on their software supply chain guidance page for Critical Software at `www.nist.gov/itl/executive-order-improving-nations-cybersecurity/critical-software-definition`. Tools such as OWASP's Threat Dragon exist as an OSS option for organizations looking to get going and can assist with activities such as data flow diagrams, ranking threats, and suggesting mitigations.

The NSA's guidance strongly recommends security test plans and release criteria. Test plans and requirements often include common security testing methods like SAST/DAST, SCA of third-party software, and penetration testing. Several OSS and vendor tools exist in the ecosystem to conduct these testing methods. These tools are also increasingly integrated with continuous integration/continuous delivery (CI/CD) pipelines to enable *shift-left* security efforts, conducting security earlier in the SDLC, where some argue it is more economical and effective. Shift-left is a term often used to emphasize the need to shift security earlier in the SDLC and catch vulnerabilities and flaws prior to their introduction to production or runtime environments.

Having these tools and testing methods in place allows organizations to determine their release criteria. These criteria could include things such as vulnerabilities exceeding the organization's risk tolerance, a lack of secure development practices, or, with the increased calls for software transparency, particularly in the public sector, producing, correlating, and validating an SBOM.

While it's critical to have established release criteria to mitigate risk to downstream software consumers, it is not an easy feat and requires acknowledging that

- Widely pervasive vulnerability scoring methodologies such as the Common Vulnerability Scoring System (CVSS) are not foolproof.
- Tools generate plenty of false positions that impede velocity.
- Many published Common Vulnerabilities and Exposures (CVEs) are not exploitable.

For a deeper dive into concerns with CVSS, check out the article "CVSS: Ubiquitous and Broken" at `https://dl.acm.org/doi/pdf/10.1145/3491263`. Shifting through the noise while driving down vulnerabilities and enabling velocity is a delicate art that requires an orchestration of effective people, processes, and technologies. Security researcher and writer Walter Haydock discusses some of the perils of well-intentioned but poorly effective security release criteria at `www.blog.deploy-securely.com/p/security-release-criteria`.

The NSA recommends that organizations have mature and codified product support and vulnerability handling policies and processes. These include having a vulnerability submission system, a product security incident response team (PSIRT), and secure delivery of in-field software via secure protocols such as Hypertext Transfer Protocol Secure/Transport Layer Security (HTTPS/TLS).

Given that software vulnerabilities inevitably originate from the individuals and teams writing the code, assessment and training is pivotal. It first requires defining policies that cover details such as who needs training and at what frequency they need it, and deciding what topics it should cover. Training often includes topics such as secure software development, secure code reviews, and software verification and vulnerability testing. It's also important to ensure that organizational security procedures and processes are treated as living documents that evolve and grow as the teams and organizations continue to glean lessons learned from after-action reviews.

All the mitigations and best practices discussed previously, such as threat modeling, security test plans, and release criteria, are specifically mapped in the NSA's guidance to the NIST SSDF, which we discuss in this chapter. Organizations selling software to public sector customers would be best advised to get familiar with NIST's SSDF, as it will soon be required that their software production activities align with it.

Develop Secure Code

Moving on from secure product criteria and management, there is the need to develop secure code. This process begins with the earliest decisions such as the selection of a programming language and considering the fundamentals of protecting digital systems and data, such as fail-safe defaults and least-privilege access control.

Organizations should be wary of insider threats, whether benign or intentionally malicious, both of which can modify or potentially exploit source code. This can occur as a result of developers being poorly trained or engineers intentionally inserting backdoors into products, when activities such as mapping features to requirements can alleviate some of the feature creep that can introduce risk. Engineers could be experiencing life circumstances that make them more susceptible to blackmail and compromise, or they may add development features that make their lives easier but lead to product insecurity. The NSA also warns of compromised remote development systems. With the proliferation of the remote work paradigm and dissolution of the network perimeter, remote development endpoints are prime targets for malicious actors. In addition, organizations routinely struggle with endpoint hygiene, especially in Bring Your Own Device (BYOD) environments. There is also the potential for third-party development teams to be an attack vector. Other common attack vectors include orphaned accounts and credentials, as users move on from teams and organizations but their accounts remain active and able to be compromised. This reality warrants organizations to have mature account and access control policies and processes in place.

Although these scenarios can wreak havoc on development efforts and lead to insecure products, organizations can take steps to mitigate the risk of insecure code. These involve using authenticated source code check-in processes, conducting vulnerability scans as we've previously discussed, and hardening the actual development environment, which may look different depending on the organization's operational conditions.

Something the NSA demonstrates that is also being emphasized by entities like NIST in their 800–161/Software Supply Chain guidance is the creation of a secure repository process flow. This workflow pattern (see Figure 8.5) allows organizations to select external software components while implementing a workflow that conducts scanning such as SCA to determine component makeup and vulnerability concerns. This workflow helps vet external software components for developers and development teams and ensures that an internal secure repository is established to make validated and verified components available for internal software development efforts.

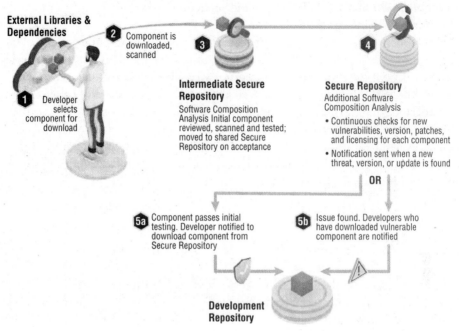

External Libraries & Dependencies

1 Developer selects component for download

2 Component is downloaded, scanned

3 **Intermediate Secure Repository**
Software Composition Analysis Initial component reviewed, scanned and tested; moved to shared Secure Repository on acceptance

4 **Secure Repository**
Additional Software Composition Analysis

• Continuous checks for new vulnerabilities, version, patches, and licensing for each component

• Notification sent when a new threat, version, or update is found

OR

5a Component passes initial testing. Developer notified to download component from Secure Repository

5b Issue found. Developers who have downloaded vulnerable component are notified

Development Repository

Figure 8.5

Source: https://media.defense.gov/2022/Sep/01/2003068942/ -1/-1/0/ESF_SECURING_THE_SOFTWARE_SUPPLY_CHAIN_DEVELOPERS.PDF, US Department of cyber security, Public domain

Using previously discussed tools such as SAST and DAST should align with security release criteria and identify and mitigate vulnerabilities appropriately. Teams should also conduct nightly builds, including security and regression testing, to ensure that flaws or malicious changes are identified and addressed. As we've mentioned, developers may add features to make their lives easier, but that can lead to backdoors. With the proliferation of remote development, the NSA recommends that organizations harden their development environment. That means hardening not only the build environment but also the endpoints or systems involved in the developmental activities or workflows—where controls such as virtual private network (VPN) access, MFA, EDR software, and more can ensure that remote development risk is mitigated to some extent.

Secure development practices should be used to generate, test, and preserve source code. This includes the above-mentioned activity of securing the development environment and involves using secure development build configurations and secure third-party software toolchains and components.

Components and software will be integrated into the delivered product, and therefore, mature and secure code integration practices are followed. This includes testing third-party components for CVEs listed in NIST's National

Vulnerability Database (NVD) and using security dependency analyzers when performing code integration.

As customers report defects or vulnerabilities, the development teams must be poised to respond to these incidents and reports. This includes having a public process to accept the reporting and internally having a process to review, diagnose, and help resolve the issues. There is also the possibility that other teams could add external development extensions, which themselves could introduce vulnerabilities. Extensions such as those from solution teams or value-added resellers (VARs) should also be developed with secure practices, and SBOMs should be made available to show the addition of any packages and/or components not included in the original product.

Verify Third-Party Components

It's no secret that development teams are increasingly using third-party software components for their code and products. This is often done to save time, cost, and effort by using available software components, whether commercial-off-the-shelf (COTS) or free and open source (FOSS). Discussing the code integration process earlier can reduce the risk of introducing insecure third-party code. Other challenges include having third-party binaries, which then require conducting binary or SCA scanning to determine unknown files and OSS components that are included, along with any potentially associated vulnerabilities. SBOM verification against source code from the third party can help as well.

When selecting and integrating third-party components, an evaluation of any associated risk should occur through SCA, along with other scanning methods such as SAST and DAST when source code is available. Development teams should also understand the provenance of the code they ingest and the assurance of its delivery method. Provenance is performed by tracing software back to the source and defining the path of the supply chain from the beginning. Note that varying levels of provenance requirements may be warranted, depending on the organization's security requirements. For example, in the OWASP Software Component Verification Standard (SCVS), provenance requirements are stricter.

The NSA recommends obtaining components from known and trusted suppliers. While we have a rich ecosystem of software producers and providers, this doesn't mean they are equal when it comes to the quality of security of their software components. Software supply chain leaders such as Joshua Corman have been advocating for mimicking automobile manufacturing leaders and using better and fewer suppliers that use higher-quality components, as detailed in his USENIX talk "Continuous Acceleration: Why Continuous Everything Needs a Supply Chain Approach" at www.youtube.com/watch?app=desktop&v=jkoFL7hGiUk&feature=youtu.be.

The OSS is adding to the challenges of third-party component governance. As Sonatype's 2021 State of the Software Supply Chain (www.sonatype.com/resources/state-of-the-software-supply-chain-2021) report points out, we have seen a 73 percent year-over-year (YoY) increase in developer downloads of OSS components (2.2 trillion+ downloads) as well as a 650 percent YoY increase in software supply chain attacks through methods such as dependency confusion, typosquatting, and malicious code injection, each of which we discussed in Chapter 2, "Existing Approaches—Traditional Vendor Risk Management," as malicious actors also realize the efficiency of this attack vector (see Figure 8.6).

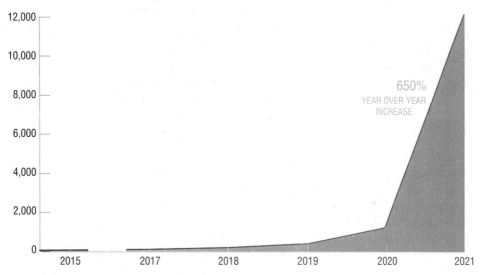

Next Generation SoftwareSupply Chain Attacks (2015–2020)

Dependency Confusion, Typosquatting, and Malicious Code Injection

Figure 8.6

When selecting and ingesting third-party components or OSS software, organizations need to understand any inherent risks and vulnerabilities associated with it. They may choose to take paths such as establishing a list of known trusted suppliers as well as vetted third-party components. Considerations include the quality of not just the component but also the supporting artifacts such as an SBOM, as well as the component owner's historical responsiveness to vulnerability reports. Organizations should also understand that component maintenance is not to be neglected. Suppliers may release updates to address reported vulnerabilities, for example, warranting updating the component if you are a downstream consumer.

Harden the Build Environment

In addition to hardening the development environment and systems, the build environment itself must be hardened. Build environments enable reproducible deliverables, but when compromised serve as a highly efficient method to deliver compromised software, such as with SolarWinds, for example. The NSA's guidance stresses that the build system be developed and maintained with the same level of security, integrity, and resilience as that of the source code and the product itself.

Malicious actors use a variety of exploits to compromise the build chain, such as infiltrating networks, scanning for vulnerabilities, and crafting and subsequently deploying an exploit. This exploit or malicious code can now be efficiently distributed to downstream software consumers without their knowledge.

The NSA's guidance recommends that not just the build pipeline but also any systems involved in the development and build process be locked down and protected from unauthorized network activities and that secure configurations be used. There are also calls to implement controls like version control, network segmentation, and the auditing and logging of any access and activities.

Building on these mitigations, the NSA recommends that advanced mitigations include items like *hermetic* and *reproducible builds*. Hermetic builds are fully declarative, immutable, and able to run without network access, and they could also include hash verification. Reproducible builds validate that binary products are built from the same source, despite variable metadata. Here, reproducible means that they identify input artifacts that lead to identical bit-for-bit outputs. There are also emerging frameworks such as in-toto (`https://github.com/in-toto/in-toto`), which strives to protect the integrity of the software supply chain by verifying that each task in the chain is carried out as planned, by authorized personnel only, and that the product is not tampered with in transit.

Several processes and practices defined by the NSA build upon not just the SLSA framework but on another emerging framework known as Software Component Verification Standard (SCVS) from OWASP.

While software signing is seeing increased adoption and recognition as a crucial part of securing the software supply chain, with efforts such as Sigstore growing in adoption (`www.sigstore.dev`) by major projects such as Kubernetes, there's also the possibility of an *exploited signing server*. Cryptographic signatures help protect the integrity of software artifacts and provide assurances for their consumers. However, if the signing server and mechanism itself is compromised, those assurances are not trustworthy or useful and are considered to be exploited. This allows malicious actors to legitimately sign potentially malicious artifacts and outputs that are ingested by unsuspecting software consumers. To mitigate this risk, the NSA recommends measures such as strong MFA and physical access control of signing infrastructure, as well as signing on isolated network segments and hardening the actual signing infrastructure.

It's worth noting that some practices such as hermetic builds may limit the use of timestamp authorities (TSAs), which is required to determine if the signing occurred at a time when the certificates involved were valid. Looking at recent incidents, such as the one that impacted Twillio and many other software-as-a-service (SaaS) providers (www.darkreading.com/remote-workforce/twilio-hackers-okta-credentials-sprawling-supply-chain-attack), demonstrates how MFA is not enough, and organizations should be implementing phishing-resistant forms of MFA such as YubiKeys.

Deliver the Code

Finally, let's consider the act of software suppliers delivering code via distribution systems. Software developers should be using binary composition analysis to verify the contents of the software they ship, along with any associated metadata. By using SCA tooling, organizations can ensure that no software of unknown provenance is included and that no sensitive data like secrets have been included in the final artifacts for delivery. Once again, a call has gone out for producing an SBOM to be included in the delivery package to the software consumer.

Malicious actors may try to leverage tactics to compromise software packages and updates as they transit the software distribution systems. This could include methods like on-path attacks to attempt to inject malicious code or vulnerabilities for later exploitation. Organizations can mitigate these risks by using secure transit mechanisms, as well as using hashing and digital signatures at both the product and software component levels.

Lastly, there is the potential to compromise the distribution system directly, via the repository, package manager, and/or other methods, to ensure compromised packages are delivered to customers. Software development teams and organizations can mitigate these threats by protecting all forms of code from unauthorized access, including repositories and package managers, as well as using appropriate Transport Layer Security such as encryption for the distribution system.

NSA Appendices

Before wrapping up this part of the chapter, it is worth noting that the NSA's guidance includes a robust set of valuable appendices (see Figure 8.7) that cover the following:

A Crosswalk   The path between the threat scenarios discussed and NIST's SSDF, mapping specific practices, and mitigations to the SSDF for the developer, supplier, or customer.

Dependencies   Dependencies and artifacts that may be provided by either the supplier, third-party suppliers, or customers to benefit suppliers and developers (see Figure 8.7).

Green - Dependencies/artifacts recommended to be provided by the supplier for benefit of the developer.

Dark Green - Dependencies/artifacts recommended to be provided by third-party suppliers for benefit of the developer.

Pink - Dependencies/artifacts recommended to be provided by the customer for benefit of the supplier/developer.

#	Dependency
1	Provide issues from customers
2	Provide given hashes as required
3	SDLC policies and procedures
4	Secure architecture, high-level design
5	Qualified team assembly with code/security training
6	Independent QA individual/team
7	Independent security audit individual/team
8	Open Source Review Board (OSRB) with repository
9	Product release management/resources
10	SBOM
11	Development location and information
12	Third-party SBOM
13	Third-party license
14	Release notes (detailing vulnerabilities fixed)
15	Vulnerability notifications
16	Publish updates and patches to the customer to address new vulnerabilities or weaknesses found within the product
17	Requirements and criteria for success
18	Implied industry security requirements
19	Provide issues from operational environment, take updates and patches
20	Vulnerability notifications and reporting from the users

Figure 8.7

Supply Chain Levels and Artifacts (SLSA)   A breakdown of what SLSA is and its various requirements, descriptions, and levels.

Artifacts and Checklists   Artifact examples, descriptions, and purposes such as product readiness checklists, design documents, and build logs. The guidance offers examples of the value these artifacts can provide and to whom.

Informative Resources   A robust set of references from sources such as the following:

- The Building Security in Maturity Model (BSIMM)
- Department of Defense for Information Technology (DoD CIO)
- Cybersecurity Executive Order (EO)
- Open Worldwide Application Security Project (OWASP)

Many of these references were cited throughout the document as examples of existing guidance that the NSA leveraged and built upon.

Recommended Practices Guide for Suppliers

Building on the initial publication of the Recommended Practices Guide for Developers, next in the NSA series is the guidance for suppliers. Suppliers, or vendors in this context, are typically "responsible for liaising between the customer and software developer." This means that suppliers have responsibilities that involve ensuring the integrity and security of software through mechanisms such as contract agreements, software releases, and notification to impacted software customers.

The NSA's guidance defines some specific responsibilities for software suppliers:

- Maintaining the integrity of securely delivered software
- Validating software packages and updates
- Maintaining awareness of known vulnerabilities
- Accepting customer reports of issues or newly discovered vulnerabilities and then notifying developers for remediation

Much like the developer guidance document, this document uses various threat examples built on NIST'S SSDF publication. As a refresher, SSDF is composed of various security practices broken out across four groups: Prepare the Organization (PO), Protect the Software (PS), Produce Well-Secured Software (PW), and Respond to Vulnerabilities (RV). The NSA's guidance follows this same structure and provides specific threat scenarios for each group as well as recommendations to remediate or mitigate associated threats.

Prepare the Organization

Some of the fundamental requirements to prepare an organization to be a supplier of software include creating the requisite policies and processes to ensure they can securely deliver software. It isn't enough to merely create the policies and processes; they should be widely circulated among the organization and be something with which key stakeholders involved in the SDLC are familiar.

When organizations don't have policies and processes clearly defined and their teams are unfamiliar with implementing them, then they lack the methods to notify customers of emerging vulnerabilities and cannot provide support throughout a product's life cycle.

To avoid these issues, several mitigations can be used, including signing images and code and verifying that what was shipped is indeed what is received via hashing. Suppliers also need codified processes to patch and update impacted software across secure communication channels.

Protect the Software

Having appropriate policies and processes in place is one thing—organizations must also do the real work of protecting the software from unauthorized access, modification, and even deletion. Various threats can manifest on this front to compromise the build and delivery of software prior to delivery to a customer. Malicious code, for example, can be injected into the code prior to delivery to the customer and present scenarios where backdoors could exist that can compromise the customer.

To prevent these sorts of risks, the NSA recommends several mitigations such as these:

- Implementing role-based access control (RBAC)
- Enforcing endpoint protection measures for developers
- Conducting code reviews
- Digitally signing code during delivery to customers, which includes using keys that are compliant with Federal Information Processing Standards (FIPS) 140 or even hardware security modules (HSMs) if warranted

The NSA's guidance also recommends that suppliers have mechanisms in place to verify the integrity of software releases through digitally signing code throughout the SDLC. This facilitates trust with the software customer and provenance goals. When suppliers fail to take these measures, threats like malicious tampering prior to software delivery can occur, as we've seen in some of the past attacks we've discussed. While code signing helps with trust and provenance, it requires verifiable build processes as a checkpoint prior to signing the code, which is what the NSA recommends. Otherwise, you simply have potentially malicious or compromised code that is signed and passed off as legitimate, as was the case with SolarWinds. The NSA goes as far as to recommend mirroring production build environments to independently compile and package code and then comparing the hashes of the two build environments, which we've seen in other guidance like SLSA with reproducible builds and measures that SolarWinds now takes.

Of course, code signing requires effective key management, so the NSA recommends that suppliers securely store private keys on HSMs to mitigate the risk of code-signing key theft or tampering, and then protecting the systems that handle key materials through both least-permissive access control and infrastructure controls.

Organizations also need strategies for how they archive legacy versions of software and meet the retention requirements associated with them. Strategies may be driven by regulatory requirements depending on the industry and/or organizational specific requirements. As the NSA's guidance points out, archived software is beneficial for a variety of purposes, such as disaster recovery, digital forensics, or even restoring of previously known-good versions of software when malicious activities do occur.

Various risks exist that can threaten the archiving and protection of software releases, however, such as insecure or inaccessible storage mediums or infrequent archive reviews, leading to a false sense of assurance that may not materialize when restoration or access to archived software releases is needed.

To mitigate some of these threats, the NSA's guidance recommends mitigations that involve persistent archival storage, limiting access to read-only to avoid unauthorized modification. While organizations may shift from using legacy storage mediums such as tapes and network drives to the cloud, they need to ensure that the risks of cloud storage are accounted for as well. Organizations should also establish specific archival and retention policies and strive to automate their implementation by using available technologies to ensure they occur in alignment with established policies.

Produce Well-Secured Software

Producing secure software requires following secure design principles throughout the SDLC. It's why in this section of the guidance the NSA lists potential threats such as developers not employing secure development practices, lacking proper training on conducting threat and risk assessments, and not fully understanding the design and operational requirements for the software being created.

To mitigate these risks, the NSA's recommendations include activities such as threat modeling, which NIST has also recommended for critical software. The NSA also recommends ensuring that the intended operational environments are fully understood and that secure design specifications are included in the software's requirements.

SaaS presents some unique risks to producing secure software due to its operational model. Some specific examples that the NSA provides include the inadvertent introduction of vulnerable code into repositories that may trigger automated builds, or varying security requirements among different models of a single SaaS solution that doesn't lead to validation of all the components. These risks can be mitigated by establishing, enforcing, and verifying common security requirements between SaaS suppliers and their associated subcontractors.

As we've discussed, most modern software includes extensive use of third-party supplier software and components. Therefore, the NSA's guidance emphasizes the need to verify that third-party software suppliers are also complying with existing security requirements and not providing components exceeding an organization's risk tolerance. Various threats exist in the use of third-party suppliers, such as a lack of sufficient contractual agreements that can lead to risk and vulnerabilities; failing to account for third-party supplier ownership, control, and past performance; and not explicitly expressing security requirements to third-party suppliers related to minimum security requirements.

To avoid these issues, the NSA recommends mitigations such as the following:

- Verifying that third parties comply with security requirements
- Using contractual agreements to communicate and enforce security requirements
- Having processes in place to mitigate risk that third-party suppliers may introduce (either inadvertently or intentionally)

Contractual considerations should account for the disclosure of vulnerabilities and notifications, as well as aligning with secure software development requirements like NIST's SSDF.

Much like other guidance from sources like NIST, the NSA recommends having a location of approved third-party software that aligns with the supplier's security requirements and denying the use of third-party software not from that approved repository. To help drive this point home, the NSA recommends that suppliers update their organizational policies to outline updating third-party software when new versions become available, vulnerabilities emerge, or risks become known.

Other relevant threats that the NSA's guidance points out include not properly configuring the compilation and build process, failing to review and analyze human-readable code, and not rigorously testing executable code. These threats can allow for the introduction of malicious software into components, compromising build processes, not evaluating security requirements during software reviews, and having inadequate testing and scanning for vulnerabilities in executable code. The NSA recommends that suppliers take measures such as obtaining a clear set of security requirements from customers, understanding the governance and compliance requirements like FedRAMP or OMB policies for those involved with the U.S. federal government, and threat-modeling all critical software components and systems in the build pipeline.

Sticking with the industry themes of building security guardrails, the NSA's guidance emphasizes the need for software to have secure settings by default. Failing to do so can lead to such threats as software being installed without proper configuration, restricting administrative access, and not logging administrative activities.

To mitigate these threats, the NSA recommends that suppliers log all administrative actions and retain them for a period of at least 30 days, institute MFA for administrative access, and disable services and functionality that aren't required for software.

Respond to Vulnerabilities

Lastly, once organizations have prepared and set measures in place to protect and produce well-secured software, they need a mechanism to respond to vulnerabilities. As many practitioners believe, it isn't a matter of if, but when, incidents or vulnerabilities will occur. Vulnerabilities are almost inevitable, so suppliers having mechanisms to respond to vulnerabilities is critical.

To respond to vulnerabilities, suppliers need standardized processes to identify, analyze, and remediate vulnerabilities on a continuous basis. Failing to do this can lead to various threats, including examples the NSA guidance provides such as releasing software with known or undisclosed vulnerabilities, having inadequate measures to remove known vulnerabilities, or using components of unknown provenance.

To mitigate these, the NSA recommends a robust set of activities, such as the following:

- Having a cross-disciplinary vulnerability assessment team in place
- Establishing processes to conduct activities like fuzzing and SCA to monitor for vulnerabilities
- Having a PSIRT in place, including a public-facing PSIRT web page for customers or external researchers to report vulnerabilities that are associated with the suppliers' products

The NSA also recommends tracking all known security issues and vulnerabilities, including their associated CVSS scores and specific impacts on products or components. Following the industry momentum of acknowledging OSS third-party component risk, the NSA recommends suppliers use SBOMs to understand third-party OSS components and the vulnerabilities associated with them. This is in addition to having corporate guidance on how to upgrade those components as issues and vulnerabilities are identified to prevent passing these risks downstream to customers. This recommendation lines up with perspectives we have shared.

The NSA guidance also specifically points out that the adoption of SaaS tools and products potentially introduces risks that can impact an organization's security posture. We have discussed those extensively in our section on SaaS in Chapter 6, so we will not repeat too much here, except to emphasize some of the key NSA recommendations for suppliers using SaaS. These include having stringent policies in place toward SaaS applications (e.g., SaaS governance), implementing identity access and management (IAM) control mechanisms, and developing mature security assessments so that security gaps between the CSP and the cloud customer (suppliers, in this case) are addressed.

As previously mentioned, the NSA's guidance for suppliers, much like the previous one for developers, has several appendices, including a crosswalk of the threat scenarios presented and NIST's SSDF.

Recommended Practices Guide for Customers

Closing out the NSA series on software supply chain guidance is the publication focused on software customers or *acquiring organizations*, as they are sometimes called. Customers are typically the organizations that procure and deploy software products in their respective environments and architectures. They should consider software supply chain risks during the acquisition, deployment, operations, and maintenance phases of the SDLC for software in their environments.

The customer's role in the software supply chain, as the NSA points out, begins during procurement and acquisitions. It starts with having requirements present during procurement that are derived from internal organizational requirements as well as relevant external regulatory considerations.

To mitigate the risk associated with not ensuring security requirements are accounted for during procurement and acquisition, the NSA proposes a variety of measures for the customer to take:

- Keeping organizational security requirements updated and integrated into business processes
- Ensuring that individual roles are assigned with associated security responsibilities throughout the procurement life cycle
- Independently verifying hashes and signatures of both original software products and any subsequent updates that occur from the supplier
- Having acquisition security (ACQSEC) teams in place to contain known risks about foreign ownership, control, or influence (FOCI) for suppliers in their supply chain

The NSA's guidance stresses the importance of customers conducting product evaluations of both the current market and proposed supplier solutions. These activities typically occur during requests for information (RFIs) or requests for proposals (RFPs), where customers have an opportunity to determine if security and SCRM requirements have been met by potential suppliers (see Figure 8.8).

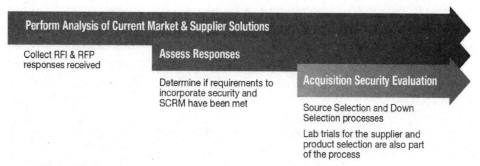

Figure 8.8

The NSA emphasizes that threat evaluation is key to assessing and managing risks with specific products and vendors. Some of the examples they provide that can impact customers include receiving a product that was not the evaluated product, discovering vulnerabilities overlooked during initial evaluations, and making changes in ownership that lead to potentially unknown external influence on the product or supplier.

The guidance points out that one critical concern for customers is a lack of visibility into product components to be able to both conduct proper evaluations and make informed risk decisions. This includes embedded components, libraries, modules, and so on, all of which tie to the broader conversation about software transparency and a need to understand software component inventory, including when evaluating products from software vendors.

To address these risks, the NSA's guidance for customers makes key recommendations like verifying the contents of software via methods such as SBOMs, and going so far as to vet external evaluation labs that may have been involved with the supplier to ensure they are genuinely independent and objective. This vetting also can involve ensuring that any external labs or evaluators that are involved have the requisite domain expertise to validate requirements as part of their evaluation activities. Another recommendation by the NSA is to ensure that third-party suppliers identified in SBOMs undergo the same evaluation as first-party suppliers. This is an example of understanding the risk that the expansive software supply chain presents and that risks can manifest from nth-tier suppliers, not always via first or even third parties.

Contracts are a key mechanism that customers can use to mitigate risk when it comes to their software supply chain and suppliers. This mechanism requires customers to integrate supply chain requirements into contractual language such as statements of work (SOWs) and RFIs and RFPs. It also requires having an educated acquisition workforce with the knowledge necessary to address software supply chain security concerns and requirements to be able to drive the contractual language in the direction needed.

Some potential threats and risks that the NSA guidance highlights include entering into contract agreements with suppliers under foreign control or who have subcontractors that can introduce risk. This situation can also lead to a broader problem where contracts lack SCRM requirements, such as requiring an SBOM from software suppliers. It also can occur when customers don't exercise proper due diligence of suppliers and a supplier has compromised software products, particularly if supporting artifacts such as hashes and signatures give a false sense of security.

To mitigate these risks, the NSA recommends practices such as requiring visibility into the provenance of products and self-attestation of security hygiene for development processes and supporting infrastructure involved in product development. These self-attestations should include a summarization of secure development practices as well as a signature by an official from the supplier who is responsible for the security of the development process and infrastructure. Hashing/signatures for the delivered products should also be included. Customers should also strive to include requirements for greater transparency and visibility into supplier sourcing and the ownership of products and upstream suppliers.

Furthermore, customers should require that suppliers send all artifacts in a standardized SBOM format (e.g., SPDX or CycloneDX), provide SBOMs for software upgrades, and supply continuous reporting for key attributes related to the supplier's ownership, location, and foreign control. Customers should require suppliers to notify them of cyber incidents, investigations, mitigations, and any impacts to the product or development environment involved in the products they are consuming.

Another key aspect for the customer is the actual deployment of software products into their environments and systems. This starts with the acceptance of a product from a supplier and requires precautions from customers prior to acceptance. If customers don't take the proper precautions, then risks such as accepting a product other than what was ordered can occur, as well as falling victim to product tampering or accepting products with missing documentation and artifacts to accompany it. Customers should have both policies and mechanisms in place to mitigate the risk of compromised products from suppliers. Methods include customers verifying the security of the infrastructure suppliers used for distribution and the integrity of the delivered product via hashes and signatures, including its components, and verifying the SBOM against the product that was delivered.

Functional testing is called out as a key consideration for software customers. Functional testing typically involves processes for creating tests and testing environments for products and executing and reporting the associated tests. If functional testing doesn't occur, customers may fall victim to threats such as a product's functionality unknowingly changing or containing unverified or unknown components. Such threats can be avoided by customers saving and storing their tests and test environments for future reference and use, as well as verifying the SBOM's contents against the product being evaluated.

The NSA recommends that customers have a configuration control board (CCB) in place as part of effective IT service management (ITSM) to carry out activities such as reviewing functional and assurance findings, determining the software's risk, and making go/no-go decisions for product use. That said, threats can occur through poor CCB implementation and processes, such as the CCB receiving inaccurate or incomplete product reports from suppliers or having a CCB that is biased by various factors or lacks the domain expertise on products and technologies to make informed decisions. To mitigate these risks, customers should ensure their CCB is composed of subject matter experts or has access to them. Customers should also ensure that organizational SCRM requirements are integrated into their CCB process and that they are documented, and that reports delivered to the CCB occur over secure communication channels.

Other phases of product adoption that present risks to customers include product integration, rollouts, upgrades, and the end-of-life (EoL) phase. Customers need to have sufficiently documented processes to use software products throughout each of these phases to avoid risks associated with compromised product integrations. Malicious actors may look to disable defensive measures prior to malicious functionality being activated, as occurred in cases such as SolarWinds, and product developers may look to either intentionally or unintentionally introduce backdoors into products that place customers at risk.

It also isn't enough for customers to have measures in place for product integration, rollouts, and upgrades; customers must not overlook the product end-of-life (EoL) phase. This phase occurs for many reasons, including customers deciding to use an alternative product, products no longer being needed, or products no longer being supported by suppliers. However, product integrations are often associated with trust relationships into customer environments, and they can involve credentials, permissions, network access, and more. Customers can mitigate these risks by ensuring that credentials, permissions, and access associated with the supplier and their products are appropriately removed from the customer environment. Furthermore, customers can also take measures such as removing supplier products from application allow lists and even explicitly denying software products through networking and security tooling. Security operations (SecOps) teams are often positioned well to create and implement plans to mitigate risk associated with EoL products within customer environments.

As the NSA's guidance points out, another key area that customers must address is the training and enablement associated with the safe deployment and use of software products. This point is supported by several security studies that often cite customer misconfiguration as a key attack vector that introduces risk and leads to customer data breaches. Even if software from the supplier isn't intentionally malicious or insecure, or due to the involvement from malicious actors, customers may unknowingly put themselves at risk by not following vendor guidance and industry best practices associated with the software's use. Malicious actors aren't often as concerned with how the risk and attack vectors materialize as with if they exist and can be exploited, period.

Lastly, and arguably most important, the NSA's guidance makes the case that supply chain risk management (SCRM) operations are pivotal to reduce the overall risk associated with the software supply chain to an organization. Mature SCRM teams and processes can help customers maintain secure baselines for software and products on their networks and infrastructure and implement effective continuous monitoring to watch for product changes and security events that introduce risk.

Without effective SCRM operations in place, customers can fall victim to malicious software that avoids security and monitoring tools and fails to have appropriate logging in place to perform effective continuous monitoring. The NSA closes out the customer guidance with a robust set of recommendations related to SCRM operations, which include enabling integrity protections on all deployed security agents, deploying out-of-band security tools for monitoring, and implementing threat modeling based on a software product's specific risks and threats coupled with adversary and threat intelligence.

While it is evident that all of these measures can't be taken by every organization, particularly SMBs, many software customers can begin heading down the path of maturing their secure consumption of software products by implementing the practices and processes outlined in the NSA customer guidance.

Summary

In this chapter, we covered existing and emerging guidance related to the public sector and government entities. This included guidance for organizations such as NIST and the NSA. While some of the requirements and guidance may only be applicable to U.S. federal agencies and their industrial base, it is still important to understand how the public sector is approaching software supply chain security. In the next chapter, we will discuss key considerations associated with software transparency for operational technology (OT) and industrial control systems (ICSs).

Software Transparency
in Operational Technology

Operational technology (OT) runs the most critical processes in the world, from missile platforms and defense missions, to water treatment plants and electric power, to critical manufacturing, airports, and more. Frequently these environments are highly isolated using air-gapped networks and may have restrictions against external connections, cloud, or mobile capabilities. Because of this, many of the techniques we rely on for software validation may not be useful here.

For instance, how does one validate the certificate revocation list (CRL) for a code-signing certificate against a signed firmware update when the Internet is not accessible? How does one look up and identify a component hash in a software bill of materials (SBOM), if it matches known malware repository entries? Do you still consider overly long expiration dates for Transport Layer Security (TLS) certificates to be an issue when you can't easily update trust information?

Additionally, when considering concerns with nation-state adversaries, many of these products are manufactured in or supported by operations in areas of the world we may consider adversarial. Topics of provenance for software become especially challenging as compliance requirements from the National Defense Authorization Act (NDAA) and various executive orders have sought to retract which nations are allowed to supply products to critical infrastructure.

For instance, in 2020, Executive Order 13920, Securing the United States Bulk-Power System (www.energy.gov/ceser/securing-united-states-bulk-power-system-eo-13920), was issued that addressed concerns with procurement from foreign adversaries destined for the U.S. power grid. This order was later followed by a prohibition order forbidding acquisition of equipment for the grid from the People's Republic of China.

These orders have since been rescinded and are now under the auspices of Executive Order 14017 on Securing America's Supply Chains (`www.whitehouse .gov/briefing-room/presidential-actions/2021/02/24/executive-order- on-americas-supply-chains`). Regardless, it remains clear that setting policy on supply chain risk management for critical infrastructure and defense is a national priority.

Executive Order 14028, which prompted a flurry of activity around software transparency, including SBOM and software labeling, was split into three primary stakeholders, one of those the mission of the National Telecommunications and Information Administration (NTIA), to define SBOM attributes. This mission and others, such as the definition of Vulnerability Exploitability eXchange (VEX) formats, has since transitioned to the Cybersecurity and Infrastructure Security Agency (CISA), whose primary mission is to secure critical infrastructure. It becomes very clear that OT environments will remain at the forefront of this software transparency movement within the United States for the foreseeable future.

The Kinetic Effect of Software

One of the most peculiar actions of EO 14028 was the move to define "critical software." As we've covered previously, these definitions can be tricky to unpack. One could argue that all software has the potential to be critical—it just depends on how you use it. One example we've used in the past is an image-rendering library used to display cute kitten pictures or videos on the Internet. Very few would consider this critical software. But what if that same library is used to render telemetry data in an electric power environment? That's a very different scenario. The same software, used in diverse ways, has a very different criticality.

One OT aspect that intrigues so many practitioners is the ability for these systems to escape their traditional virtual boundaries and create real-world kinetic impacts. Software controls the gates that keep a prison on lockdown, maintains the chemical mixtures that sanitize your drinking water, operates the power grids, and even runs kinetic military defense systems. If that kitten-rendering library was used in a missile targeting system and soldiers' lives depended on it, that, too, could be considered extremely critical. In OT, the potential for software defects to result in loss of human life can be catastrophic.

In the past several years, there have been multiple reports of ransomware creating delays in hospital care, and in Germany in 2020, it was suggested that a patient's death was caused by ransomware. While this was largely unsubstantiated, it is clear from research, such as that performed by Pew Charitable Trusts (www.pewtrusts.org/en/research-and-analysis/blogs/stateline/2022/05/18/ransomware-attacks-on-hospitals-put-patients-at-risk), that these events have the potential to cause the loss of human life. As our software-controlled society and remote telemedicine systems create opportunities for enhanced medical care, they also provide new opportunities for attackers.

So, too, have attacks on the power grid increased. We have seen firsthand how the military strategies of countries such as Russia have used a combination of cyber- and kinetic attacks to cripple a nation. For example, in removing their ability to create safe drinking water or provide electricity, the health of a nation's citizens can be compromised. Additionally, the war machine of a nation, from ports, railroads, electricity, water, and other dependencies, creates a network effect that makes cyber sabotage incredibly attractive to an adversary. How else can you create physical sabotage scenarios from around the world?

The Stuxnet attack might be one of the best examples in which a kinetic result was carried out through software. While analysis showed that the initial attack was borne by an infected USB drive, it was malware that produced a massive delay of Iran's nuclear enrichment capabilities. Some analysts have suggested this may have created as much as a two-year setback across 984 centrifuges (http://large.stanford.edu/courses/2015/ph241/holloway1).

Perhaps the most thorough analysis of the Stuxnet attack was performed by Langner, Inc., an industrial control system (ICS) asset management company with a long history of deep expertise in the ICS security space. In 2013, with later updates in 2017, they released the paper "To Kill a Centrifuge" (www.langner.com/wp-content/uploads/2017/03/to-kill-a-centrifuge.pdf), which described how the attack was ultimately carried out and what it means for both Iran's nuclear enrichment program and the rest of the industry, as we look to prevent future attacks against critical infrastructure.

Stuxnet was designed to reduce the efficiency of the centrifuges. While the infection took place at multiple sites, the Natanz enrichment facility is widely thought to have been the initial target. In the summer of 2010, it was discovered that there were an abnormal number of failures in the centrifuges, but not so overtly as to arouse suspicion. It was clear that the level of sophistication here was designed with some degree of subtlety, as it just as easily could have been engineered to outright destroy the centrifuges.

The initial infection is thought to have been facilitated by an infection of Windows machines, likely the same mobile assets used by control engineers to program and manage the Siemens software and equipment responsible for the enrichment program. The malware did not get identified as malicious by antivirus vendors until a number of years later, when it utilized several zero-day exploits. It did not transit the network until initial infection, and so the traditional measures to analyze network traffic and rely on antimalware solutions to prevent the spread were largely ineffective.

But what is noteworthy, even beyond the challenges in using traditional methods to detect and prevent infection, is that the malware was designed with logic to stealthily degrade the performance of and ultimately introduce frailty to the rotors used in the pressure system. By alternating the slow and fast cycles, it pushed the boundaries of what the system was designed to do by testing the system's physical limitations. This type of logic behavioral change is indicative of how a legitimate code change can introduce major consequences into a system.

Legacy Software Risks

Similarly, as we have discussed previously, much of this software is very old and comes with similar challenges as it relates to validating legacy products. A key characteristic of OT systems is the need for resilience. As the noted ICS security expert Daniel Ehrenreich is known to say, these environments are all about safety, reliability, and productivity, not confidentiality, integrity, and availability (www.cisa.gov/uscert/sites/default/files/ICSJWG-Archive/QNL_JUN_21/Understanding%20ICS%20Cyber-Attacks%20and%20Defense%20Measures_S508C.pdf).

So, how do we achieve these goals? We achieve them largely through exhaustive engineering mapped against an extremely strong culture of safety engineering, where system characteristics are threat-modeled against safety impacts. Standards such as ISA84 (www.isa.org/technical-topics/safety) are heavily applied in these environments, and safety is more commonplace than cybersecurity as a design driver. For the critical infrastructure company, every meeting starts with a "Safety Moment" exercise to get employees thinking about safety, hard hats and protective gear are the norm, and it's not even an option to think otherwise. Additionally, these environments tend to be very static, because change implies risk. Once an engineer has performed a Factory Acceptance Test (FAT) to ensure that the system works as designed and a Site Acceptance Test (SAT) where safety and controls have been evaluated, the system is largely considered to be "change locked," meaning no additional changes should be made. Normal changes occur, such as minor changes to the programmable logic controller (PLC), some patching may occur for noncritical or redundant systems, and new jobs may be queued for processing, but major changes usually do not occur.

While this limits the ability to introduce security controls, it also reduces the likelihood of failure through planned change as it relates to supply chain compromise. The combination of the absence of change, as well as the perception that the environment is isolated or "air-gapped" when this might not truly be the case, can sometimes lead to a false sense of security. But it is true that reducing change events lessens the likelihood of a dependency confusion attack creating an impact for the OT system, at least until there is a planned change. One further complication here is that for truly air-gapped systems, or sites without Internet access, it can be challenging to validate the authenticity and security of software. It is quite common that software is walked into the facility on an engineer's laptop and not downloaded from a trusted site. In some situations, such as nuclear facilities, it is common to require a kiosk-based antimalware scanning capability, but as we saw in the Stuxnet example, this is unlikely to be an effective approach.

Regardless of the lack of change, the traditional mindset in the early 2000s was that the OT systems were so complex and proprietary that nobody outside the factory knew how they worked. Very few attack tools existed and the documentation was largely nonexistent to aid an adversary in attacking the thousands of potential ICS protocols that might be in place. The increasing digital transformation and standardization of the OT protocol stack, as well as information sharing within Internet communities, have lessened the value of this security by obscurity. There are now stable exploits and attack tools in frameworks such as Metasploit, regular hacking competitions for ICS such as Pwn2Own at the annual S4 ICS Security Conference held in Miami Beach, and many other similar events.

The landscape is changing and new approaches to securing software are largely ignoring the legacy software space. Most software supply chain security advances are applied to software as a service (SaaS), containers, and modern software development frameworks but are largely uninterested in addressing the legacy software problem beyond reverse engineering tools focused on ICS firmware vulnerability discovery. The challenge then becomes how do we address these issues for an end-of-support product—one where the supplier is no longer in business? The choices are typically reduced to spending lots of money to rip and replace or apply virtual patches or mitigating controls, and hoping that we have reduced the attack surface in all the right places.

Ladder Logic and Setpoints in Control Systems

Programmable logic controllers (PLCs), remote terminal units (RTUs), and similar OT devices run basic automation programs, often programmed using ladder logic, function block diagrams, or other methods. They describe a series of inputs and outputs and include logic or parameters used to make decisions. It might be as simple as an on or off switch, or it might include conditional logic such as using auxiliary inputs like temperature, rotations per minute, voltage, pressure, or other sensor inputs tied to that logic. The program will often define a range of acceptable values, and the concept of a setpoint is used to identify what normal (or not normal) looks like.

When discussing the kinetic software effects, it may be noteworthy to discuss what constitutes a vulnerability. Do we need an exploit or Metasploit module to create damage? What if a simple data integrity condition can trigger the catastrophic impact? We don't need a Common Vulnerabilities and Exposures (CVE), but perhaps we can manipulate sensor data so that it reports a false condition. Or perhaps we can manipulate the setpoint that defines what normal is. If we know the failure condition for an overpressure event occurs at 500 pounds per square inch (PSI), and the setpoint falls safely below it at 350 PSI but an unauthorized change modifies the setpoint to 1,000 PSI, that might be more catastrophic than a Log4Shell exploit to that system when it causes the boiler to explode.

Programmable logic controllers (PLCs) typically include basic safety mechanisms such as the physical key that determines whether the device is in a run state or a program state, which is required to make changes. For instance, the Trisis malware that impacted Schneider Electric Triconex Safety Instrumented System was one of the first known attacks targeting a safety system. This attack was carried out in part because the device was set in program mode so that changes were possible, and in part because the organization did not fully understand what normal looked like and ignored failures. But the authors have seen situations where a firmware change can be implemented on many OT devices that bypasses the physical key for programming control. While a best practice is to keep the device in run state, this is not a guarantee that a combined supply chain compromise of the firmware couldn't facilitate similar attacks in the future.

In the case of Triton, the attack was delivered via a multistage activity as documented by Idaho National Laboratory Cybersecurity for the Operational Technology Environment (CyOTE), which seeks to address a methodology around triaging of observable indicators and taking action upon those indicators. CyOTE, in their case study of Triton (`https://cyote.inl.gov/cyote/wp-content/uploads/sites/2/2023/01/Triton-CyOTE-Case-Study.pdf`), established the chain of events as listed here:

Step 1—IT Network Exploitation: This step was enabled through a poorly configured firewall allowing access to the IT network.

Step 2—Pivoting from the IT to the OT Network: An engineering workstation inside the OT network was compromised and a payload was deployed, mimicking a legitimate Triconex application, `trilog.exe`.

Step 3—OT Attack Capability Development: The attackers then established a point of control where they identified target systems for further attack, including establishing the running state of target safety instrumented system (SIS) systems.

Step 4—OT Attack Capability Delivery: Unauthorized code was transferred to the Triconex device multiple times, first to test and then ultimately to inject malicious shellcode and new ladder logic that changed the device's behavior.

Step 5—Supporting Attack—Hide: Leveraging mechanisms to evade detection, the malware disabled random access memory/read-only memory (RAM/ROM) checking, and only targeted devices in a program mode but only after an infection modified the firmware to allow for execution even in a run state.

Step 6—OT Attack Execution and Impact: The end result was the complete disablement of safety controls for the system, with options to selectively disable or not, based on program logic.

While this attack followed a traditional approach to first compromise IT and move into OT, the lack of firmware and code validation that facilitated this attack is no different than the multitude of software supply chain attacks we have seen. The authors feel this is a landmark case in understanding how a lack of software and firmware validation could lead to downstream safety impacts, potentially leading to the loss of human life. There are many other takeaways from this case, such as the need for proper segmentation, effective monitoring, and baselining environments for anomaly detection and incident response processes, but had the product required a signed binary to execute, this attack would likely have been prevented.

ICS Attack Surface

As mentioned previously, the ICS attack surface is typically minimized when compared to enterprise IT. Most environments are heavily segmented, and the Department of Energy sponsored a study through the Security Energy Infrastructure Executive Task Force at the direction of Section 5726 of the National Defense Authorization Act (NDAA) for Fiscal Year 2020. This effort produced a series of reference architectures, including specifying a recommended segmentation strategy for electric power based on the site type, an example of which can be seen in Figure 9.1.

Substation Profile

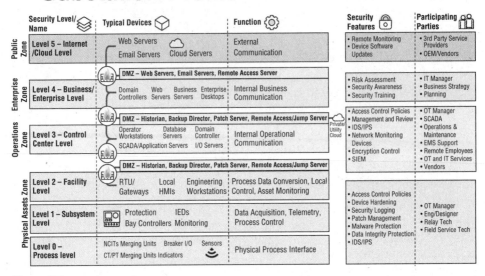

Figure 9.1

Source: `https://inl.gov/wp-content/uploads/2022/03/SEI-ETF-Reference-Architecture-for-Electric-Energy-OT-and-Profiles.pdf`, US Department of Energy, Public domain

Additionally, recommendations from the North American Electric Reliability Corporation (NERC) Critical Infrastructure Protection (CIP) regulatory standards governing the North American Bulk Electric System and requirements from the International Electrotechnical Commission (IEC) 62443 family of standards prescribe segmentation approaches to protect OT systems from being directly exposed, and enterprise IT environments untrusted by these networks.

There are still thousands of ICS assets exposed to the Internet, many of which have weak or no authentication. The popular attack surface browser site Shodan has an entire page dedicated to identifying these systems (`www.shodan.io/explore/category/industrial-control-systems`). As you can see from looking at this site, even searching for specific ICS products yields thousands of hits, many of which are vulnerable and used in critical processes.

With the focus on segmentation for those assets not exposed to the Internet, what does this mean for critical infrastructure organizations? Many attacks still proliferate from an initial intrusion into enterprise IT networks via phishing or other means and then pivot. But if these environments are truly separated, it behooves organizations to look at how software is introduced into the environment through contractors introducing foreign universal serial bus (USB) keys or CD-ROMs shipped from a vendor for firmware updates. These vectors tend to be tightly coupled to physical security, which necessitates a holistic strategy to control what software can be introduced. Likewise for the product vendors, they need to provision mechanisms for operators to perform offline validation of images when online methods are not available.

Smart Grid

The smart grid is a modernized, digital version of the traditional electrical grid that uses advanced technology to improve the efficiency, reliability, and flexibility of the power system. It includes the use of sensors, communication networks, and control systems to monitor and control the flow of electricity, allowing for the integration of renewable energy sources and the management of demand. This allows for greater use of distributed energy resources (DERs), such as solar and wind power, and the implementation of demand response programs to manage energy usage during periods of high demand.

Following the efforts within the Biden administration to fund advances in renewable energy and infrastructure improvements, DER is quickly becoming a big topic as billions of dollars are invested into the grid for renewables over the next few years. These systems are small-scale energy generation and storage systems, such as rooftop solar panels and larger solar farms like what we have seen invested in by NextEra Energy, wind turbines, and battery storage systems that are connected to the grid at the distribution level. The smart grid allows for the integration of these DERs by enabling real-time communication and control between the grid and these distributed resources. This increased connectivity is in stark contrast to the traditionally disconnected and isolated grid infrastructure, and the exposure risks of these devices in the field creates new cybersecurity challenges for grid operators.

Inverter-based technologies within DER, such as solar panels and wind turbines, are becoming an increasingly important part of the smart grid. These technologies convert direct current (DC) power generated by the DERs into alternating current (AC) power that can be used by the grid and can also provide grid services such as voltage and frequency control. Inverters and other DER control systems are connected to the Internet and can be remotely controlled and monitored. This can increase the attack surface and create potential vulnerabilities for cyberattacks.

In addition to DER, advanced metering infrastructure (AMI) is used to measure and communicate detailed information about energy usage to both utilities and consumers in real time, which allows for more accurate billing and the implementation of demand response programs. Furthermore, advanced analytics and machine-learning algorithms are used to analyze large amounts of data generated by the smart grid to detect patterns, predict equipment failures, and optimize the grid's operation.

This increase in complexity brings new capabilities to dynamically correct when risky conditions are detected, but this also brings new opportunities for software to introduce catastrophic consequences. Advanced warning times for issues may be shorter, especially due to the weather-dependent nature of DER resources and new attack patterns like those focused on battery capacity and discharge, which may create energy shortages when grid operators aren't ready. This is where logic-based attacks may become the new norm for adversaries seeking to impact the new and improved grid we are designing today.

With this complexity comes the need for technology standardization. IEC 61850 is an international standard that defines the communication protocols and data models used in the substation automation systems of electric power systems. It plays a key role in the smart grid by providing a common language and framework for the different devices and systems that make up the grid to communicate with each other. One of the main benefits of IEC 61850 is that it enables the integration of different devices and systems from different vendors, which allows for a more efficient, cost-effective deployment of smart grid technologies. IEC 61850 also provides a common data model for different devices and systems, which makes it easier to exchange information between different systems and to perform advanced analytics on the data collected from the grid.

As we start to look at the proliferation of IoT devices that make up the smart grid, our security posture may start to look a lot like typical IoT attack surfaces. An article from 2021 by Gonda Lamberink explored the supply chain risk surface related to IoT and specifically the smart grid (`www.power-grid.com/executive-insight/securing-smart-grid-supply-chains-with-a-zero-trust-mindset`).

In the article, Lamberink calls for a zero trust-based mindset to reduce the risk to the smart grid, which is particularly interesting because in traditional grids an implicit trust is frequently the case. Most systems have no authentication, no encryption communications demanding zero to low latency and network convergence times that traditional security technologies cannot keep up with. The increased exposure of the smart grid means that traditional walled-garden approaches are not feasible to protect this infrastructure.

Furthermore, as we look to standards frameworks aligned with these environments, the traditional NERC CIP and IEC 62443 set of standards still apply, but many are looking to more traditional IoT frameworks from NIST and others as well.

Summary

In this chapter, we discussed the kinetic effects of software and the potential to cause physical impacts in our society. We also covered risks associated with legacy software and ladder logic in industrial control systems. We expanded on the topic of the ICS attack surface and the risk it poses to critical infrastructure, defense, and society as well as the role that the smart grid plays. In the following chapters, we will discuss some practical guidance for both software suppliers and consumers.

CHAPTER 10

Practical Guidance for Suppliers

While we have discussed many of the emerging sources of industry guidance from private and public sector organizations, the next couple of chapters will strive to give some practical guidance to both suppliers and consumers. This will include a synthesis of guidance from the sources we've discussed, as well as industry best practices and advice based on the author's professional experience as well.

Not all the recommendations, best practices, and processes may be practical to implement for all suppliers. Just like the diverse ecosystem of software consumers, software suppliers exist on a spectrum as it relates to resources, expertise, and constraints. It will often be a dichotomy between software consumers and suppliers, depending on the industry, business relationship, regulatory requirements, and contractual aspects at play to come to terms with what does or doesn't get implemented, provided, or disclosed and under what circumstances.

Vulnerability Disclosure and Response PSIRT

We've spoken quite a bit about industry frameworks such as NIST's Secure Software Development Framework (SSDF) in other chapters of this book, so it makes sense to cite it as an example here as well.

As discussed, SSDF calls for organizations to implement sound practices to help aid secure software development. It lays out the practices across four groups:

Preparing the Organization, Protecting Software, Producing Well-Secured Software, and Responding to Vulnerabilities. One key theme across these four groups is the ability for organizations and suppliers to both disclose and respond to vulnerabilities that impact their consumers. This is emphasized in areas such as having policies in place that address vulnerability disclosure and remediation activities. Having these policies and processes in place produces several key benefits for software suppliers, such as being able to inform researchers about their vulnerability management practices and report potential vulnerabilities they may discover to the supplier.

As anyone who has been in cybersecurity or software development long enough knows, it isn't a matter of *if* vulnerabilities will emerge, but *when*. Therefore, it is key for organizations to have codified security response processes and mature capabilities when it comes to disclosing vulnerabilities to software consumers. This traditionally has occurred through static notification measures such as websites, emails, and PDF documentation. However, as we have discussed elsewhere in the text, the industry is now moving toward automated machine-readable notification advisories. This is most prominently showing up through avenues such as the Common Security Advisory Framework (CSAF) and the Vulnerability Exploitability eXchange (VEX), which is considered by many to be an accompanying document to SBOMs that will show the actual exploitability of vulnerabilities associated with software and products from suppliers. CSAF aims to allow stakeholders to automate the creation and consumption of security vulnerability information and is striving to support VEX, although as of this writing, that capability is still maturing. Another notable example is CycloneDX, the industry-leading SBOM format we have discussed, which also has something they refer to as a "Bill of Vulnerabilities" (`https://cyclonedx.org/capabilities/bov`) that allows the sharing of vulnerability data between systems and sources of vulnerability intelligence.

The emergence of methods and standards such as CSAF and VEX shows a continued industry momentum to shift from the traditional static vulnerability advisory and notification processes to one of machine readability and automation, which allows the process to be more efficient, less error prone, and ultimately more scalable as well.

Having a Vulnerability Disclosure Program (VDP) in place is a sign of maturity from software suppliers and builds trust with consumers while empowering them to be aware of ongoing vulnerabilities and incidents as well as take remedial action to address vulnerabilities associated with the products in their environment before they can be exploited by a malicious actor. It is also becoming a requirement in some industries, such as the U.S. federal sector, that third-party software providers self-attest to aligning with SSDF practices, such as the existence of a VDP.

Having a VDP in place that is responsive to security researchers and that communicates openly and effectively with consumers builds consumer trust and helps mitigate risk to suppliers that may come in the form of financial ramifications such as regulatory consequences for poor practices or reputational harm. While you may find yourself in the position of being a software supplier, the inevitable reality is that you are also likely a software consumer or use third parties to some extent when it comes to providing your software and products to your own downstream consumers. This means you need to take steps to understand your own supply chain and the security measures that your suppliers take. This may come in the form of attestations and vetting software components you use from third parties in your software. If it is a proprietary supplier, you can use contractual measures to enforce a level of rigor that your organization or downstream consumers require. If the components are provided using OSS, you need to implement OSS governance, as we have discussed elsewhere and as recommended by leaders such as NIST. Failing to do so creates risk for your downstream consumers and potentially business challenges as savvy consumers will inevitably push back on insecure software passed on to them either by seeking to understand your secure software development practices or asking for artifacts such as SBOMs that can expose risk embedded in your products or applications.

Product Security Incident Response Team (PSIRT)

Another key recommendation, tied to both SSDF and industry best practice around being a product and software supplier, is implementing a product security incident response team (PSIRT). A PSIRT is like a cybersecurity incident response team (CSIRT) but instead of being inward facing and focused on the organization's infrastructure and systems, a PSIRT is product-focused and concerned with vulnerabilities and threats to an organization's product. PSIRT makes an appearance in the NIST SSDF in the Respond to Vulnerabilities (RV) group and is listed as an implementation example that allows organizations to handle responses to vulnerability reports and incidents, and handle communication among the organization's stakeholders, which may be internal and external.

Whether you're looking to start a new PSIRT team or assess the maturity of an existing one to identify gaps for improvement, one great resource to do so is the PSIRT Maturity Document from FIRST, the same organization that leads CVSS and EPSS, which we have discussed in other chapters (www.first.org/standards/frameworks/psirts/psirt_maturity_document). FIRST's PSIRT Maturity Document provides three maturity levels for PSIRT teams to benchmark against, going from Basic, Intermediate, and Proactive levels of maturity (see Figure 10.1). Let's take a brief look at each maturity level to understand the associated capabilities per level.

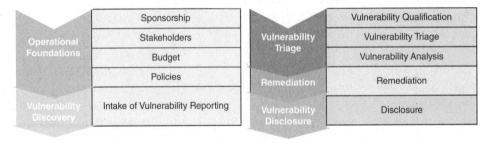

Figure 10.1

Source: `www.first.org/standards/frameworks/psirts/psirt_maturity_document`

Before diving into the levels of a PSIRT, one of the most foundational steps is creating a PSIRT charter that captures the PSIRT's mission statement, stakeholders, affiliation/sponsoring organization, and scope.

At the Basic level, a PSIRT is likely just being established and trying to get to a baseline level of functionality. This requires things such as executive sponsorship, stakeholder identification, and budget and baseline procedures. This means the PSIRT needs to have the support of the organization's leadership; have identified who the stakeholders are, both internal and external; have a budget for initial staffing and establishment; and have created policies and processes to codify how the PSIRT will functional fundamentally.

Example policies and processes that FIRST's document provides include a vulnerability management, information handling, and remediation service level agreement. Beyond that, the PSIRT needs some basic capabilities to meet its intent. This includes the ability to create vulnerability reports, which involves publishing contact information and how to go about reporting vulnerabilities to the organization's PSIRT.

Receiving vulnerability reports is just the first step, though; going beyond that, PSIRTs need the ability to triage and analyze vulnerability reports. This involves key steps such as qualification of vulnerability reports, asking whether a vulnerability is valid and whether it should be accepted or rejected. FIRST recommends that PSIRTs capture key vulnerability information and adopt machine-readable formats to aid efficiency and scale. Resources they cite include the Common Vulnerability Reporting Framework (CVRF), CSAF, and the Common Vulnerabilities and Exposures (CVE) program, the last of which ultimately is supported by NIST's National Vulnerability Database (NVD) and enables vulnerability communication to consumers, often through the support of vulnerability scanning tools that integrate and query the NVD for vulnerability data such as CVEs.

Once the PSIRT has qualified a vulnerability as valid and accepted, they need to move on to vulnerability analysis, which involves understanding how vulnerability works, how it can be exploited, what versions of their products and services are impacted by the vulnerability, and what the ramifications of exploitation generically can be. Ramifications will vary depending on the environment and mitigating controls that may or may not exist, which is often left to consumers to determine due to their inherent knowledge of their operating environment.

During analysis PSIRTs will often perform prioritization and scoring. FIRST's documentation recommends the use of CVSS, which is logical given their relationship with CVSS, but as we have discussed elsewhere, CVSS also has several strong critiques from academia and industry alike. Despite those criticisms, CVSS experiences broad adoption in the industry, and if a PSIRT chose another scoring methodology, as FIRST notes, they will likely need to explain the decision to consumers who are often familiar with CVSS.

Now that a vulnerability has been qualified and analyzed, the supplier needs to remediate the vulnerability. Remediation may involve activities such as a code fix and product patch or guidance for consumers to mitigate the risk of a vulnerability, or theoretically choosing not to fix the vulnerability whatsoever, based on a cost–benefit analysis by the PSIRT and their peers among the supplier firm.

Lastly, the Basic level of maturity of vulnerability disclosure involves notifying the consumers of the product or service of the vulnerability. This notification is ideally accompanied by guidance on how to remediate the vulnerability or mitigate it if a code fix or resolution doesn't exist. FIRST also recommends crediting the security researcher or entity responsible for notifying the supplier of the vulnerability to begin with. It provides attribution to the reporting party and builds trust among the community.

Moving beyond the basic and foundational level of maturity, a PSIRT would then advance to Maturity Level 2 or Intermediate. This is where the PSIRT starts to provide more comprehensive services, engage with more stakeholders both internal and external to the organization, and mature existing fundamental capabilities (see Figure 10.2).

As FIRST mentioned, PSIRTs at the Intermediate level have a clear understanding of their stakeholders, establish processes, and can optimize their analysis and response to vulnerabilities. Intermediate-level PSIRTs are also able to use tooling to improve their vulnerability intake and processing capabilities. FIRST recommends that PSIRTs at the Intermediate level begin understanding the components that go into a released product, capturing this data in a product manifest or bill of materials, often called an SBOM if the product is software centric.

	Sponsorship			Vulnerability Qualification
	Stakeholders			Vulnerability Triage
	Charter		Vulnerability Triage	Vulnerability Analysis
	Organizational Model			Established Finders
Operational Foundations	Management & Stakeholder Support			Vulnerability Reproduction
	Budget			Security Remedy Management Plan
	Staff		Remediation	Remediation
	Resources & Tools			
	Policies			Notification
	Internal Stakeholder Management		Vulnerability Disclosure	Disclosure
Stakeholder Ecosystem Management	Downstream Stakeholder Management			Vulnerability Metrics
	Incident Communication Coordination			Training the PSIRT
	Intake of Vulnerability Reporting		Training & Education	
Vulnerability Discovery	Identifying Unreported Vulnerabilities			Provide Feedback Mechanisms

Figure 10.2

The possession of the BOM not only helps with software component visibility and vulnerability management for communication to consumers downstream, but also enables the organization to understand what third parties they may need to engage with, such as OSS projects.

FIRST's guidance points out that more mature PSIRTs have clear roles and responsibilities for understanding where each stakeholder fits into the vulnerability triage and analysis activities and have begun to build rapport with the security researchers who may be reporting vulnerabilities or flaws to the PSIRT. This rapport is built by having functional processes and tools such as ticketing systems in place to facilitate the vulnerability reporting process.

In addition to the use of CVSS and severity scoring, PSIRTs often mature to use the Common Weakness Enumeration (CWE) labeling for vulnerabilities. As we discussed in Chapter 3, "Vulnerability Databases and Scoring Methodologies," CWE is a system managed by MITRE that provides a community-developed list of software and hardware weakness types that allows quick labeling and categorization of vulnerabilities.

Intermediate PSIRTs are also able to lean on previous vulnerability remediation activities to avoid starting from scratch each time and have codified processes to aid in vulnerability remediation activities and, subsequently, vulnerability disclosure as well. This means improving how the PSIRT works with various parties as part of disclosure, and FIRST recommends the use of their Guidelines and Practices for Multi-Party Vulnerability Coordination and Disclosure to facilitate a mature approach to vulnerability disclosure (www.first.org/global/sigs/vulnerability-coordination/multiparty/guidelines-v1.1).

Part of this disclosure maturity will involve standardized avenues for disclosure, metric tracking, and iterative process improvement as the disclosure activities go on. FIRST also points out that there may be cases where the PSIRT decides to provide customer notification prior to the actual public disclosure. This makes sense given that once the information is public, it isn't just defenders who are watching but also malicious actors who inevitably will look to exploit the vulnerability before consumers can remediate the flaws.

Finally, the PSIRT ideally progresses to Maturity Level 3, also known as Advanced (see Figure 10.3).

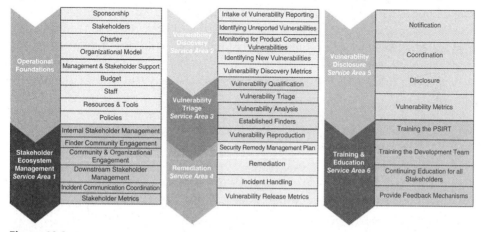

Figure 10.3

One quick look at Figure 10.3 reveals that the PSIRT has now built a robust portfolio of services and capabilities as well as advancing on foundational capabilities. This infers that the process of vulnerability reporting ingestion, analysis, and the subsequent delivery of security updates for the products the PSIRT is responsible for is understood across the organization and its stakeholders.

One of the biggest differentiators for Advanced PSIRTs from others is the shift from a reactive culture to a proactive one. This means actively looking out for vulnerabilities or flaws in products, over-communicating to stakeholders, and being engaged and working cohesively with product engineering teams.

Much of the truth of being advanced means excellent execution of the fundamentals. This includes strong relationships with stakeholders to provide and receive feedback to optimize the function and performance of the PSIRT. This active improvement process is tied to tangible metrics and key productivity indicators (KPIs). Examples include customer satisfaction and service-level objectives and agreements (SLOs/SLAs).

Keeping with the theme of DevSecOps, FIRST mentions that another hallmark of advanced PSIRTs is tight integration and relationships with the Development team to understand the product roadmap and upcoming features and releases. The PSIRT also will have optimized their tooling to handle vulnerability intake, analysis, and reporting processes. The PSIRT also has actively influenced the software development life cycle of the organization's products and services to ensure that vulnerability analysis and scanning is a standardized activity embedded into the development workflow and life cycle.

Given that a PSIRT is constantly engaging with security researchers, often with the same one more than once, they begin to understand the proficiency and validity of the vulnerability reports from the research community and can prioritize reporting and escalations based on this knowledge. Advanced PSIRTs can embody the "shift-left" mantra of the industry by getting engineering teams to take feedback early in the product development life cycle. This includes not just the identification of vulnerabilities but also prioritization and remediation activities.

It is also crucial that the PSIRT understand the ecosystem they operate in, not just downstream to consumers but upstream to their own providers. This awareness is accompanied by clear and actionable communication and expectations in each direction of the software supply chain.

Lastly, given a PSIRT's proficiency in dealing with vulnerabilities and product flaws, the PSIRT can begin to teach others. This could manifest in internal training and communication on product security and vulnerability management practices to optimize not only the PSIRT's performance but also the performance of the development and product teams they support. This not only improves the product and PSIRT's operations but also ideally leads to more secure products for downstream consumers, which is the goal at the end of the day.

To Share or Not to Share and How Much Is Too Much?

One thing a software supplier may find themselves asking in the push for software transparency is what exactly they need to share, or if they should be sharing this data at all. While this decision-making process and analysis will look different for every organization, one thing that is clear is that the push for software transparency from consumers, customers, governmental agencies, and regulatory bodies is continuing to grow due to the increased prevalence of software supply chain attacks and concerns from consumers and the broader industry regarding the risk of unknown and potentially insecure software component consumption.

Factors that dictate what a supplier may be required or compelled to share will be driven by a myriad of factors such as contractual language, consumer requests, and applicable regulatory requirements. Some consumers or industries may require or request that suppliers provide a first-party list of software components, whereas others may require or request an exhaustive, to the extent practical, list of transitive dependencies involved in software and products. Using the NTIA SBOM Minimum Elements Report as an example, with regard to *depth*, the report states that "[an] SBOM should contain all primary (top level) components, with all their transitive dependencies listed. At a minimum, all top-level dependencies must be listed with enough detail to seek out the transitive dependencies recursively."

Obviously, this requirement will only apply to entities in the U.S. federal ecosystem that fall under the NTIA minimum elements requirements, but it can also serve as a useful guide. One thing to note is that the level of effort involved in seeking out transitive dependencies can be extensive, so suppliers not providing this depth to consumers leave the burden on consumers, which is of course exponential across all consumers, rather than being done by the suppliers directly and then communicated to their consumer base. In addition to leaving the work to consumers when it comes to identifying transitive dependencies, only providing top-level dependencies to consumers leaves them blind to vulnerabilities and risks associated with transitive dependencies. As discussed in the "State of Dependency Management" report from Endor Labs, which we have discussed in other chapters, the report found that 95 percent of vulnerable dependencies are transitive dependencies. This means that if an SBOM fails to include transitive dependencies, most vulnerabilities won't be communicated or visible to consumers without them doing the legwork to identify them on their own. This doesn't cover the nuanced analysis and detail of whether the dependency, either direct or transitive, is reachable and exploitable, but it at least provides further context into all dependencies related to the application or product, and their vulnerabilities, rather than just top-level details.

Another key consideration for software suppliers providing SBOMs is whether the SBOMs they provide will be useful and contain enough rich metadata to make them valuable to downstream consumers. One early emerging tool to aid in this activity is the SBOM Scorecard project, provided by eBay (`https://github.com/eBay/sbom-scorecard`).

Another emerging option is a project from the OWASP SCVS project that we discussed in Chapter 6, "Cloud and Containerization." While the project is still underway, it strives to help organizations evaluate BOMs for alignment with organizational policies, formatting, and taxonomy.

Tools such as this along with SBOM Scorecard will be necessary as the industry's adoption of SBOMs continues. As we have discussed, the level of depth, completeness, and accuracy of SBOMs currently varies and organizations will want to ensure alignment with their specific requirements based on their organization or regulations to ensure that the SBOMs they distribute or consume meet their needs (`https://scvs.owasp.org/bom-maturity-model`).

This tool can be used to determine some key criteria, such as whether the SBOM specification is compliant, whether it provides information about how it was generated, as well as information associated with packages, such as having IDs, licensing information, and versioning.

We discussed the NTIA–defined minimum elements for an SBOM in Chapter 4, "Rise of Software Bill of Materials." These minimum elements will be important for federal software suppliers and consumers, given that it is likely to be mandated to align with the minimum element requirements in the federal sector. A useful tool to aid with this is the `ntia-conformance-checker`, which can verify whether SBOM documents have the NTIA–defined minimum elements (`https://github.com/spdx/ntia-conformance-checker`).

Building on these two tools are efforts by organizations such as Chainguard, through their Chainguard Labs endeavor, which in late 2022 looked at a collection of publicly available OSS SBOMs to determine their quality and contents, using methods such as the tools we've discussed (`www.chainguard.dev/unchained/are-sboms-any-good-preliminary-measurement-of-the-quality-of-open-source-project-sboms`).

While their research found that some OSS SBOMs did contain quality data, many did not. None complied with the NTIA minimum element requirements, and a large portion of them lacked package licensing and version information. While this isn't great news, it also should be contrasted with the reality that SBOM adoption, including generation, requirements, and quality, is in its infancy across the industry. However, it is good to have these early research efforts and tools for suppliers to understand existing gaps and how to ensure the SBOMs they provide to downstream consumers are high quality and useful. The push for software component inventory, transparency, and efforts such as SBOMs revolve around data. Without high-quality data, both suppliers and consumers will be overwhelmed with insufficient insight to make risk-informed decisions and drive the sort of organizational outcomes that can help bolster the state of the software supply chain.

Copyleft, Licensing Concerns, and "As-Is" Code

As we have discussed in Chapter 5, "Challenges in Software Transparency," licensing is also a key concern for many suppliers, particularly as it relates to OSS and the licensing applied to it. One licensing method that many software suppliers may be concerned with is what is referred to as *Copyleft*. Copyleft is largely understood to be a licensing method to make a program or software free and requires all subsequent modifications and extended versions of the program to also be free. Copyleft licensing manifests in a variety of licensing

formats, most notably GNU General Public Licensing (GNU GPL; www.gnu
.org/licenses/copyleft.en.html).

With the additional push for software transparency, some vendors likely
have additional concerns around copyright violations, including violations of
Copyleft licensed software. While suppliers should be taking steps to ensure
they are not violating licenses currently, the additional transparency of measures such as SBOMs will disclose OSS components in vendor products and
software. The visibility of licensing will be evident not only for the suppliers,
but also for consumers as free and open source software (FOSS) project maintainers and contributors. Copyright holders, such as FOSS project creators and
maintainers, are the entities that can initiate legal action based on perceived
violations of copyrights, such as Copyleft.

Suppliers should be sure to take additional steps to inventory their software
component usage and ensure they are not violating any applicable copyrights
based on the FOSS software they may be using in their products and software
to avoid potential legal challenges and issues, as well as questions of ethics.

As discussed in the preceding section, insufficient SBOM data, including a lack
of licensing information, will leave suppliers in a position to not fully understand
their licensing compliance. Suppliers need to ensure that they understand the
full extent of their FOSS usage and the associated licensing requirements for
any components involved in the versions of their software.

In addition to being a legal concern, licensing is a potential security concern.
Given the voluntary nature of most OSS, many maintainers make their projects
and code available as is. This means they may not be able or willing to fix concerns raised by downstream consumers. Therefore, consumers and organizations
making use of OSS must be prepared to fork the projects and begin taking on
the responsibility of fixing issues or vulnerabilities they identify since there is
no onus of responsibility or responsiveness on the OSS maintainer. Many in
the industry still do not understand this, and it isn't uncommon to see unrealistic expectations levied toward OSS maintainers to address issues or provide
support when nothing binds them to do so in most cases.

While the use of OSS projects and components has seen tremendous growth,
some organizations seem to misunderstand the dynamics of OSS. When it comes
to software supply chain security, most OSS maintainers should not be considered "suppliers." Your organization generally has no business or contractual
relationship with them, and you are using their code as is, with no expectations
for maintenance, updates, or responsiveness. Therefore, organizations using OSS
in their products, applications, and services need to understand the extent of
their OSS usage and be prepared to take responsibility for components if needed.

This dynamic is captured very well in a blog article by OSS maintainer Thomas Depierre, titled "I am not a supplier" (www.softwaremaxims.com/blog/not-a-supplier).

Depierre lays out how despite the pervasiveness of FOSS in the digital economy, OSS maintainers are not "suppliers" in the traditional sense and downstream consumers are not able to make any demands of them.

Open Source Program Offices

As we have discussed, organizations of every shape, size, and sector have embraced OSS. The financial, medical, and manufacturing industries—and even national security—now use OSS to power their most critical applications and activities. This includes software suppliers, who commonly use OSS as part of their product and application development.

However, this widespread adoption comes with pitfalls: a corresponding increase of almost 800 percent in software supply chain attacks according to the State of the Software Supply Chain Report from Sonatype.

With the rapid growth of OSS adoption, organizations have begun to create open source program offices (OSPOs) to help codify strategies around OSS use and contribution and to foster collaboration with the broader OSS community. These OSPOs often have key responsibilities such as cultivating an OSS strategy, leading its execution, and facilitating the use of OSS products and services across an enterprise (www.linuxfoundation.org/resources/open-source-guides/creating-an-open-source-program).

As organizations continue their adoption and use of OSS, they would benefit tremendously from the beginning to implement an OSPO. The OSPO can help address some of the issues we have discussed in the previous section, as well as some we will discuss next.

While both suppliers as well as enterprise consumers, who are often doing their own internal development activities, can benefit from an OSPO, we will discuss it from the perspective of a software supplier, who often makes use of OSS in their products and software (https://fossa.com/blog/building-open-source-program-office-ospo).

The OSPO's unique position in leading OSS management and strategy makes it a key player in an organization's approach to security and governance of OSS, an increasingly critical role. Studies show that modern applications include more than 500 OSS components. With such widespread use, it's important to recognize some alarming statistics concerning OSS components.

According to a 2022 Synopsys survey, 81 percent include at least one vulnerability, 88 percent haven't had new development in the past two years, and 88 percent of those used were not the latest version. All these metrics culminate in one alarming reality: organizations are making extensive use of outdated and insecure components. This means we have a massive attack surface in modern enterprise environments that are poorly governed and rich in pathways for malicious actors (`www.synopsys.com/content/dam/synopsys/sig-assets/ reports/rep-ossra-2022.pdf`).

By now, readers should be familiar with the U.S. Cybersecurity Executive Order (EO), including Section 4, "Enhancing Software Supply Chain Security." As a result of the EO, NIST has produced comprehensive software supply chain guidance, including open source software controls, which we will discuss here, as well as how OSPOs can advocate for their implementation (`www .nist.gov/itl/executive-order-14028-improving-nations-cybersecurity/ software-security-supply-chains-open`).

NIST lays out its suite of OSS controls in three maturity tiers: foundational, sustaining, and enhancing capabilities. Among those controls are things such as using aspects of the NIST Secure Software Development Framework (SSDF) and ensuring OSS components are acquired via secure channels from trustworthy sources. The reality of the modern enterprise environment is that most organizations don't have full visibility and governance of their own OSS use, let alone ongoing monitoring of the vulnerabilities associated with it. This is a perfect example of where the OSPO shines: as an evangelist for the effective use of commercial OSS products and services, advocating vigilance for the vulnerabilities associated with OSS, and ensuring that these security practices are codified into organizational policies and processes.

NIST's recommended OSS security controls also include establishing internal repositories of known and vetted OSS components that developers can use to reduce organizational risk. Rather than allowing an environment in which developers are free to pull and use all OSS components without insight into their vulnerabilities and risk, internal repositories create a robust library of OSS components that enable developer velocity while also driving down organizational risk due to vulnerable OSS component usage.

Another key recommendation of the NIST SSDF is to implement supporting toolchains, including specifying which tools must be included in the CI/CD pipelines to mitigate risks. Examples could include integrating things such as software composition analysis (SCA) and SBOM tooling into modern CI/CD toolchains to ensure that the enterprise gets full visibility of vulnerable OSS components moving through toolchains and into production environments. This also facilitates the push to "shift security left," ensuring security scans occur earlier in the software development life cycle and that vulnerabilities are identified and remediated prior to introducing them into production, where they can be exploited by malicious actors. Policies and processes that OSPOs can evangelize and codify in this area include not only vulnerability scanning and SBOMs but also enabling signing capabilities that help create immutable records and logs to support both integrity and auditability of software development activities.

The most mature tier laid out by NIST—enhancing capabilities—includes prioritizing the use of secure programming languages and ultimately automating the collection, storage, and scanning of OSS components into the previously mentioned hardened internal repositories. This is perhaps the most critical step to help drive down risk while also not impeding the velocity of development teams, which if hindered would certainly just work around organizational policies and processes to accomplish their tasks.

Among the commonly filled roles in an OSPO are developer relations, advocacy, and evangelism. While these groups often build enthusiasm and interest among the company's development teams, they're also often about forging critical relationships. Those relationships can be leveraged to encourage buy-in to emerging OSS security best practices, which many organizations simply haven't implemented yet despite broad OSS usage in their applications, software, and products. This creates multiple benefits, such as ensuring the organization minimizes use of insecure dependencies and produces more secure applications, whether for internal or external purposes.

Research, such as that from Chinmayi Sharma, also suggests that software vendors are the primary beneficiaries of OSS and are therefore in the best position to help address OSS supply chain risk. This places software vendors in a great position to become more involved in OSS communities, scan for vulnerabilities, and contribute to OSS projects to mitigate them. This would be a shift from the current model in which the OSS community largely shoulders this burden with a lack of equal participation and contribution from the software vendor community. Software suppliers benefit tremendously from the use of OSS in their products and services, and by implementing and maturing an OSPO they can both better understand their OSS usage and its associated risks as well as contribute to the community that they rely so heavily on.

This places OSPOs in a perfect position to lead a paradigm shift and ultimately bolster the security of the broader OSS supply chain. OSS has led to innovations and capabilities in nearly every industry. OSPOs are now positioned to lead the charge of those industries and associated organizations becoming more involved in the OSS community while also addressing the current system risk that OSS poses due to disjointed involvement and investment. This will help drive down some of the risk passed on to downstream consumers of a supplier's software through better governance and security of OSS components used in the supplier's software.

Consistency Across Product Teams

No push for software transparency and providing artifacts such as SBOMs and attestations can be effective if it isn't implemented consistently across the organization's various product teams. It is not uncommon for very large organizations or those with a global presence to have multiple product teams, some with their own tools and SDLC processes.

The authors are aware of at least one automation manufacturer that creates a new legal entity for each product line. So, in essence there are tens or hundreds of legal entities, all producing software under very similar-sounding names that are not always clear to the end consumer. As such, security assessments against one company and its associated development processes do not apply to the other companies and their associated product lines. This can get very complex.

At one point, one of the authors managed application security for a global manufacturing company where there were over 100 different development teams, most of them adopting different practices. The push for standardization was met with a great deal of resistance, some of it due to regional prejudices such as European versus North America opinions of who had the better process.

As the industry at large is still making up its mind about CycloneDX, SPDX, VEX, and VDR, it is no surprise that we may be seeing these inconsistencies within organizations for some time to come. Therefore, it is important that consumers get very specific in the security addendums for contracting as to the practices they expect and intend to hold suppliers accountable.

As software consumers look to both implement standardized processes, governance and customer experiences across their various applications and products, it is important to come to some level of consensus on what those entail. For example, perhaps specific CI/CD tooling may look different but standardized outputs and artifact formats are agreed upon by the different teams.

Manual Effort vs. Automation and Accuracy

One key point that suppliers must consider is the role of automation contrasted with the need for accuracy in the information provided to consumers. Doing software assurance becomes an exercise in scalability for large software companies, especially those with very rapid deployment schedules across hundreds or even thousands of software products. In some instances, the automation may fail to identify a critical software component. For example, a Docker image that loads a component dynamically at runtime or that does not include the component in the Dockerfile may require that the component be manually identified. But it may be helpful to determine what is "good enough" for an initial capture of the SBOM.

If the supplier can produce an SBOM or other artifact that exceeds a certain confidence level, say, 80 percent, is this sufficient for the consumer of that artifact? There will always be some possibility of error, and when automating the process this margin may potentially increase. If not 80 percent, what is your expected confidence level? Who are your customers? Have you spoken to them about realistic expectations? Do you have a process to update and correct a previously erroneous supply chain artifact? To notify your customer? To update any analysis based on this new information? What if the artifact was correct but new analysis insights such as a new CVE are discovered? It's not only the artifact you produce that must be correct, but the insights gained from analysis as well.

One common issue we see, especially with reverse-engineered SBOMs, is a failure to understand what is being analyzed. There are a variety of techniques to identify a component, but some are no more sophisticated than a string match within the file. A comment that says "cve_x was patched in component_version_1.2.3" may be interpreted as the installed component is 1.2.3 when it is in fact 2.0. Doing an exhaustive reverse-engineering exercise for every version is not realistic, so what is your confidence level in these cases? It is probably lower than 80 percent. In the authors' experience, it is frequently closer to 60 percent. So, understanding the method for artifact creation may also factor into the equation.

Does the phase at which the SBOM is produced matter? Design, build, and deployment may also produce SBOMs for the same application that differ substantially. Early-phase SBOMs may not be helpful for the end consumer, and trying to get perfectly automated SBOMs of the build may be an exercise in futility. Perhaps it's good enough for the supplier's internal software assurance practices, and perfection can be reserved for what is ultimately delivered to the customer. This moves much of the manual effort to the end as a quality assurance process and an opportunity to correct any detected deviations.

Summary

In this chapter we encouraged consumers to think broad and deep about the challenge of software supply chain security and the role of the SBOM. We explained why organizations need, or should desire an SBOM and more broadly, software transparency from suppliers as well as recommended potential use cases of how to make use of an SBOM and managing them at scale. We also discussed that while an SBOM may help address some challenges in software supply chain security and transparency, it is far from a panacea and has a ways to go in terms of tooling, automation, standardization and maturity as well. In the next chapter we will discuss software transparency predictions, international efforts and where we're headed as a society with regard to software supply chain security.

CHAPTER 11

Practical Guidance for Consumers

On the flip side of software suppliers are software consumers. These consumers are trying to make sense of the array of guidance, best practices, and requirements that are emerging and inevitably involved in the push-and-pull dynamic of the relationship between suppliers and consumers. Each have different perspectives, incentives, and goals as well and potentially differing regulatory requirements. While some software consumers may be large enterprise environments with robust cybersecurity staff and expertise, this isn't always the case, as many consumers are small and mid-sized businesses (SMBs) with limited to no internal cybersecurity expertise and resources. These smaller organizations often must rely on outside managed service providers and partners, and simply prioritize activities that are realistic based on their resources when it comes to secure software consumption. In this chapter, we discuss some practical guidance for consumers, building on many of the recommendations made in Chapter 7, "Existing and Emerging Commercial Guidance," and Chapter 8, "Existing and Emerging Government Guidance."

Thinking Broad and Deep

While this chapter on guidance for consumers includes discussions and recommendations associated with software bills of materials (SBOMs), we want to emphasize that the SBOM is merely one emerging tool and resource in the broader discussion of software supply chain security. However, given its heavy focus in the industry, we feel compelled to provide some relevant guidance.

As discussed in our landmark cases such as SolarWinds, Log4j, and Kaseya, the risks associated with the software supply chain may be associated with propriety software vendors, open source software (OSS) components, managed service providers, and cloud service providers, among others.

Additionally, as evident by the existing and emerging guidance from sources such as NIST, CNCF, NSA, and others, software supply chain best practices and considerations for consumers involve key activities, including understanding their suppliers, the shared responsibilities in those relationships, the organizational governance surrounding software consumption, as well as internal practices and processes accompanying tooling to ensure the secure consumption, development, and use of software to enable their organizations' unique business and mission needs.

Furthermore, as discussed in Chapter 4, "Rise of Software Bill of Materials," in the section "SBOM Critiques and Concerns," much remains to be resolved in relation to SBOM tooling and operationalization to help organizations successfully ingest, analyze, enrich, and store SBOMs to use as part of their software supply chain and broader Cybersecurity Supply Chain Risk Management (C-SCRM) activities. In addition, some insight must be provided about the current state and maturity of SBOMs for some communities like OSS projects, based on research by various organizations and available tooling evaluation.

As we have touched on in this book, depending on the industry and relevant regulatory factors at play, SBOM adoption rates and the depth of SBOM data differ across the ecosystem, as suppliers aren't necessarily incentivized to provide these artifacts to consumers without either a business benefit or regulatory or procurement/acquisition requirement to do so. Due to these reasons, we want to emphasize that while SBOMs are useful in the push for software transparency and software supply chain security, they should not be viewed as a silver bullet, as is the case with almost any area of cybersecurity. It is a complex problem set with no singular solution, hence the long-standing phrase *defense-in-depth*. The threats facing IT systems involve users, endpoints, data, complex interdependent systems, and more, creating a situation where no single solution or technology can solve all of its associated challenges and threats.

Do I Really Need an SBOM?

With all the hype and confusion surrounding SBOMs, some software consumers may be asking themselves if they even need an SBOM. While the software industry has, of course, existed without the use of SBOMs for decades, it doesn't mean there haven't been challenges, and those are only accelerating with the increased use of OSS and third-party components.

SBOM interest has grown tremendously among both suppliers and consumers in the software industry, and it doesn't appear to be a trend that will slow. According to surveys such as "The State of Software Bill of Materials (SBOM) and Cybersecurity Readiness" from The Linux Foundation, SBOM use increased by 66 percent in 2022 and forecasts project almost 88 percent of organizations will use SBOMs to some extent in 2023 (`www.linuxfounda tion.org/research/the-state-of-software-bill-of-materials-sbom-and-cybersecurity-readiness`).

Modern software and applications are primarily composed of OSS and third-party software components, and without the use of an SBOM or rigorous activities with their own challenges such as software composition analysis (SCA), consumers don't have a strong understanding of the software's components or dependencies they consume. This means consumers currently are and have traditionally consumed software from suppliers with little to no understanding of what components are involved or their vulnerabilities, exploitability, and the risk they potentially pose to the organization and their partners, customers, and stakeholders. As discussed in Chapter 2, "Existing Approaches—Traditional Vendor Risk Management," traditional procurement/acquisition and vendor risk assessment processes simply haven't had the level of depth to include software component inventory and risk management.

While mature and proactive suppliers ideally will publish patches or updates to address vulnerable components in their software, this isn't always the case, as studies suggest by vendors like Veracode in their "State of Software Security" report from 2017 (`www.veracode.com/sites/default/files/pdf/resources/ reports/report-state-of-software-security-2017-veracode-report.pdf`). In this study, Veracode found that only about half of suppliers develop patches for the third-party component vulnerabilities identified in their software. This isn't to say all vulnerable components are exploitable, but it still leaves consumers without context and guidance, and the accompanying residual risk.

Consumers are then left with potentially vulnerable software that they have no idea is vulnerable. Unless they have an SBOM from the supplier for the software in question, showing its included components, consumers cannot correlate for vulnerabilities associated with those components, inquire about their exploitability with their suppliers, or independently assess and validate their vulnerability exploitability. The transparency that an SBOM brings helps alleviate this current gap of visibility and awareness that most software consumers have.

Another reason for the consumer's use of SBOMs is that databases such as the National Vulnerability Database (NVD), which we have discussed in other chapters, show product-level vulnerabilities but typically lack detailed insight into the components involved in the product and the vulnerabilities associated with those specific components. Consumers can't simply rely on legacy approaches of strictly using the NVD and a product's Common Platform Enumeration (CPE) name for visibility or awareness of vulnerable components within the product.

As we have discussed, other vulnerability databases are emerging that provide better capabilities around OSS vulnerabilities as well as support for a package URL (PURL), which can be a more effective approach for identifying component-level vulnerabilities (`https://github.com/package-url/purl-spec`).

As you'll recall, we've discussed efforts by the SBOM Forum in their white paper "A Proposal to Operationalize Component Identification for Vulnerability Management," which called on MITRE and the NVD to adopt PURL for the identification of OSS and commercial software. To some extent, this would help resolve the current gaps that NVD has for component-level vulnerabilities associated with products. As pointed out in the white paper, full-scale automation and the effectiveness of SBOMs will be inhibited until this naming challenge is resolved or at least significantly improved.

While suppliers may frequently be proactive in identifying vulnerabilities in their components and products, remediating them, and notifying their consumers, this isn't always the case. Having component visibility allows the consumer to maintain awareness of component-level vulnerabilities and notify suppliers of new component vulnerabilities as the consumer identifies them (if not previously notified from the supplier, which would be ideal). It also empowers the consumer to inquire about the exploitability of identified vulnerabilities, if the supplier isn't actively providing that context. As we will discuss soon, it also enables consumers to implement methods like virtual patches for when there are circumstances of known vulnerabilities for which a supplier hasn't yet issued a remediation or patch and may never.

This places the onus on the supplier knowing consumers are aware of and concerned with component vulnerabilities. The reality is, identifying and remediating vulnerabilities has a cost associated with it, and suppliers aren't necessarily incentivized to do this proactively over other revenue-generating activities, for example, such as product and feature development.

Asset inventory has been a security best practice and critical control in sources such as SANS and Center for Internet Security (CIS) guidance for years. However, the conversation has matured to software asset inventory and now software component asset inventory as the industry realizes the risk that a single software component can cause to not just an organization but entire industries.

Knowing that it isn't practical for organizations to adopt all security controls or prioritize their implementation equally, CIS provides a list of critical security controls correlated with the most pervasive attacks in the ecosystem. CIS states the list is a "must do, do first" starting point for every enterprise seeking to improve their security defense (`www.cisecurity.org/controls`).

The CIS Critical Security Controls are mapped to other industry frameworks such as Payment Card Industry Data Security Standard (PCI DSS), Health Insurance Portability and Accountability Act (HIPAA), North American Electric

Reliability Corporation Critical Infrastructure Protection (NERC CIP), and Federal Information Security Modernization Act (FISMA), all of which also discuss the need for software inventory to some extent. While traditionally this may have meant applications, it is increasingly moving to a more granular software asset inventory with the proliferation of software supply chain attacks and vulnerable software components.

As the CIS guidance points out, the inventory and control of software assets is a critical foundation for preventing attacks. Malicious actors often seek out vulnerable software versions that they can exploit. This can lead to various impacts on the organization, including moving laterally to other enterprise assets and even a cascading scenario where they pivot outside of the initial targeted organization to business partners, customers, or other organizations to which the target has access.

Without having a robust and accurate software asset inventory, consumers will not be able to determine where or if vulnerable components exist in their environment or if there are other concerns such as those related to licensing.

In addition to playing a pivotal role on the software component asset inventory front, SBOMs aid other use cases for consumers as well, such as incident response teams. In the wake of the Log4j incident, for example, it was reported by the Cyber Safety Review Board (CSRB), as we've discussed, that some federal agencies spent tens of thousands of hours investigating the incident and trying to find the presence of vulnerable Log4j components in their enterprise environments.

While incident responses in large complex environments will inevitably take time regardless of the context, if the incident is tied to a vulnerable software component such as Log4j and your organization lacks a comprehensive software component inventory, it will be incredibly difficult to determine where and to what extent your organization is vulnerable.

Procurement and acquisition are other examples where an SBOM is valuable from the consumer's perspective. As consumers often go through processes to vet new applications and suppliers for use in their enterprises or to facilitate business processes, it is key to understand the potential risk that those suppliers pose.

It isn't uncommon for organizations to use methods such as requesting vulnerability scans, penetration test reports, compliance artifacts such as SOC 2, and so forth to help them determine the suitability of using a specific vendor or supplier. However, this activity historically doesn't include software component inventory data, leaving consumers largely unaware of the software component makeup of the products included, in addition to being uninformed as to the vulnerabilities associated with the third-party software components suppliers may be using in their products.

By requesting SBOMs and Vulnerability Exploitability eXchange (VEX) documents from suppliers, consumers are empowered to understand any vulnerabilities associated with their suppliers' products, their exploitability, and the potential impact these products could have on their organizations' security posture before moving too far in the procurement and acquisition process.

Another key SBOM consideration for consumers is to ensure that they work with their suppliers to receive SBOMs in a format the consumers can support (for example, if their internal tooling and capabilities are oriented around SPDX or CycloneDX, rather than having the capability to support both). Consumers can use methods such as contract terms to require that suppliers provide specific formats based on their individual needs and capabilities. Consumers can also use their contract terms to define not just the format of SBOMs they require but also the frequency, delivery method, required fields, and more. Examples of this include the U.S. federal sector, which is rallying around the National Telecommunications and Information Administration (NTIA)–defined minimum elements for an SBOM that define the required field and contents.

What Do I Do with It?

Great—you have received SBOMs from your software suppliers or begun creating them yourself based on your internal development efforts. Now, what do you do with the SBOMs to make them valuable and actionable?

As we previously discussed, an SBOM can be valuable for a variety of use cases such as vulnerability management, dependency hygiene, incident response, licensing, and procurement. The key to making them actionable involves integrating the SBOMs into your organizational policies and processes and involving the relevant stakeholders who can help make the artifacts valuable related to their respective roles and responsibilities.

While the industry has quickly seen the proliferation of tools to help create SBOMs as we discussed in Chapter 4, when it comes to ingesting, analyzing, enriching, storing, and reporting on SBOMs and their associated data-at-scale, the industry still has quite a bit of maturing to do.

This maturation also applies to other challenges such as legacy software or cloud environments, the latter of which has the industry yet to come to a uniform consensus on what an SBOM in the cloud context looks like due to the complexity of cloud environments and the myriad of interdependencies between services and providers.

Without having a coherent plan of what to do with SBOMs upon their creation or reception, organizations will be left with artifacts that potentially could provide insight into vulnerabilities, risks, and dependencies, but they won't become valuable unless they're made actionable through the organization's use of technology and supporting policies and processes. SBOMs have tremendous use cases, as we have discussed, but organizations must have a plan in place to make proper use of them to avoid adding additional cognitive load, both individually and organizationally, for little return on investment.

Receiving and Managing SBOMs at Scale

While viewed individually, the idea of an SBOM and its use to illuminate the software components involved in products and being consumed seems logical. Yet the idea of doing it at scale in large enterprise environments across hundreds or thousands of development teams and many third-party software suppliers can quickly become daunting. How does an organization manage all this data-at-scale? How do you ensure you have a robust and comprehensive approach to continuously handle SBOMs to drive decisions around risk, procurement, and some other use cases we have discussed?

There are a variety of methods in which a consumer can receive or obtain an SBOM. One useful resource that expands on these options is the NTIA white paper titled "Sharing and Exchanging SBOMs" that came out of the NTIA multistakeholder process on Software Component Transparency that we have discussed in other chapters (https://ntia.gov/sites/default/files/publications/ntia_sbom_sharing_exchanging_sboms-10feb2021_0.pdf).

In the context of the NTIA guidance, the SBOM exchange includes advertisement or discovery and access. Advertisement or discovery involves publishing and locating the SBOM or registering an endpoint to receive SBOM updates.

Access is at the other end of the process of retrieving or transmitting the SBOM itself. Some examples include websites, emails, File Transfer Protocol (FTP), application programming interfaces (APIs), or source code management (SCM) systems. Some examples in the guidance expand on the URL included in product literature or packaging from suppliers, where consumers can navigate to view the SBOM. While this may be useful to understand the initial components involved in a product, it is easy to see where challenges will occur as product updates and new components are introduced. It will require that the product's URL be kept up-to-date with the latest components across the various versions of the product.

Package management tools also can facilitate the distribution and retrieval of SBOMs, appearing as an SBOM in the top-level directory of a software repository or as the SBOM for a container manifest file.

Another example provided by NTIA is the ability to establish a publish and subscriber system for SBOMs. This system creates a situation where upstream suppliers can regularly publish updated SBOMs for downstream consumers to retrieve the information, either manually or via automation. This situation enables a constant flow of communication on the software component's makeup to downstream consumers from suppliers providing near-real-time SBOM flow.

SBOMs are oriented around the two data interchange formats of JSON and XML, which enable machine readability and automation that's critical to scale. While these artifacts can be understood by humans, using computers to ingest and parse the SBOM data is far more efficient and scalable. It also enables enrichment through processes like performing vulnerability analysis or integrations with databases and other storage systems. It can aid in integrating SBOM data into existing organizational tooling and workflows to make more informed decisions driven by software component and vulnerability data.

The modern enterprise environment involves several internal development teams as well as a myriad of external and third-party software suppliers. Given that industry guidance recommends the creation and reception of a new SBOM with every software release, it's easy to see why the idea of a static-based artifact and delivery mechanism for SBOMs isn't scalable or logical in most modern technology environments.

Large enterprise organizations have and will continue to develop organic capabilities oriented around APIs and automation to facilitate the creation, ingestion, enrichment, analysis, and storage of SBOMs at scale. We will see the continued growth of managed service providers (MSPs) and vendors providing platforms to aid in the SBOM's use and governance for organizations who either don't want to do it internally or lack the resources and expertise to do so. Some of these may take the form of escrow organizations to function as a trusted third party or intermediary between suppliers and consumers.

In addition to obtaining an SBOM, consumers should verify the integrity and origin of the SBOM to determine its validity. This includes making use of digital signatures and hashes for SBOMs and their associated components and attestations to the extent that they exist, which can provide insight into the actual build environment and processes used to develop and distribute software in addition to its components and makeup.

As SBOMs increasingly become a key artifact used by organizations as part of their software supply chain practices, malicious actors will inevitably seek to exploit them and their associated practices to bypass organizational security measures and compromise organizations across the ecosystem.

As pointed out by NTIA in their "Software Consumers Playbook: SBOM Acquisition, Management, and Use" guidance (www.ntia.gov/files/ntia/publications/software_consumers_sbom_acquisition_management_and_use_-_final.pdf), organizations can often make best use of SBOMs by having their data fed into organizational workflows. This takes SBOMs from being a singular artifact viewed in isolation, and reframes them as a collection of data that can be parsed, extracted, and loaded into other automated organizational processes. This reframing can be facilitated by internally developed OSS tooling that facilitates extracting data from SBOMs or commercial tooling providers.

The guidance points out that a variety of commercial solutions and specific industry use cases ranging from medical devices, fleet management, and others, are currently moving toward SBOM adoption. This movement creates a situation where subsets of SBOM data such as specific components, suppliers, versions, and other data can provide relevant insights across an organization's environment for specific use cases and purposes. It will allow organizations to couple SBOM data with other relevant data and insights to improve a variety of business and mission decisions.

When it comes to SBOM reception and storage by software consumers, there should be an expectation of safe storage and access control on the consumer's part, unless otherwise authorized by the software supplier. Many software suppliers understandably have concerns around broadly disclosing their SBOMs because it exposes vulnerabilities in their applications and products that can be taken advantage of by malicious actors.

Ideally, suppliers are actively addressing vulnerabilities in their products, but as with any organization, many suppliers are dealing with constraints around resources such as time, budget, and expertise, which means having products that are entirely free of vulnerabilities isn't often likely or practical. For this reason, consumers who have been provided SBOMs by their suppliers should take the appropriate steps to safeguard their artifacts and data to avoid unauthorized access or disclosure. Examples include the OMB 22-18 memo, which calls for specific U.S. federal agencies to implement appropriate mechanisms for information protection and the sharing of artifacts like SBOMs that they receive from third-party software suppliers.

Reducing the Noise

Having an SBOM is a great beginning, but without context around the actual exploitability of vulnerabilities, it will largely become additional noise, straining consumers and their various stakeholders. Therefore, it is key to acquire granular information around software components like exploitability.

Previously discussed in Chapter 4, the Vulnerability Exploitability eXchange (VEX) is quickly becoming a non-negotiable companion document for SBOMs among the practitioner community. The reason is that without the context of exploitability, software consumers will have no guidance or insight to help drive their vulnerability prioritization activities as part of vulnerability management. When software consumers are empowered with information about the exploitability of their vulnerabilities, they can better understand what components of an application warrant additional attention and present actual risk.

This empowerment and context creates a situation in which, although VEX may accompany an initial SBOM, it's possible for additional VEX documents and communication to occur even without a change to the underlying software components communicated via the SBOM. The reason is because new vulnerabilities are constantly being discovered and reported without changes to the VEX–associated software. A new vulnerability may be discovered for a preexisting software component, which would mean a new VEX would need to be provided to software consumers informing them of the exploitability of that new vulnerability. Open source, industry-driven efforts such as the OpenVEX specification have begun to gain momentum in the industry, in an attempt to meet the VEX requirements and use cases as discussed by CISA and others and to provide a minimal SBOM format-agnostic method to create, merge, and attest to VEX documents to communicate exploitability of vulnerabilities associated with SBOMs and software (`https://github.com/openvex/spec`).

One bill of material (BOM) format is CycloneDX, which boasts robust support for providing context as it relates to vulnerable components to help consumers better prioritize their vulnerability management efforts. CycloneDX provides additional capabilities outside of an SBOM, including support for VEX to convey the exploitability of vulnerability components used in products. It can also support vulnerability disclosure reports (VDRs) to communicate known and unknown vulnerabilities affecting components and services and even a bill of vulnerabilities (BoV) that can be used to share vulnerability data between systems and sources of vulnerability intelligence.

Lastly, knowing that we have a complex modern ecosystem of software, services, and components, CycloneDX provides support for what is known as a *BOM-Link*, which enables us to reference components, services, or vulnerabilities in BOMs from other systems.

Consumers should be adamant in requiring that suppliers supply accompanying artifacts like VEX documents to provide insight into the exploitability of vulnerable components in their products and applications. Failing to do so leaves the consumer with a significant amount of effort and guesswork related to trying to address vulnerabilities in the software they consume.

In addition to using VEX and other methods previously discussed, software consumers can leverage industry vulnerability databases we have discussed beyond NVD, such as OSV, OSS Index, and more, along with enriching vulnerability data with the Exploit Prediction Scoring System (EPSS) and threat intelligence to improve the fidelity of vulnerability insights and prioritize the vulnerabilities posing the greatest risk to an organization.

The Divergent Workflow—I Can't Just Apply a Patch?

As we have discussed in the previous sections, the reality is that despite vulnerabilities being present in suppliers' software and products, these vulnerabilities often may not have available fixes or patches that consumers can simply apply. This could be due to resource constraints the supplier has, patching and remediation timelines, competing feature backlogs, or simply a lack of further support and sustainment from a software supplier or project.

Studies from groups like Aberdeen Strategy & Research, for example, found that out of over 20,000 vulnerabilities discovered in 2020, vendors didn't issue patches for almost 20 percent of them by the end of the year. This included thousands of vulnerabilities with publicly available exploits as well. The reality is that much like software consumers who historically struggle to apply patches even when available to vulnerable applications, vendors often struggle to keep up the pace when it comes to issuing patches for known vulnerabilities in their products and software.

As a result, it creates a situation where consumers must take other measures to address the risks which those vulnerabilities or flaws present that don't involve patching the suppliers' software directly. Often, it culminates in what the industry refers to as *virtual patching*, which is defined by the Open World-wide Application Security Project (OWASP) as "a security policy enforcement layer which prevents the exploitation of a known vulnerability" (`https://owasp` `.org/www-community/Virtual_Patching_Best_Practices`).

In the case of web applications, this generally involves being able to intercept transactions and data flows and ensuring that malicious traffic looking to exploit the known vulnerability doesn't make it to the web application. This often takes the form of web application firewalls (WAFs), which are generally deployed to protect web applications from malicious attacks like cross-site scripting (XSS) or SQL injection that look to compromise flaws and vulnerabilities in the application.

Numerous studies show that nearly half of vulnerabilities disclosed have no patch available from their supplier upon the vulnerability's disclosure. This shows a progressive attempt to communicate quickly with the consumer community regarding known vulnerabilities and risks, but it inevitably also creates a situation of widely disclosing a vulnerability with no patch for consumers to use to remediate the risk.

In addition to the constraints from the suppliers' end with having patches available, it is also common for there to be business or mission constraints that don't always allow traditional patching to be an option, even if a patch is available from a supplier. For example, there may be concerns about taking mission or business-critical systems offline or the potential to disrupt systems generating revenue for the organization. Organizations may also defer applying available patches from vendors and suppliers until a scheduled maintenance window, instead deferring to using a virtual patch in the interim to mitigate the risk.

It's situations like these where the practice of virtual patching comes into play for software consumers. In addition to methods such as WAFs, software consumers can make changes to environments, systems, and configurations to try to mitigate the exploitability or impact of a vulnerability based on the specific details of the vulnerability being discussed.

While some organizations may have mature approaches to virtual patching in place already, many others often do not. One great resource to use is the "Virtual Patching Cheat Sheet" from OWASP (`https://cheatsheetseries.owasp.org/cheatsheets/Virtual_Patching_Cheat_Sheet.html`). It proposes a virtual patching methodology of six steps that includes preparation, identification, analysis, virtual patch creation, implementation/testing, and recovery/follow-up. Let's look at each of these steps next.

Preparation

The preparation phase involves prepping the organization to establish a virtual patching process prior to needing to deal with vulnerabilities or intrusion. As OWASP points out, incidents can be tense, chaotic periods and trying to establish a process during chaos is a recipe for disaster. Organizations must ensure that they are monitoring for alerts from their suppliers and vendors using sources like mailing lists and public vulnerability disclosures. You'll recall that we discussed this being a key capability in Chapter 9, "Software Transparency in Operational Technology." Consumers also need to obtain pre-authorization to sidestep traditional organizational patching and governance processes to apply the virtual patch as quickly as possible. Consumers will need to deploy their virtual patching tooling *prior* to incidents or activities so that they can respond quickly. Lastly, they will need to establish HTTP audit logging to monitor web traffic fields like the request URI as well as request-and-response headers and bodies. This data will enable consumers to identify applicable traffic and respond in future phases.

Identification

Once consumers have prepared to implement virtual patching, they can begin identifying vulnerabilities in their environment. OWASP defines identification as either proactive or reactive. On the proactive front, an organization is actively assessing their web security posture using methods like penetration testing and automated web assessments or by reviewing the source code of their applications to identify flaws. Reactive identification, which is the norm for all but the most mature organizations, involves identifying vulnerabilities through methods like being contacted by the vendor, coming across a public disclosure, or worst of all, experiencing an actual security incident.

Analysis

During the analysis phase, several activities are involved to ensure that the organization can properly respond to an identified vulnerability, including determining the applicability of a virtual patch. What is the actual vulnerability or flaw? Do the organization's tools and capabilities provide the proper mechanism to address it? The vulnerability also must be captured in the organization's tracking or ticketing system and have a proper vulnerability identifier applied. It may be a CVE name and number, an identifier defined during the vulnerability's announcement from a supplier, or even one assigned to it through the organization's vulnerability scanning tools. The key here is to internally use a uniform name for any vulnerability to ensure a coherent response and tracking process.

In addition to properly identifying and tracking the vulnerability, the organization must understand the impact level of the vulnerability. Not all vulnerabilities are created equally and they come in varying levels of severity. Organizations will need to capture which specific versions of software are impacted, and then determine where these versions of the software exist within their environment. While the version and presence of the software is key, an organization must also document the specific configuration required to allow the vulnerability to be exploited. For some vulnerabilities, this may be something as trivial as their mere existence, while others may require specific configurations or environmental factors to exist for the vulnerability to be exploited. Lastly, OWASP recommends capturing the proof of concept (PoC) exploit code if it was made available in the vulnerability's announcement. This exploit code can be used by organizations as they start to create their virtual patch to address the vulnerability.

Virtual Patch Creation

You've prepared, identified the vulnerability, and analyzed it, and now you're prepared to create the virtual patch. What does this involve? OWASP defines two overarching tenets that virtual patching is bound by, which include no false positives and negatives. This means you don't want to block legitimate traffic, which could negatively impact the mission, business, revenue, customers, and so on. In addition, you don't want false negatives, which allow malicious traffic through, potentially due to the malicious actor evading detection. Obviously achieving these goals 100 percent of the time is a lofty goal, but it's one worth striving for in order to avoid your attempts at virtual patching having a negative impact on your organization.

Virtual patches can be created either manually or automatically. On the manual front, it may look like creating allow lists to perform input validation and denying anything that doesn't align with the defined criteria. Another manual method is the use of a block list based on a set of rules and criteria related to the attack and vulnerability that blocks any traffic meeting the criteria. OWASP points out that this method, while an option, isn't ideal. In this case, the potential for false negatives is higher, and the chance that malicious activity can slip by, avoiding the specific criteria, is present. For example, we previously mentioned PoC exploit code that may have been made available during the vulnerability's announcement. Organizations can use this code to create block lists.

OWASP's Virtual Patching Cheat Sheet points out that both approaches of allow or block lists have pros and cons. Block lists are easier/quicker to come up with but also allow for more potential to be evaded. Allow lists are more restrictive but also require more precision given that anything not aligned with it will be blocked, including legitimate business and mission-oriented traffic that can cause organizational disruptions. These sorts of situations can hinder trust from the business to security and risk the authority to quickly apply virtual patches in the future.

Beyond manual virtual patch creation processes, it is also possible in some cases to implement automated virtual patches. OWASP points to several examples such as OWASP's ModSecurity Core Rule Set (CRS) Scripts, ThreadFix Virtual Patching, and direct importing to the WAF device. These options use methods such as taking imported XML vulnerability data from tools and converting it into virtual patches to protect systems. While these patches are ideal and a key part of scaling virtual patching practices, they often also require some manual involvement, tuning, and oversight to ensure their effectiveness.

Implementation and Testing

Once a virtual patch has been created, organizations must begin testing and implementing it to protect their organizations from malicious actors looking to exploit the associated vulnerabilities. Organizations may make use of various applications during this phase like the web browser, command-line interface (CLI), and proxy servers, among others. OWASP recommends testing virtual patches in a log-only configuration initially to not block legitimate user traffic and to ensure the virtual patch's effectiveness. Once this is completed and verified, the virtual patch can block traffic that could be malicious. If it aligns with the previously defined allow or block lists, it can be fully implemented while having a level of assurance that it won't impede the business and its operations.

Recovery and Follow-up

The last phase OWASP identifies for virtual patching is the recovery and follow-up phase. This phase involves activities like updating data in the organization's ticketing system, performing periodic reassessments, and running virtual patch alert reports. Proper updating of ticketing systems allows organizations to gauge metrics associated with vulnerability management for virtual patching and capture relevant data for future incidents. Reassessments can be used to determine when and if the virtual patch can be removed (e.g., if the web application source code has been fixed directly). Reports can be used to provide information when a virtual patch has been triggered, providing insight into potential malicious activity and traffic underway looking to impact the organization.

Long-Term Thinking

One thing to keep in mind is that a virtual patch can be thought of as a bandage—a temporary solution to a permanent problem. While it's an excellent method to protect vulnerable applications that can't be patched directly or can't be remediated due to concerns around business interruption and mission impacts, a virtual patch should be viewed as a temporary remediation. Organizations must be conscious of the fact that malicious actors can bypass a WAF using a variety of creative methods as well. For example, in 2022, application security firm Claroty demonstrated that they could bypass five of the most popular vendors in the WAF space by using JSON to obfuscate database commands and evade detection by the WAF tools (`www.darkreading.com/application-security/popular-wafs-json-bypass`).

This reality means that organizations must have long-term plans set in place to remediate application vulnerabilities at the source, as well as have sound security architecture and engineering practices like zero trust in place, to mitigate the risk of lateral movement or further limit the blast radius and business impact if malicious actors bypass the virtual patch mechanisms.

Summary

In this chapter, we provided practical guidance for software consumers, which includes thinking broadly and deeply about the extent of their software consumption and the various sources and potential attack vectors associated with it. We also discussed the emergence of SBOMs and their relevance from the perspective of software consumers, while also highlighting some potential gaps and areas of improvement that need to be addressed by software consumers seeking to operationalize SBOMs as part of their cybersecurity supply chain risk management (C-SCRM) strategies and processes. We discussed how software consumers must be prepared to use methods like virtual patching to address vulnerabilities, especially when it comes to their OSS consumption but also when dealing with vendors who may not have addressed vulnerabilities in a timely fashion. In the next chapter, we lay out where we are headed as an industry and as a society, along with some predictions of what is on the horizon for the software transparency movement.

Software Transparency Predictions

By now it should be clear that the topic of software transparency and efforts to bolster the security posture of the broader software supply chain are anything but fleeting. We are seeing a myriad of efforts across the public and private sectors worldwide in terms of regulations, tooling, technologies, and frameworks.

Because of the exponential increases in software supply chain attacks, including the landmark cases we have discussed, the emerging frameworks, and the growing maturity of the vulnerability database and scoring ecosystem, software supply chain security is an area experiencing tremendous attention and innovation.

In this chapter, we discuss emerging regulations, requirements, and potential solutions that could play a significant role in this innovation, and explore where we may be headed next.

Emerging Efforts, Regulations, and Requirements

On the emerging regulations and requirements front, it should be clear now that governments around the world are waking up to the criticality of software to their institutions, agencies, and overall societies. Software has become inextricably linked to nearly every aspect of modern society, woven into everything from simple daily leisure activities to even the most critical infrastructure and national security. Throughout this book, we have cited testimony from elected officials, defense leaders, and technology giants, emphasizing how important software is to modern society across every critical industry and sector.

Governments are finally beginning to acknowledge the societal dependence on software and starting to make investments to recognize open source software (OSS) as a public good, due to its pervasiveness across every aspect of modern society. Germany has recently made efforts to launch a sovereign technology fund to support OSS (`https://sciencebusiness.net/news/germany-launch-sovereign-tech-fund-secure-digital-infrastructure`). Their leadership has commented on the importance of OSS in modern digital infrastructure despite its fragility as an ecosystem.

In the UK, a group called OpenUK launched a "Summer of Open Source Software Security" in 2022. Leaders involved in the initiative emphasized the reality that modern national critical infrastructure is being built on OSS. The effort focused on the need to secure and maintain OSS due to the national critical infrastructure's dependence on it (`https://openuk.uk/launching-the-openuk-summer-of-open-source-software-security`).

Another notable piece of legislation worth mentioning is the "Securing Open Source Software Act of 2022," which was introduced to the U.S. Senate in September 2022. This bill set forth duties for the Cybersecurity Information Security Agency (CISA) regarding OSS security. Among the responsibilities for CISA are performing industry outreach and engagement, supporting federal efforts to secure OSS, and coordinating with non-federal entities to ensure the long-term security of OSS. CISA was tasked to publish a framework that would include government, industry, and the OSS community itself, focused on securing OSS and the best practices associated with doing so. The bill also included language for a critical infrastructure assessment study and pilot to determine the role OSS plays in U.S. critical infrastructure (`www.congress.gov/bill/117th-congress/senate-bill/4913`).

While some of these references, as well as items such as the Department of Defense's (DoD) OSS memo, which we have previously discussed, may make it seem like the push for and interest in both using and governing the use of OSS is accelerating, studies from sources such as the Center for Strategic and International Studies (CSIS) published in early 2023 point out that the U.S. government has been publishing policies related to OSS for several decades. The report cites 669 OSS policy initiatives across governments around the world between 1999 and 2022 (see Figure 12.1).

That said, the accelerated use of OSS, which appears in 97 percent of the codebases we have discussed, coupled with the accelerated attacks against the software supply chain, are spurring interest—and will continue to do so—from governments and industry in securing the software supply chain.

In the United States, we have seen tremendous government activity around securing the software supply chain. While various efforts were underway, the publication of Executive Order (EO) 14028, "Improving the Nation's Cyber-security," inarguably accelerated this reality. Section 4 of the EO, "Enhancing Software Supply Chain Security," specifically focuses on this challenge and tasks various governmental entities across the United States with producing guidance, requirements, and more to address the risks across the software supply chain.

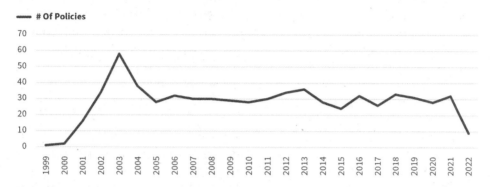

Figure 12.1

Source: www.csis.org/analysis/governments-role-promoting-open-source-software, Center for Strategic & International Studies

Among the requirements in the EO was one for the National Institute of Standards and Technology (NIST) to produce "guidance identifying practices to enhance the security of the software supply chain." NIST went on to update their Secure Software Development Framework (SSDF) (https://csrc.nist.gov/Projects/ssdf) along with providing dedicated software supply chain guidance per the EO (www.nist.gov/system/files/documents/2022/02/04/software-supply-chain-security-guidance-under-EO-14028-section-4e.pdf).

Building on that guidance, the Office of Management and Budget (OMB) produced a memo titled "Enhancing the Security of the Software Supply Chain through Secure Software Development Practices" (M-22-18). This memo mentions the U.S. government's reliance on technologies and digital products as well as the persistent threats they face that may impede the government's ability to provide services on which the public relies.

The memo requires U.S. federal agencies to comply with the NIST guidance previously mentioned when using third-party software on agency information systems or that impacts agency data. It applies to all the agency's use of software after the date of the memo's publication, including not just new procurements but any major version changes to existing third-party software use as well.

It is worth noting that the memo specifically excludes agency-developed software, which of course raises concerns about the security of said software and requires internal agency measures to ensure that appropriate secure software development activities occur. Federal agencies are far from being immune to security incidents, with examples such as the breach of the Office of Personnel and Management (OPM) that occurred in 2015 and exposed the data of over 21 million Americans.

The memo states that agencies must *only* use software provided by software producers who are able to self-attest compliance with the previously mentioned NIST guidance. It calls on the agencies' chief information officers (CIOs) and chief acquisition officers (CAOs) to ensure these requirements are met. Software producers must be able to provide self-attestations in the form of *conformance statements*, and these self-attestations must be obtained by the agency for *all* third-party software under the memo's requirements. The memo also empha-sizes the need to make their attestations inclusive of their product portfolios to enable the reuse of the attestations across all purchasing agencies, which can drive efficiencies and data sharing across the U.S. federal ecosystem.

Knowing that software producers may not be able to meet aspects of SSDF and the NIST software supply chain guidance in their entirety (either initially or potentially ever), the memo also allows for the use of what are known as plans of action and milestones (POAMs). POAMs allow software vendors to document gaps in their attestations of compliance, explaining mitigating controls/measures, planned dates to close them, and so on. It's a mechanism that exists in other compliance programs like the Federal Risk and Authorization Management Program (FedRAMP) and internal agency system authorizations under the NIST Risk Management Framework (RMF).

Vendors will need to provide details about the organization and the product(s) being covered under the attestation, and then document their alignment with secure development guidance and capture it in a standardized self-attestation form. Agencies will have the option to request a third-party assessment if the service or software is considered critical and the risk warrants it. These third-party assessments may include groups like FedRAMP third-party assessment organizations (3PAOs).

Something worth pointing out in the case of both self-assessments and even more likely 3PAOs is the potential for reducing the number of available software vendors with which the federal government can work. As previously mentioned when discussing FedRAMP, the FedRAMP Marketplace (`https://marketplace .fedramp.gov/#!/products?sort=productName`), which is where FedRAMP authorized cloud service offerings are listed, has roughly 300 authorized cloud services at the time of this writing that the federal government can use, despite the marketplace having been around for a decade and there being tens of thou-sands of cloud providers in the broader commercial market for consumption. So, while these 3PAO efforts are well intended and potentially identify more secure vendors and offerings, they also constrain the number of available ven-dors and offerings for consumption due to the prohibitive cost and requirements that compliance incurs.

Many argue that the risk of losing access to innovative vendors and solutions should be considered in the broader discussion of risk and not isolated to strictly cybersecurity. That means the business/mission risk of failing to innovate and modernize is also considered in the equation. That said, as we have mentioned, some leaders, like Joshua Corman, have also argued for "fewer better suppliers" as well, in attempts to have a more secure supply chain of reliable and secure offerings and components. Both arguments, of course, have merit and will vary depending on the individual's and the organization's risk tolerance.

In addition to self-attesting or being assessed by a third party for conformance with the NIST software supply chain and secure development guidance, agencies also may require software bill of materials (SBOMs) in their solicitation requirements, particularly if it is deemed "critical software" as defined by NIST, which we have previously discussed and that is captured in another OMB memo titled "Protecting Critical Software Through Enhanced Security Measures" (www .whitehouse.gov/wp-content/uploads/2021/08/M-21-30.pdf).

The SBOMs the vendors provide must align with the National Telecommunications and Information Association (NTIA)-defined SBOM formats and include the minimum elements also defined by NTIA discussed in Chapter 4, "Rise of Software Bill of Materials." Much like the self-attestations, the OMB memo emphasizes the need for reciprocity/reuse of the SBOMs across agencies to avoid duplicative work by both the agencies and the vendors. Building on the potential for using SBOMs, agencies may require other artifacts such as vulnerability and integrity outputs related to code and proof of participation in vulnerability disclosure programs.

Leaders in the Federal Energy Regulatory Commission (FERC) have also begun voicing desires to update critical infrastructure protection (CIP) standards tied to protecting electrical utilities and other energy sector entities. These desires include calls for increased software transparency and pointing out concerns with self-attestations, rather than artifacts such as SBOMs, which provide machine-readable evidence of vulnerable software components, or lack thereof (www.nextgov.com/cybersecurity/2022/12/ ferc-chairman-wants-update-cybersecurity-requirements/380666).

This seems to be the direction of organizations such as FERC and the North American Electric Reliability Corporation (NERC) based on documents from organizations like the Edison Electric Institute, which in October 2022 published Module Procurement Contract Language Addressing Cybersecurity Supply Chain Risk 3.0. This document lists a requirement R.1.2.5, "Proposed EEI Contract Language," which focuses on hardware, firmware, software, and patch integrity and authenticity. Section (e) specifically states that "Contractor shall provide a software bill of materials for produced (including licensed) products consisting of a list of components and associated metadata that make up a component" (www.eei.org/-/media/Project/EEI/Documents/Issues-and-Policy/Model--Procurement-Contract.pdf).

Another place software supply chain security and SBOMs showed up was in the initial version and language of the U.S. 2023 National Defense Authorization Act. In Section 6722, titled "DHS Software Supply Chain Risk Management," the text called for a bill of materials to be included when submitting bid proposals and a certification that each item listed on the submitted BOM be "free from all known vulnerabilities or defects affecting the security of the end product or service." It requires using sources such as NIST's National Vulnerability Database (NVD), which we've discussed along with other databases that track security vulnerabilities and defects of OSS and third-party software. Many in the industry immediately jumped on this language to point out the impracticality of having vulnerability-free software; however, it is worth mentioning that the language also allows notifications for plans to mitigate, repair, and resolve each security vulnerability or defect that did exist in the BOM.

One notable example of industry pushback came from a letter published by the Alliance for Digital Innovation, a group that represents industry tech giants like AWS, Google Cloud, and VMware. The letter petitioned Congress "to remove the SBOM language from the NDAA and give industry and agencies more time to develop solutions that will better secure the country's cybersecurity supply chain." For those interested in the letter, it can be found here: https://alliance4digitalinnovation.org/wp-content/uploads/2022/10/NDAA-FY23-Letter-Final.pdf.

While early versions of the 2023 National Defense Authorization Act (NDAA) did include language for SBOMs and further software supply chain transparency, it appears industry lobbying efforts and concerns prevailed, with SBOM and vulnerability language being removed from the final text of the 2023 NDAA. (See www.congress.gov/117/bills/hr7776/BILLS-117hr7776enr.pdf). It will remain to be seen if SBOM and software supply chain language makes its way back into future-year versions of the U.S. NDAA. That said, as we have discussed elsewhere, individual entities in the defense community, like the U.S. Army are making their efforts around SBOM with a request for information (RFI) and other contractual avenues and signals to industry that they are committed to pursuing software transparency.

In addition to U.S. federal-wide emerging requirements, specific branches of the Department of Defense (DoD) have signaled intentions to adopt SBOMs at scale for use cases not around just vulnerability management but acquisition as well. In late 2022, the U.S. Army released an RFI that aims to seek industry feedback on "the acquisition, validation, ingest, and use of Software Bills of Material (SBOMs) and closely associated matters." The RFI acknowledges that the U.S. Army runs on hundreds of thousands of software components brought together to achieve mission outcomes. This echoes earlier sentiments we've touched on that were stated by senior federal, military, and industry leaders who emphasized the role software plays in the future of military conflict.

The U.S. Department of State also signaled its intention to make SBOMs a core component of its deliverable's contractual activities and services. In July 2022, the Department of State issued a draft request for proposals as part of its acquisition program. The contract vehicle, called "Evolve," is estimated to be valued up to $8 billion to $10 billion USD. In Section H.14.7, there is a specific requirement for a "Bill of Materials," requiring contractors to provide an SBOM in an industry-standard format like Software Package Data Exchange (SPDX) or CycloneDX to capture the various components included in the software. The delivered SBOM must align with the minimum elements defined by NTIA, and the requirements state that they apply to *all* task orders on the contract. The required frequency was defined as being tied to any updates to the software and its component makeup (`https://sam.gov/opp/bee1b04eda40442bbdfbca21774d55ce/view`).

The momentum around software transparency and SBOMs isn't just limited to the United States. In the European Union (EU), an effort titled the EU Cyber Resilience Act was proposed in 2022 that serves as regulation on cybersecurity requirements for products with digital elements. It is aimed at ensuring more secure hardware and software products are used across the EU (`https://digital-strategy.ec.europa.eu/en/library/cyber-resilience-act`).

The Cyber Resilience Act states that the estimated global annual cost of cyber-crime was 5.5 trillion euros in 2021. The act points out that the primary problem of poor cybersecurity among products rife with vulnerabilities and insufficient access to information for users is understanding what products are secure or the extent to which they are. The act's primary objectives are creating developmental conditions for secure products with digital elements by reducing vulnerabilities, and for manufacturers to address security throughout a product's life cycle as well, allowing users to make informed choices on a product's security with digital elements.

In the text of the Cyber Resilience Act, specific language calls for suppliers to identify and document the components contained within the product by using an SBOM. It states that "in order to facilitate vulnerability analysis, manufacturers should identify and document components contained in the products with digital elements, including by drawing up a software bill of materials." The act specifically calls out the need for vendors to identify vulnerable third-party components in products.

The Power of the U.S. Government Supply Chains to Affect Markets

While the numbers vary depending on the source, there's no denying that the U.S. government market for IT and software spending is significant. Some sources estimate that the U.S. federal government budgeted over $65 billion for the 2023 Fiscal Year (FY) (`www.whitehouse.gov/wp-content/uploads/2022/03/ap_16_it_fy2023.pdf`). This is an increase over the previous 2022 budget of $58 billion and demonstrates a continued growth of federal IT spending among the civilian branch agencies (see Figure 12.2).

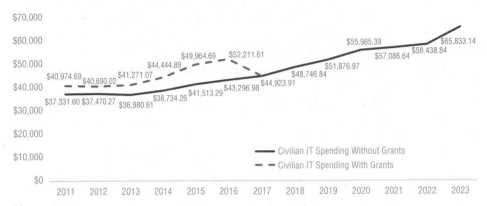

Figure 12.2

On the defense front, the 2023 FY DoD budget request was $773 billion USD. While a significant portion of this budget isn't technology and software specific, a portion of it is, and as discussed, an increasing portion of modern warfare systems and platforms are powered by technology and software as well.

Of course, this spending is isolated to the U.S. federal government DoD and doesn't include other U.S. government markets such as state and local government entities, who have their own IT spending budgets and consumption. This isn't to say all this IT spending is tied to software, but as we have discussed throughout this book, almost all modern technology is powered by software in some shape or form. This means when new policy, regulatory, or contractual requirements emerge in the U.S. governmental space, those changes end up touching a significant portion of the overall technology and software industry.

Many have made the argument that since the U.S. government buys software from many of the same vendors that broader society does, their emerging requirements will have an industry-wide impact, even outside of the government sector. Requirements we have discussed, like requiring the use of secure software development practices, providing insight into the components within software, and having mechanisms in place, like vulnerability disclosure programs, will impact not only hundreds and thousands of software vendors who work with the U.S. government but also those who work with thousands of commercial software consumers and inevitably millions of people worldwide as well.

Others have also made the case that the NIST standards that are adopted by the government, such as the Secure Software Development Framework (SSDF) and other software supply chain guidance, is likely to become voluntarily adopted by commercial sector entities as well.

One popular example is the Cybersecurity Framework (CSF) published by NIST in 2014, as a result of a previous Executive Order (EO) issued by then-President Obama, titled "Strengthening the Cybersecurity of Federal and Critical Infrastructure." This EO made the use of CSF mandatory for U.S. federal government agencies, but as NIST points out in their CSF FAQ, a CSF is now used by many private sector organizations, despite being voluntary for them, unlike the U.S. federal government (www.nist.gov/cyberframework/frequently-asked-questions/framework-basics).

Other examples include guidance and frameworks such as FedRAMP, which is only required for cloud service providers (CSPs) working with the federal government but that has served as a leading example for cloud security in the commercial sector, being cited in commercial frameworks and guidance like the Cloud Security Alliance's (CSA) Cloud Controls Matrix (CCM).

We've also discussed the DoD's emerging Cybersecurity Maturity Model Certification (CMMC), which impacts over 300,000 defense industrial base (DIB) vendors working with the DoD and that has contributed to a broader discussion around supply chain risk management when it comes to vendors in organizational supply chains beyond just software. One thing worth pointing out here is that a survey published in late 2022 found that most of the DIB vendors were unprepared to meet these emerging requirements and that 87 percent of contractors had a failing score with the Defense Federal Acquisition Regulation Supplement (DFARS) requirements, which is where contractors self-report their scores in what is known as the Supplier Performance Risk System (SPRS).

There have also been reports of self-attested scores not aligning with reality once assessed by a third party, which should be concerning when we look and see emerging software supply chain requirements such as OMB M-22-18 also requiring self-attestation by third-party software suppliers regarding their use of secure development practices. Self-attestation suffers from challenges like subjectivity and transparency when contracts and revenue are involved (https://cybersheath.com/more-than-87-of-pentagon-supply-chain-fails-basic-cybersecurity-minimums).

Many believe that the size and scope of the government tends to create scenarios where commercial industry follows its lead in terms of requirements and approaches. This means that while things like SBOMs and attestations related to secure software development may only be hard regulatory requirements in the federal sector, it is likely that they will make their way into commercial practice, too, particularly among other regulated and security-conscious industries such as the finance and medical communities.

Acceleration of Supply Chain Attacks

While we discussed some of these metrics in Chapter 1, "Background on Software Supply Chain Threats," it is worth reemphasizing as we bring the book to a close that we believe the trend of software supply chain attacks is one that will only continue to accelerate. This is due to a variety of factors, such as the increased complexity of the modern digital environment and ecosystem and expansive use of OSS and third-party software, coupled with the realization by malicious actors of just how efficient and effective software supply chain attacks can be.

Among the most alarming metrics we've cited is the 2022 Sonatype State of the Software Supply Chain report. This report found that there was a 742 percent average annual increase in software supply chain attacks over the previous three-year period. The report also cited that six out of seven vulnerabilities occur due to transitive dependencies. This is corroborated by other sources, such as the State of Dependency Management report we've cited from security vendor Endor Labs in Chapter 4, when we discussed challenges with transparency and OSS.

A single vulnerable component or piece of code can be reused by other projects as well, leading to an exponential distribution of its presence in the ecosystem and ultimately an increased risk profile. For example, vulnerable code from Log4j was reused by hundreds of projects and made its way into tens of thousands of other components in over 150 million downloads and is still being downloaded tens of thousands of times a day as of this writing, according to Sonatype (www .sonatype.com/resources/log4j-vulnerability-resource-center). Researchers are now identifying hundreds of thousands of malicious packages making their way across the ecosystem, showing an increased focus by malicious actors on the software supply chain and contributing to the exponential growth in software supply chain attacks that we continue to see as an industry.

The same Sonatype report shows that one correlating factor is the massive growth of OSS supply and consumption. As shown in Figure 12.3, taken from the report, across the major ecosystems surveyed there are now over 3 million projects, 47 million versions, and an annual request volume of over 3 trillion, which has all culminated in a more than 30 percent YoY growth in the ecosystems surveyed.

While the growth and consumption of OSS accelerates speed, efficiency, and innovation across nearly every industry through code reuse, it also proliferates significant systemic risk due to vulnerabilities in the third-party code being reused everywhere. These widely used projects and dependencies are also some of the most vulnerable. In a sense, the widespread success and adoption of OSS projects can also contribute to their risk profile, due to their expansive use and contribution to the attack surface of the industries using them.

Ecosystem	Total Projects	Total Project Versions	2022 Annual Request Volume Estimate	YoY Project Growth	YoY Download Growth	Average Versions Released per Project
Java (Maven)	492k	9.5M	675B	14%	36%	19
JavaScript (npm)	2.06M	29M	2.1T [1]	9%	32%	14
Python (PyPI)	396K	3.7M	179B [2]	18%	41%	9
.NET (NuGet)	321K	4.7M	96B [3]	-5%	23%	15
Totals / Avgs	**3.3M**	**47M**	**3.1T**	**9%**	**33%**	**14**

Figure 12.3

Source: `www.sonatype.com/state-of-the-software-supply-chain/open-source-supply-demand-security`, Sonatype

The problem is further exacerbated due to the existence of transitive dependencies, with the average library having 5.7 transitive dependencies and 62 percent of those having vulnerabilities in their third-party dependencies. Therefore, it's key to ensure that dependencies are chosen under careful consideration due to the vulnerabilities and potential risk that may be associated with them. Several vendors are beginning to integrate features to help developers make risk-informed decisions when it comes to their component selection processes during software development.

Continuing the theme of dependency management, the Sonatype report raises several concerns with which the average developer must wrestle. This includes tracking and managing 150 initial dependencies, up to 1,500 dependency changes per year per application, and then being able to have enough security and legal expertise to choose the safest versions. In an environment where many developers are often evaluated or incentivized based on speed to delivery, this level of analysis and nuance often isn't a key consideration, let alone practical and realistic.

While among the most reputable, the Sonatype report is far from the only source that corroborates an exponential increase in software supply chain attacks. The accelerated use of OSS, coupled with increased focus on this attack vector from malicious actors and the cognitive overload of many of the entities in a position to make more secure decisions, such as software developers, creates a perfect storm.

We unfortunately do not see this trend declining as malicious actors have realized how fruitful and effective it can be. In fact, we anticipate the novelty and creativity of attackers to continue to evolve, targeting not just OSS components but service and software providers as well, as demonstrated in some of our landmark cases.

In another nod to the validity of this trend, in 2022 the European Union Agency for Cybersecurity (ENISA) listed supply chain compromise of software dependencies as the number 1 threat to emerge by 2030 (see Figure 12.4). It ranks this threat ahead of other critical areas like disinformation, skills shortages, and the potential for AI abuse. This shows that the software supply chain threat is not only critical right now, as evident by the trends we have discussed and historical context and catalogs of software supply chain attacks, but that it will remain a relevant threat to organizations and nations for some time into the future.

Figure 12.4

Source: www.enisa.europa.eu/news/cybersecurity-threats-fast-forward-2030, The European Union Agency for Cybersecurity

The Increasing Connectedness of Our Digital World

Among the most evident trends in society is the rapid and continued growth of digitally connected devices. As we have stated throughout this book, nearly every aspect of our society is tied to digitally connected devices and software, from benign lifestyle items like home devices, smart watches, and medical devices to critical infrastructure and military systems.

While much of the connectivity traditionally was driven by computer devices such as servers, endpoints, and mobile devices, this trend is being exponentially accelerated through the incredible growth of the Internet of Things (IoT).

IoT devices are often defined as objects connected to the Internet and capable of transferring data, and they can include devices such as wireless sensors, household objects, industrial tooling, and manufacturing equipment.

In modern society, there's a nearly limitless number and type of devices that can be connected. Numerous factors have contributed to the growth of connected devices, including low-cost sensor technologies, cloud computing, and innovative networking protocols. We have also seen a tremendous growth in what is called Industrial IoT (IIoT). IIoT uses cloud, analytics, and machine learning to power a variety of use cases such as smart manufacturing, cities, power grids, and digital supply chains.

This connectivity brings a tremendous potential for analytics, efficiency, innovation, and capabilities that were not possible in our previously disconnected world. This pervasive connectivity also bring benefits such as new business models and revenue streams, improving efficiency and operations and even providing an improved quality of life in the personal setting. That said, it also brings an exponential and system risk unlike anything we have ever seen.

Common security challenges associated with IoT devices include hard-coded and weak credentials, a lack of regular and timely firmware updates, and an overall limited visibility when it comes to the footprint of IoT devices that organizations may be using.

As we have seen from sources like Verizon's Data Breach reporting, compromised credentials are a common attack vector for malicious actors. This doesn't bode well when many Internet of Things (IoT) and Operational Technology (OT) devices often use default credentials from their manufacturers, making them an easy target for malicious actors. Another common challenge for IoT devices is a lack of regular firmware updates or even malicious actors compromising patches and software updates delivered to IoT devices. When looking at the scope and scale of the growing IoT footprint, it is easy to see how its growth can exacerbate the challenges associated with the software supply chain and how one compromised patch can have an outsized impact.

Some sources projected that there were over 13 billion connected devices at the end of 2022, and that number is anticipated to grow to as many as 75 billion in just a few short years by 2025. With this prolific growth of connected devices, governments and regulatory agencies have struggled to keep pace. That said, some efforts are underway to try to improve the regulation for IoT devices, with a focus on privacy and cybersecurity, but more so the former of the two.

A UK consumer champion group named "Which?" released their findings in 2023, highlighting how many leading smart device manufacturers may abandon software support for the devices after just a couple of years. The group points out how this not only causes concern for operational support and longevity of the "smart" devices, but also how this can pose security risks as well, due to their widespread use and presence in society and lack of digital support throughout their life cycle.

A look at the EU and the United States shows some of the relevant regulatory efforts underway when it comes to privacy and cybersecurity, some of which are specific to IoT but others that are broad while still applying to IoT. On the EU consumer privacy front, the most notable is the General Data Protection Regulation (GDPR), which took effect in 2018 in the EU and UK. The GDPR focuses on how individuals' data can be handled and provides a framework around the key principles of fairness, lawfulness, and transparency.

While EU-based, the GDPR can and does apply to organizations out of the EU, if those organizations are in control of EU citizens' data. We previously have discussed the emerging Cyber Resilience Act in the EU. This act requires manufacturers to implement security as part of the design and production process and provides visibility into the software components involved with devices including IoT.

In the United States, recent efforts are underway to create a cybersecurity labeling program for IoT devices (www.nist.gov/itl/executive-order-14028-improving-nations-cybersecurity/cybersecurity-labeling-consumers-0). This program is aimed at American consumers and seeks, much like the EU Cyber Resilience Act, to lead to more transparency and better information for consumers to make better choices when it comes to the security of the products they purchase and use. It also is aimed at incentivizing IoT device manufacturers to consider security as part of their product development. The White House, building on the momentum of the Cybersecurity Executive Order (EO) we've discussed throughout this book, has been having discussions and engagement with some of the industry's largest Internet-enabled manufacturers to advance the effort. As of this writing, the cybersecurity labeling program is scheduled to be published in spring 2023 (www.whitehouse.gov/briefing-room/statements-releases/2022/10/20/statement-by-nsc-spokesperson-adrienne-watson-on-the-biden-harris-administrations-effort-to-secure-household-internet-enabled-devices).

In addition to the cybersecurity labeling program, NIST has a robust Cybersecurity for IoT program that provides standards, guidance, and related tools. This includes information for manufacturers of IoT devices, along with information for federal agencies looking to use IoT devices and for consumers as well. In fall 2022, the U.S. Department of Commerce appointed an Internet of Things Advisory Board to help drive efforts to secure the IoT landscape and provide key insights and recommendations based on expertise and industry experience (www.nist.gov/itl/applied-cybersecurity/nist-cybersecurity-iot-program).

Another notable example comes from the 2023 appropriations bill signed by President Biden, specifically Sec. 3305, which includes language requiring the makers of Internet-connected medical devices to reasonably ensure that the devices and their related systems are cybersecure. Among the specific language are requirements to monitor, identify, and address cybersecurity vulnerabilities in the devices and provide post-market updates and patches to address vulnerabilities. These requirements for covered devices are set to be enforced by the Food and Drug Administration (FDA; `www.congress.gov/117/bills/hr2617/BILLS-117hr2617enr.pdf`).

It is not difficult to see how the growth of the IoT landscape in society, being used in nearly every industry and in both professional and personal settings, opens the door for a massive growth in the attack surface and opportunity for malicious actors looking to facilitate software supply chain attacks and disruption. These IoT devices are powered by software, pervasive across society, slated for tremendous growth, and largely not yet focused on from the cybersecurity perspective by most organizations, either as suppliers or consumers. We anticipate language like that found in the 2023 appropriations bill and elsewhere will continue to evolve as it relates to the security and software used by IoT devices.

What Comes Next?

While predicting the future is difficult to impossible, the growing push for software transparency is nearly palpable. The risk that vulnerable software poses to everyday citizens, governments, and societies can no longer be ignored.

Software is ingrained in everything from our most basic personal luxury activities to our most critical infrastructure, civic services, and national security systems. As we have stated throughout this book, software presents nearly limitless potential for innovation and ingenuity, but it also presents a level of systemic risk to our modern way of life that cannot be overstated. In addition to the many industry and governmental efforts we have discussed, we anticipate increased efforts by governments, academia, and industry to bring increased transparency and safety to the software industry.

In a recent interview at the start of 2023, the director of CISA, Jen Easterly, stressed the need for government and industry to come together to improve the cyber safety of society. Pointing to the ongoing attacks against not just technology firms but also hospitals, school districts, and critical infrastructure, Easterly explained that the current approach to cyber safety is not sustainable.

She emphasized that companies need to take steps to create products and software that are secure by design, going as far as to say that "cyber is a social good" and that efforts to improve software security should have a direct tie to societal resiliency. Aligning with messages we have heard from researchers like Chinmayi Sharma in her piece "A Tragedy of the Digital Commons," Easterly stated that the burden can no longer fall to consumers and everyday citizens, and instead needs to be on the companies and software suppliers who are in the best position to do something about it (`https://finance.yahoo.com/`

news/us-cybersecurity-director-the-tech-ecosystem-has-become-really-unsafe-222118097.html).

In a sign of the changing approach to cybersecurity, the *Washington Post* was cited in January 2023 as stating that the forthcoming national cyber strategy is unlike any before it, and that "for the first time, regulation is on the menu of a national cybersecurity strategy" (www.washingtonpost.com/politics/2023/01/06/biden-national-cyber-strategy-is-unlike-any-before-it).

Jim Dempsey, an expert on privacy and Internet policy as well as a lecturer at UC Berkeley, unpacks the topic of an increase in cybersecurity regulation in an excellent article from January 2023 titled "One Small Legislative Step for Cybersecurity" (www.lawfareblog.com/one-small-legislative-step-cybersecurity). In the article, Dempsey points out that the previously discussed requirement for connected medical devices in the 2023 appropriations bill was arguably the first time since 2005 that Congress has expressly authorized any agency to regulate the cybersecurity of privately owned and operated systems of any kind.

Dempsey points out that, to date, most cybersecurity measures related to critical infrastructure have been voluntary. Many critics have pointed out that cybersecurity can be classified as a market failure, and that leaving it to the market to self-regulate and prioritize cybersecurity has failed and continues to do so. If this perspective is true, it is concerning given that most U.S. critical infrastructure is privately owned and operated, often uses vulnerable software components, and is heavily targeted by malicious actors.

Many suspect that the national cyber strategy and associated efforts in the United States, which has traditionally been based on voluntary efforts, beginning to shift toward regulatory requirements. With these emerging requirements will come increased liability and accountability for suppliers and entities who neglect their cybersecurity responsibilities when it comes to software, products, and digital systems. As we have touched on previously, some consider cybersecurity a market failure and a challenge that voluntary efforts alone cannot resolve. This increased push for regulatory requirements and ramifications strives to level the playing field to address current gaps in national security and public safety, both of which are now underpinned by software.

In the United States, there are 16 critical infrastructure sectors, which span areas including communications, energy, emergency services, transportation, IT, and the defense industrial base, among others. As the nation has continued to see an acceleration of malicious cyberattacks against critical infrastructure entities, key security leaders have increased their focus on these sectors and the state of their regulation. One such example is the Deputy National Security Adviser, Anne Neuberger, and her associated team. While the team identified that many of the critical infrastructure sectors have some regulatory measures in place related to cybersecurity, this is not the case for all the sectors. Gaps were identified among several areas in the United States, including food, agriculture, and schooling.

As cited by the Federal Emergency Management Agency (FEMA), the private sector owns most of the nation's critical infrastructure and key resources at 85 percent. The report also points out that this critical infrastructure is becoming more prone to failure as the average age of the structure increases (`www.fema .gov/pdf/about/programs/oppa/critical_infrastructure_paper.pdf`).

In support of the report's validity, in early 2023 the U.S. Federal Aviation Administration (FAA) was forced to halt all U.S. flights on January 11 due to an outage of its Notice to Air Missions (NOTAMs) system. A 2022 report from the FAA explains their challenges with legacy hardware and software (`www .faa.gov/sites/faa.gov/files/2022-02/FAA_FY22_Business_Planv2.pdf`).

As cited in studies like the 2022 Synopsys Open Source Security and Risk Analysis Report, the United States was being hit with 10 million attempted exploits per hour, with attacks specifically targeting critical infrastructure sectors. Half of critical infrastructure codebases have been found to contain OSS. As cited in the same study, nearly all codebases included OSS more than four years out of date or with components with no new development in two years. Software, much like our physical infrastructure, becomes increasingly fragile with age, particularly due to the emergence of new vulnerabilities.

When you consider the aging physical infrastructure, often powered by outdated and potentially vulnerable software that's regularly undergoing a constant barrage of malicious activity, you can see where things begin to become concerning. This is supported by sources such as the 2023 World Economic Forum (WEF) Global Risks Report, which cited cyberattacks on critical infrastructure as one of the highest ranked risks. When surveyed, nearly all cybersecurity leaders cited a strong concern for a devastating global cyberattack within the next two years (`www3.weforum.org/docs/WEF_Global_Risks_Report_2023.pdf`).

In addition to other areas of emerging regulatory efforts, such as cybersecurity data breach reporting requirements and device labeling, there is a growing push for the increased transparency of the software provided by suppliers. This includes providing transparency for the software components, dependencies, and their associated vulnerabilities. While not perfect, these efforts help to address the current information asymmetry that exists between software suppliers and consumers.

It is unrealistic to expect everyday citizens and businesses whose core competency and profession is not cybersecurity to be experts in software security, secure software development, and vulnerability management. We do not ask this in other areas of society such as automobiles, airplanes, pharmaceuticals, and food. As a society, we have baked measures into these industries to address information asymmetries between suppliers and consumers to ensure safety, responsibility, and accountability, while also still allowing for consumers to make risk informed decisions. We are now seeing efforts to do something similar with software and technology.

As we have pointed out by citing efforts from other nations around the world, this issue is not limited to just the United States. Governments and nations around the world are waking up to the systemic risk that insecure software, a lack of transparency, and a lack of accountability for secure products and technologies pose. They are responding with similar efforts to address these issues as well.

We fully anticipate that contrasted with software transparency and security efforts by governments and regulatory bodies, there will be pushback from industry groups, lobbyists, and commercial entities. For example, the U.S. Chamber of Commerce has stated that they are actively anticipating reviewing the new national cyber strategy and determining the impact on their respective members. Efforts by lobbyists and industry groups have had some success pushing back on other historical efforts for increased transparency and accountability for software suppliers as well as recent efforts such as the 2023 NDAA and its inclusion of SBOMs.

There is, of course, merit to the concerns these groups raise, such as the maturity of some of the artifacts and insights being required as well as a need to reconcile the patchwork landscape of regulatory requirements that govern their activities. Disjointed regulations and requirements cause confusion among industries, can lead to wasted time and investment, and can stifle innovation and speed. The ability for governments and citizens to use innovative technologies and capabilities is key for not just quality of life but also economic prosperity and national security. Efforts to regulate software must be contrasted with the constraints and impacts the regulatory efforts impose. Many in the DoD, for example, have cited broken and antiquated requirements and regulations impeding their ability to execute at the speed of relevance.

This is emphasized in the latest DoD's Software Modernization Strategy, which explains the key role that software modernization plays in national security. In the opening lines of the document, it states:

> **The Department's adaptability increasingly relies on software and the ability to securely and rapidly deliver resilient software capability is a competitive advantage that will define future conflicts. Transforming software delivery times from years to minutes will require significant change to our processes, policies, workforce, and technology.** (https://media.defense.gov/2022/Feb/03/2002932833/-1/-1/1/DEPARTMENT-OF-DEFENSE-SOFTWARE-MODERNIZATION-STRATEGY.PDF)

So, while the push for software transparency and increased software supply chain security rigor is warranted based on the historical lack of transparency into software consumption, exponential increase in OSS use, and accelerating attacks from malicious actors, these efforts must be contrasted with the burden and friction they impose upon teams, organizations, and the industry.

We also anticipate that much more maturing needs to occur as it relates to tooling to facilitate these goals. This applies to the areas of IoT, OT, legacy software, and even cloud environments when it comes to software component asset inventory, higher-fidelity vulnerability data, and automation to support the exchange of data between software suppliers, consumers, and other industry entities involved in the software ecosystem. Insights from tooling and artifacts must be automatable and actionable for development teams, for example, to not excessively impede their velocity to deliver code to production and help organizations deliver on software-enabled business and mission outcomes.

Another trend we anticipate continuing to evolve is the shift from traditional static form-based vendor risk assessment to one that is API-centric, facilitated by technologies such as the cloud, and that enables automation and near-real-time assessment. This automation trend will also be key to successful scaling and achieving the desired outcomes related to SBOMs and communicating exploitability, particularly in large, complex development environments that follow Agile and DevSecOps methodologies with frequent software releases, leading to an increased velocity in associated artifacts like SBOMs and their accompanying exploitability context.

For years, compliance and security has lagged behind broader trends across the industry to push for DevOps, increased velocity, speed to market, and rapid software development and release. We are now seeing momentum and maturity with accompanying movements like DevSecOps and improved innovative security tooling and processes in environments such as cloud and CI/CD toolchains to provide the security and compliance controls required while limiting the impact on developer velocity. As we see the increased trend toward codification (e.g., as-code), declarative infrastructures and microservices, security, and compliance must continue to innovate to keep pace, function as an enabler, and still provide the level of transparency and accountability needed as it relates to the software supply chain.

As we discussed in Chapter 11, "Practical Guidance for Consumers," we also anticipate further efforts by both software suppliers and consumers to mature their software supply chain governance and security efforts. From the supplier's perspective, this will manifest in areas such as improved governance of OSS, transparency related to software components in products for downstream consumers, and a reckoning with the actual expectations they can levy on the OSS maintainers and communities of which they make extensive use.

From the consumer's perspective, we anticipate that software consumers will continue to demand increased transparency from their upstream software suppliers and vendors. This includes areas such as seeking assurance that secure software development practices were followed and requesting software artifacts like SBOMs and accompanying artifacts that show not just vulnerabilities but their exploitability. Further communications will need to occur between suppliers and consumers to help clarify not just the presence and exploitability of vulnerabilities but also timelines for remediation as well as mitigating measures consumers can take to reduce risk prior to vulnerability remediations.

Organizations of all shapes and sizes will also continue to take a hard look at their software supply chains. This hard look will extend well beyond just OSS and third-party software vendors whose software is installed and running in their environments but also to as-a-service providers like managed service providers (MSPs), cloud service providers (CSPs), and software-as-a-service (SaaS) providers who've also been an increased target for malicious actors looking to exploit the tangled and complex software supply chain ecosystem in which we currently operate.

These efforts may lead to some reconciliation in the software ecosystem as more mature and security-savvy consumers look to make use of mature and secure software suppliers and service providers to mitigate risk to their organizations, stakeholders, and customers. We suspect this trend will be most prevalent among communities including national security and other regulated industries such as finance and aerospace.

In addition to changes among the teams developing, supplying, and consuming software, we anticipate further involvement and oversight of cybersecurity concerns at the most senior levels of organizations, going beyond just the CISO and the boardroom. This is, in part, being driven by the realization that nearly every business is in the realm of technology and software even if it isn't their core competency, as it is often helping drive their revenue and operations. It is also being driven by emerging changes from bodies such as the U.S. Securities and Exchange Commission (SEC), which is driving boards to include cyber risk as part of their fiduciary and oversight activities.

For example, recently proposed rule changes by the SEC titled "Cybersecurity Risk Management, Strategy, Governance and Incident Disclosure" include provisions to require organizations to make disclosures related to their board of directors' cybersecurity expertise. This will facilitate a paradigm shift where organizational leadership will need to be more informed of and involved in cyber risk oversight of their respective firms, including concerns related to software supply chain security and incidents occurring due to software supply chain attacks or malicious activity (`www.sec.gov/rules/proposed/2022/33-11038.pdf`).

These changes signal a shifting regulatory landscape where the boards of organizations will now be held accountable to ensure that they have cybersecurity expertise as part of their board makeup. Given that software supply chain attacks are accelerating and a regular focus of discussion and concern for organizations over the last several years, it is safe to assume that the topic will make its way to the attention of the boards and already has in some organizations.

In this book, we've covered a wide range of applicable topics in the area of software supply chain security. These topics have included landmark software supply chain attacks, traditional assessment methodologies, emerging guidance and best practices, the rise of the SBOM and related topics, as well as practical guidance for both suppliers and consumers. We also covered the role that innovative technologies such as the cloud, Kubernetes, and containers play in the software supply chain ecosystem. While it would be nearly impossible to cover all the relevant topics given the complexity of the modern software supply chain and associated ecosystem, this content should position practitioners to both produce secure software transparently and to understand the risk of the software they consume, either from the OSS ecosystem or directly from third-party software suppliers.

As we have emphasized throughout this book, software is critical to nearly every aspect of our society, and ensuring that we're both producing and consuming secure software is paramount as we move into the pervasively digital future. Software offers an unparalleled promise of innovation, capability, and growth as well as unparalleled levels of systemic risk that can devastate our society if not addressed properly.

As Supreme Court Justice Louis Brandeis said over a century ago, "Sunlight is said to be the best of disinfectants." Society is now pushing for transparency of the digital ecosystem that surrounds every aspect of our lives and the system risk associated with it.

We are champions of this sunlight.

Index